The Gayborhood

The Gayborhood

From Sexual Liberation to Cosmopolitan Spectacle

Edited by
Christopher T. Conner and Daniel Okamura

LEXINGTON BOOKS
Lanham • Boulder • New York • London

Published by Lexington Books
An imprint of The Rowman & Littlefield Publishing Group, Inc.
4501 Forbes Boulevard, Suite 200, Lanham, Maryland 20706
www.rowman.com

6 Tinworth Street, London SE11 5AL, United Kingdom

Chapter 1 was originally published as Brodyn, A. and Ghaziani, A. (2018),
Performative Progressiveness: Accounting for New Forms of Inequality in the
Gayborhood. City & Community, 17: 307–329. https://doi .org/10.1111/cico.12298.
Chapter 2 from 2015. Urban Studies 52(16): 3144–3159; epilogue added 2020.

British Library Cataloguing in Publication Information Available

Library of Congress Cataloging-in-Publication Data

Names: Conner, Christopher T., 1981- editor. | Okamura, Daniel, 1979- editor.
Title: The gayborhood : from sexual liberation to cosmopolitan spectacle /
   edited by Christopher T. Conner and Daniel Okamura.
Description: Lanham : Lexington Books, [2021] | Includes bibliographical
   references and index.
Identifiers: LCCN 2021002378 (print) | LCCN 2021002379 (ebook) |
   ISBN 9781793609830 (cloth) | ISBN 9781793609847 (epub) |
   ISBN 9781793609854 (pbk)
Subjects: LCSH: Gays—United States. | Neighborhoods—United States. |
   Communities—United States. | Sociology, Urban—United States.
Classification: LCC HQ76.3.U5 G39435 2021 (print) | LCC HQ76.3.U5 (ebook) |
   DDC 306.76/60973—dc23
LC record available at https://lccn.loc.gov/2021002378
LC ebook record available at https://lccn.loc.gov/2021002379

Contents

Acknowledgments   vii

Introduction: Queering the Sociological Imagination   1
Christopher T. Conner and Daniel Okamura

1   Performative Progressiveness: Accounting for New Forms of
Inequality in the Gayborhood   15
Adriana Brodyn and Amin Ghaziani

2   Style and the Value of Gay Nightlife: Homonormative
Placemaking in San Francisco   45
Greggor Mattson

3   Gayborhoods as Criminogenic Space   67
Vanessa R. Panfil

4   Gay Collective Sex in New York City from the Late
1800s to Today: The Triumph of Collective Intimacy   85
Étienne Meunier and Jeffrey Escoffier

5   Disappearing: The Gay Singleton in Gay Spaces   107
Aliraza Javaid

6   Erotic Capital and Queer Men of Color   125
Omar Ali Mushtaq

7   The Whiteness of Queer Urban Placemaking   143
Theodore Greene

8 Beyond the Heteronormative Framework: How Two-Mother
      Families in Poland Deal with Social Invisibility and Related
      Anxieties   161
      Magdalena Wojciechowska

9 When the Gayborhood Isn't Enough: How Trans Youth
      Utilize the Internet to Make a Digital Trans Neighborhood   173
      Jonathan Jiménez

10 Gays under Glass: Gay Dating Apps and the Affection-Image   189
      Tom Penney

11 Gayborhood Change: The Intertwined Sexual and Racial
      Character of Assimilation in Chicago's Boystown   205
      Jason Orne

Afterword: Somewhere beyond the Gayborhood   227
C. J. Janovy

Index   237

About the Editors   247

About the Contributors   249

Acknowledgments

While ordinarily we would take the opportunity to thank one of our mentors in this case, this edited volume represents our ability to go rogue, and to prove to ourselves, and others, our ability to produce a great contribution to the discipline. We hope this edited volume makes our mentors proud.

We are also deeply indebted to the contributors of this volume (in alphabetical order of surnames): Adriana Brodyn, Jeffrey Escoffier, Amin Ghaziani, Theodore Greene, C. J. Janovy, Aliraza Javaid, Jonathan Jiménez, Greggor Mattson, Omar Ali Mushtaq, Étienne Meunier, Jason Orne, Vanessa R. Panfil, Tom Penney, and Magdalena Wojciechowska. Producing an edited volume is a labor of love and places you in close contact with the contributors. We are thankful to have had the opportunity to work so closely with a diverse group of individuals. Moreover, we intentionally sought out both recognized scholars and those whose work is just emerging. In doing so, we were also able to diversify the makeup of the contributors and the topics covered. It was our intent to produce a collection of chapters highlighting the importance of the "gayborhood" and the important work that is still left to do. We feel that this collection achieves those wishes.

Finally, there are a variety of individuals who helped make this edited volume a reality and without which we couldn't have done this work. We would like to thank Cristina Bodinger-deUriarte, Cadillac Barbie, David R. Dickens, Stephanie "DJ Deanne" Swanson, Bryan Yamasaki, our friends and colleagues at University of Nevada, Las Vegas and University of Missouri, and many others inside and outside the gayborhood too numerous to mention.

Chris and Daniel

Introduction

Queering the Sociological Imagination

Christopher T. Conner and Daniel Okamura

This edited volume brings together a collection of chapters devoted to the study of gay urban enclaves, colloquially known as "gayborhoods." Gayborhoods are urban spaces that contain a variety of residents, businesses, and social service agencies catering to LGBT+ persons. The rise in popularity and attention devoted to gayborhoods, in both scholarly and in popular media discourses, is largely a product of recent civil rights gains and recognizes that these spaces represent an essential part of LGBT+ life. Even rural residents and those who do not live in gayborhoods draw upon the cultural and sub-cultural (Thornton 1995) capital of gay urban enclaves, even if they deny their necessity (see also Brekhus 2003).

Gayborhoods are sociologically sophisticated sites of observation as they are the physical locations where sexual identity, politics, and shared group identity converge. Within this built environment, we can physically map out the history, trajectory, and ongoing issues facing LGBT+ persons. Today, some gayborhoods even contain monuments to these struggles and use other symbols to mark these areas as separate from the rest of the city. One of the most iconic gayborhoods, Chicago's Boystown, is lined with pylons dedicated to historic gay rights figures, including sociologist Jane Addams, whose sexual identity is often completely ignored (Fredriksen-Goldsen et al. 2009). Gayborhoods also illustrate the innovative ways groups of people, so marginalized, can come together to create communal space in efforts to band together for survival. However, these spaces are also filled with internal strife as organizers are called upon to negotiate the multiple hierarchies and inter-sections that make up those who depend upon the gayborhood.

We, the editors, have collaborated with scholars from a diverse array of backgrounds in the interest of covering a wide range of topics. Many of these chapters call upon us to read the gayborhood critically, and rightfully so. These chapters remind us that our greatest strength—diversity—if not safeguarded internally, can divide us. Unlike other texts, this is not an inter-disciplinary collection of papers. The work contained herein is largely socio-logical and empirically grounded in research rather than purely theoretical.[1] We hope that this text promotes an important area of sociology while also giving voice to the ongoing problems in and outside of the gayborhood.

The gayborhood then ought to be thought of as more than a collection of buildings, but also as a space where people enact a series of cultural prac-tices (Buckland 2002). The development of the gayborhood in sociology first emerged in the 1970s thanks to the work of Humphreys (1970; 1972), Warren (1974), Weinberg and Williams (1974), Martin Levine (1979), and others who utilized a symbolic interactionist approach.[2] Collectively, these schol-ars attempted to humanize gay men and other marginalized groups to show their collective struggle in a society that oppressed them.[3] Working against the moral reformers[4] who viewed homosexuality as an illness, these scholars documented how people created their own refuge within the urban environ-ment. Despite finding a great deal of insights into the struggles gay men faced how they dealt with a system structurally designed to marginalize them, and even their internal struggles to maintain group solidarity, this framework has been largely abandoned.[5]

Despite decades of research on the topic, gayborhoods, and the study of gay urban life, remain an obscure subject in sociology. As we argue in this chapter, part of this is due to the suspicion by other scholars that such an area of study may be a thinly veiled attempt at academic hedonistic debauchery.[6] However, this reflects a series of ongoing biases within sociology, whether explicit or implicit, rooted in the field's hetero-orthodoxy. As Kuhn (1962) has argued, science is a political endeavor, and what constitutes science for some may be easily dismissed by others.

The stigma of researching topics thought of as "fun" areas of research also stems from a stigma that has long plagued those operating under the rubric of the sociology of culture. As Harry Edwards (1973:8–9) has brilliantly argued:

> A fourth factor contributing to an insufficient volume of scientific knowledge about athletics is that many people have succumbed to the sports propagandist's theme that organized athletics is, for the most part, merely recreation. In short, throughout the social structure of America, people—laymen and profession-als—have traditionally accepted the "fun-and-games" image of sport to the almost total exclusion of any consider to regarding its more serious aspects.

Similar arguments have been made for the study of celebrity culture (Ferris 2007), subcultures (Anderson 2009), and sexuality scholars (Orne 2017:9).[7] However, this criticism is part of a larger critique in sociology that begins with the assault on symbolic interactionism's interest in "deviant subcultures." Critics of the approach argued that the deviance framework merely championed groups labeled as "deviant" without providing solutions on how to improve their conditions (i.e., the poor, race, and ethnic groups, and—key to this anthology—gays and lesbians).[8] Despite the dim view by certain gatekeepers, these obstacles have been overcome in those working on elevating the status of the gayborhood to a site of serious sociological inquiry.

Castells (1983) has noted that the sociological significance in studying gayborhoods emerges from how the built environment is used as a way to resolve micro-level desires while simultaneously organizing to reclaim political power. This results in an interconnected ecosystem in which the personal, communal, and political manifest themselves within a given space as a shared culture. Gayborhoods represent spaces where having a different sexuality is normalized and where LGBT+ people go to feel normal, desirable, and worthy. Some of the simple "privileges" include the right to hold hands, kiss, find lovers, and not worry about judgment by non-gays. Scholars of race talk about the struggles that racial minorities endure living in predominantly white spaces—the same processes underlie the experiences of marginalization that sexual minorities face in heteronormative spaces.

WHOSE CULTURE, WHOSE COMMUNITY?

Much of the current scholarship connects the issues facing LGBT+ persons, outlined earlier, to neo-Marxist critiques of the political economy. These scholars illustrate how LGBT+ political organizations have been made possible by movement leaders presenting an image of the group as a highly profitable consumer market (Valocchi 1999; Chasin 2000; Barrett and Pollack 2005; Guidotto 2006). However, as Chasin (2000) has shown, such notions selectively highlight the minority of privileged white gay men and further marginalize those who do not fit this homonormative image (Mulvey 1975; Chasin 2000; Wood 2004; Anderson 2011). Thus, race and other variables of one's social position become inextricably linked to LGBT+ community-building efforts in late-stage capitalism—one benefits only if they are in the top rungs of the stratified system. The image of what being gay means has become entwined within a race- and class-based system, ultimately dividing and marginalizing voices within the group and shifting the focus away from substantive changes and driving these prejudices underground.

Today, gayborhoods are increasingly under threat as urban developers displace the founders of these spaces (often creating new hip nightlife spaces to replace traditional gay venues). Urban planners such as Richard Florida

(2005; 2009) have used the confluence of gay spaces and high-income residents migrating to them to promote policies that would increase gentrifying these areas (Colbert 2007). As others have pointed out elsewhere (see Deener 2012; Lloyd 2006; Dunier 1999, Orne 2017), cultural urban renewal strategies drastically alter the makeup by displacing the residents, who often can't afford to live there due to rising housing costs, by commodifying the cultural aesthetics of those areas. The result is a reproduction of existing divisions in the larger societal framework (Willis 1977; Han 2008; Choi et al. 2011; Mattson 2015). And yet, despite the economic and political forces that threaten their existences, gayborhoods endure, often due to the participation of former and displaced populations who continue to associate gay neighborhoods as safe spaces to publicly express their sexual and gender identities (Greene 2014).

While early gay culture utilized carnivalesque cultural elements as political strategies (Rabinovitz 2012), one of the first gay organizations—the Mattachine Society—picked up on this and modeled itself on being court jesters mocking the elite (Cervini 2020). Political strategies, however, depend upon the historical context in which they are embedded. What functions as a progressive political performance today may not be politically progressive moving forward (see Conner and Katz 2020). Popular media depictions have slowly co-opted the resistance strategies employed by LGBT+ activists. RuPaul, *Queer Eye for the Straight Guy*, and Lady Gaga have colonized the gayborhood by weaponizing the very culture they created to incorporate LGBT+ politics into mainstream culture via the culture industry (Horkheimer and Adorno [1944] 1982). Some argue that the result illustrates the Frankfurt School's critique that artificially produced culture, rather than elevating human consciousness, could actually cause it to regress (see Marcuse 1964; [1977] 1978). Today, much of the gayborhood has been colonized by the culture industry as the last traces of a political movement are wiped clean.

As understood here in the United States, this divide between political organizing strategies lies between those who wish to advance an assimilationist-style strategy and those who follow a separatist approach. The best illustration of this divide occurred during the fiftieth anniversary of the Stonewall riots held in New York City. While in the middle of NYC, city officials and corporations held a parade that attracted more than one million people worldwide. Across the East River in Brooklyn, activists and community organizers marched in protest of what they felt were commodifying tendencies subverting the movement's interests. The activists' concerns are those raised by the Frankfurt School, especially by philosopher Herbert Marcuse in his seminal work, *One-Dimensional Man*, first published in 1964.

POST-GAY

Some assimilationists have gone as far as to describe the current era of LGBT+ politics as "post-gay" and encourage movement leaders to double down on assimilationist tactics (Warner 1999; Ghaziani 2014).[9] They also wish to distance themselves from and denounce separatist approaches to political organizing activities. These people see the continued existence of gayborhoods as a barrier to full assimilation and achievement of the ultimate goal: creating a parallel heteronormative (so-called homonormative) life course. Some high-profile gays and lesbians have gone so far as to argue that sexuality alone should not define them (Hicklin 2012). The most recent and extreme example of this includes statements from 2020 presidential candidate Pete Buttigieg, who argued that his sexuality mattered little in his daily life.

While market-based rights strategies have resulted in greater "tolerance," they have not achieved full equality. Thus, commodifying tendencies have obscured some of the important political policy work to be done as organizing efforts become professionalized and more bureaucratic. This has resulted in an enhanced level of visibility and accommodation for LGBT+ persons, but not without its consequences and limits (Melucci 1994; Allegretto and Arthur 2001; Movement Advancement Project 2013; Maddux 2011; see Meyer 2012). Critics argue that the symbolic forms of resistance have merely obscured inequalities that persist among LGBTQ populations (Piccone 1978; Žižek 1997; Habermas 1981; Pichardo 1997).

While some of this cultural, or even sub-cultural, capital (see Thornton 1995) is still worth something, it is quickly becoming replaced. Those with privilege do well in these spaces, and those without it are sorted out elsewhere. The culture industry maintains itself by removing politically dissident features and replacing them with those more in line with a respectable, commercially appealing style. We can observe the extent of this phenomenon in closing iconic gay spaces and their replacement with "straight-friendly" businesses (see Orne 2017). The sociological question that should be asked is how members resolve the paradox of ongoing problems and, in so doing, maintain their senses of community and culture during an era in which they are presented in visible and positive light.

THE QUEER DIGITAL FRONTIER

Digital technologies have also called into question the necessity of gayborhoods and also challenge us to think beyond the confines of a traditionally bounded physical space. On the surface, new technologies seem to be a welcome boon to gay culture, freeing us from the gay ghetto (Carter 2010).

However, empirical studies (Han 2008; Choi et al. 2011; Woo 2013; Foster-Gimbel and Engeln 2016) have shown that apps, rather than creating a utopia, amplify underlying problems within the community. One example of this is the all-too-common appearance of phrases in online gay spaces such as no Asians, no blacks, no fats, no fems (Han 2008; Choi et al. 2011; Foster-Gimbel and Engeln 2016). This has raised interesting questions about who gets to participate in the LGBT+ community if such a thing ever existed, and the Internet's role in defining community.

It would be impossible to write an opening chapter to this edited volume without considering the global pandemic created by the novel coronavirus. Many owners of business establishments that make up gayborhoods were already struggling to maintain their businesses before the pandemic hit (Mattson 2019; 2020). The result of the financial fallout for these businesses is their permanent closure and the loss of the queer public realm. However, others have seized this opportunity to reimagine a gayborhood made up of entirely online spaces. Using various software platforms (Twitch, Zoom, Facebook Live), club promoters, DJs, drag queens, and others have experimented with new ways of creating community.[10] Some have even used this as a new way to experiment with how they "do sex" (Dickson 2020; Kahn 2020). While at first glance, these new social configurations may hint at the possibility of greater equality, as Benjamin (2020; 2019) argues, new technologies merely obscure old forms of prejudice. As is generally the case with digital technologies, they offer us new possibilities and configurations of social life, but those realities have yet to be fully realized (Kellner 1989).

ORGANIZATION OF THE BOOK

Following this introduction, the book begins with Adriana Brodyn and Amin Ghaziani's analysis of what happens when straight people move into and exert entitlement onto gayborhoods. Their chapter, "Performative Progressiveness: Accounting for New Forms of Inequality in the Gayborhood," illustrates the concept of performative progressiveness, a concept they use to describe how straight patrons of gay bars use progressive attitudes while engaging in homonegative actions—this is not unlike Piccone's (1978) notion of artificial negativity, or Žižek's (1997) multiculturalism critique. As they argue, the increased presence of "outsiders" in once predominately gay spaces has undermined notions of solidarity and placemaking and allowed residents with more power and privilege to redefine cultural enclaves in the city. Thus, this volume opens by asking the critical question of for whom do "gayborhoods" serve in this era of heightened visibility.[11]

In the next chapter, Greggor Mattson's historical exploration of San Francisco's three gay bar districts illustrates that we must be wary of reductionist claims that institutionalize and homogenize gay placemaking initiatives. As Mattson shows, the success or failure of gay urban enclaves remains a complex issue and that the cosmopolitan shift that helped popularize one district may do so at the expense of another. Moreover, he reminds us of the power of homonormativity to create hierarchies placing some gays at the forefront of popular culture vis-a-vis respectability politics while rendering invisible other forms of gay self-expression. Finally, his revised version of this chapter, originally appearing in *Urban Studies*, fulfills the notion of immanent critique (see Antonio 1980) by offering us possible new configurations for gay urban nightlife.

Vanessa R. Panfil reminds us in the following chapter that before spaces like Boystown or the Castro were inhabited by the highly affluent, gayborhoods were thought of as "deviant" or even criminal spaces due to laws criminalizing same-sex behaviors, police harassment, and the actions of outside agitators (i.e., gay bashers). Moreover, as Panfil argues, the history of the gay rights movement has been one of transgressing authority as a political organizing strategy, making gayborhoods criminogenic sites understood through the lens of cultural criminology. While most studies of gayborhoods focus on their cultural aspects about either sexual or consumer behaviors, this chapter provides us with a refreshing take on how to theorize gay urban spaces.

Étienne Meunier and Jeffrey Escoffier analyze the changing attitudes toward collective sex venues within New York City across four distinct periods: pre-Stonewall, post-Stonewall, the AIDS crisis, and contemporary context. In so doing, Meunier and Escoffier illustrate how societal shifts impact our views on sex and sexuality—and how larger historical shifts are experienced by sexual minorities. Additionally, they remind us that while we live in an era of unprecedented gains in civil rights in the United States, this has not necessarily translated to solving issues of finding intimacy. Moreover, as they further show, finding intimate relationships means navigating a range of sociological variables that are intertwined with one's racialized, classed, gendered, and embodied perspectives.

In "Disappearing: The Gay Singleton in Gay Spaces," Aliraza Javaid gives us an autoethnographic account for how status, privilege, and ultimately, stigma manifest themselves within "gayborhoods." As Javaid shows, there is a homonormative assumption of coupledom in gay spaces that has emerged within recent years. He reveals that one's access to the freedoms alluded to by the gayborhood is experienced differently the farther a single person is placed from the cultural ideal. His account shows us the subtle reminders that exist within gay spaces when one is "other." While Javaid's focus is on his role as a "gay singleton" and how this has become a stigma in an era of heightened civil rights gains, he also reminds us the role that ethnicity plays in navigating gay spaces. Moreover, social actors often do not talk in strictly sociological terms. His chapter captures a personalized tale of how inequalities are experienced within the realm of intimacy and gay social life.

In "Erotic Capital and Queer Men of Color," Omar Ali Mushtaq investigates how gay men of color navigate predominantly white spaces, using the perspective of dark-skinned go-go dancers to understand how they perceive their bodies within these spaces and in relation to white bodies in those spaces. His chapter interrogates notions of sexual and cultural capital and how gay men of color attempt to leverage their bodies to access sexual capital. Mushtaq's chapter illustrates how these men occupy lower levels of sexual and cultural capital based on their race and attempt to overcome this by engaging in bodybuilding practices that allow them to display their muscularity and masculinity to compensate. Moreover, due to his subjects' occupation as go-go dancers, this eroticized capital impacts their actual capital—perhaps making these interview subjects some of the best equipped to examine this phenomenon.

A 2013 Pew Survey study of LGBT Americans found that 56 percent of participants felt it was important to maintain LGBT neighborhoods and bars, even while most (72 percent) say they have never lived there. Thus, while the "coming out" narrative may lead to a migration into urban gay enclaves (Weston 1995), such experiences are not necessarily enjoyed equally by all who would hope to find refuge and shelter. Theodore Greene's chapter, "The Whiteness of Queer Urban Placemaking," draws our attention to the unequal ways in which means is embedded into the queer urban environment and complicates our understanding of such processes that have traditionally focused on white subjective experiences. Conventional scholarship, as he argues, "tends to erase or marginalize the experiences of queer communities of color, whose subcultural practices and traditions might not align with those familiar among mainstream queer communities." Greene's chapter calls upon us to consider the racialized nature of queer cultural practices and how such erasure reflects the different trajectories and life histories for non-white queer-identifying individuals. Thus, Latinx and Muslim queer communities' spatial practices following the Pulse nightclub shooting in 2016 found a more welcoming and receptive audience due to the homogenization of certain cultural practices that appealed to white queer residents. Rather than sacrificing their racialized cultural practice in favor of greater inclusion within the confines of the gayborhood, Latinx and Muslim queer geographies provided a platform to "create sanctuaries of collective mourning and healing while simultaneously critiquing their erasure from mainstream discourses around the tragedy." Greene's analysis here also shows how macro-level cultural practices also shape individual, interpersonal narratives for queer citizens of color, showing how the two interact and sometimes reinforce each other.

While most of the chapters in this text are written about and by those living in the United States, Magdalena Wojciechowska's chapter on lesbian mothers reminds us that, while many countries are experiencing civil rights gains, this is not the case everywhere. This ethnographic study involving twenty-one same-sex couples, who she followed over six years, illustrates the complex social dynamics that lesbian mothers in Poland have to navigate daily. For her participants, the "gayborhood" becomes a space not rooted in a physical location but upon which same-sex couples can connect and not have to "pass" according to heteronormative standards. Moreover, within this unfavorable political climate, passing as "normal" is a survival strategy done out of love for their families to maintain their existence. This chapter also reminds us that not everyone experiences the benefits of "passing."

The unprecedented era of civil rights gains epitomized in the 2015 Supreme Court decision *Obergefell v. Hodges*, allowing gays and lesbians the right to marry, has helped popularize and mainstream an image of "homornormativity" that obscures and exacerbates other forms of inequality. Moreover, neoliberal policies and practices have aided efforts to gentrify "gayborhoods" and exacerbated racialized inequalities that have always existed within these spaces. Jonathan Jiménez explores an understudied dimension of gayborhoods, which is the estrangement and exclusion of trans-youth from supposedly LGBT+ spaces. Jiménez's chapter documents how trans-youth negotiate the transition of both gender and age in the face of these greater historical trends and utilize digital tools to create new forms of community.

In "Gays under Glass," Tom Penney explores digital impression management in how men seeking sex with other men construct photorealistic but artificially embodied masculinities in the popular cruising app, Grindr. He argues that the very structure of the user experience (UX) functions to fetishize men as objects and reproduce hierarchies of masculinity through the use of the grid layout, the demand to approve or reject, and the divide between the face and the body. In swiping at images of masculinity, separated by a glass barrier between us and artificial affect, and submitting to such an inhuman system, Penney argues that men tacitly identify with and call forth from within a "microfascist" culture.

The current era of heightened visibility and, to an extent, increased acceptance brings new challenges. Jason Orne uses the familiar sociological frameworks of assimilation and intersectionality in his examination of Chicago's Boystown. He examines the assimilation of sexual identity into mainstream straightness via gentrification, arguing that queer people "clean up" nonwhite residential areas, making it too expensive for its original residents, only to then see the area turn into a destination for straight people, thereby pricing themselves out as well. His data also reveal, however, that only particular brands of gayness have mainstream market appeal, where queer people of color must often commute into the gayborhood to consume its sexually liberated atmosphere, and are not always welcomed.

While not a sociologist, C. J. Janovy's chapter is no less impactful, concluding this volume with an exploration of rural residents in Independence, Kansas. An unlikely spot to find expressions of queerness, Janovy nonetheless points out some of the linkages that can be found outside of iconic gayborhood locales. Moreover, in this chapter, we can see how to restore the political potential for queer activism and organizing. Beyond this, Janovy shows us how much sociology has to learn from other fields of inquiry and other social worlds that remain underexplored.

We are pleased to have had the opportunity to work with the authors on these articles. Moreover, we thank them immensely for their patience and in trusting us with their prose. As with any project of this nature, we have enjoyed strengthening our relationships with other scholars and providing them with an opportunity to advance their work.

NOTES

1. Note the final chapter has been written by C. J. Janovy who is a journalist and author of *No Place Like Home: Lessons in Activism from Rural Kansas*. Our choice here is intentional, and points to the fact that there is a metro-normative bias in these studies (see Conner and Okamura forthcoming). It also was done to show how much sociology can benefit from other sources—art, journalism, philosophy, and elsewhere.

2. For more on this, please see Waskul, Dennis D. and Rebecca F. Plante. 2010. "Sex(ualities) and Symbolic Interaction." *Symbolic Interaction* 33(2):148–162.

3. Sociologically speaking, these studies were classified under the subheading of deviance and applied the framework of early symbolic interactionists (see Tannenbaum 1938, Lemert 1951, Kitsuse 1962, Erikson 1962, and Becker 1963).

4. This is not dissimilar to other studies in deviance such as Stanley Cohen's (1972) seminal work *Folk Devils and Moral Panics*.

5. While the editors of the text have been criticized for their overly thorough documentation at conferences, they feel it necessary to make a connection to this early scholarship, which may allow for a connection into other areas of sociology.

6. As suggested, by some, to the editors of this volume at conferences and in other professional settings.

7. The editors often find themselves in awkward positions having to defend the notion that the sociology of sport, subcultures, computer hackers, or other deviant subcultures are serious sites of academic inquiry.

8. One example is a particularly vicious attack made by Dusky Lee Smith (1965, 1973). See also Craig Calhoun's (2007) *Sociology in America: A History* (pp. 376–377).

9. This is similar to arguments that we live in a post-racial society (see Dawson and Bobo 2009).

10. Though, for many of these individuals, this has been to make up for income that has been lost due to the closure of gayborhood entertainment venues. Many drag queens, DJs, and others were hired as private contractors and paid below minimum wage. Likewise, bar owners who do not own the land they do business on are subject to the demands of landlords and are unable to withstand dry spells in the economy.

11. This chapter also picks up on a number of significant points on the importance of categories. As Ridolfo, Miller and Maitland (2012) have shown, this is a significant issue in survey data trying to ascertain an accurate picture of the LGBT population. However, such changes also have important political implications. We would also need to add to the references: Ridolfo, H., Miller, K. & Maitland, A. Measuring Sexual Identity Using Survey Questionnaires: How Valid Are Our Measures?. Sex Res Soc Policy 9, 113–124 (2012). https://doi.org/10.1007/s13178-011-0074-x.

REFERENCES

Adorno, Theodor W. 1975 [1967]. "Culture industry reconsidered." Translated by Anson G. Rabinbach *New German Critique* 6 (Fall):12–19.

Allegretto, Sylvia A. and Michelle M. Arthur. 2001. "An empirical analysis of homosexual/heterosexual earning differentials: Unmarried and unequal?" *Industrial and Labor Relations Review* 54(3):631–646.

Anderson, Elijah. 2011. *The Cosmopolitan Canopy: Race and Civility in Everyday Life*. New York: WW Norton and Company.

Anderson, Tammy. 2009. *Rave Culture: The Alteration and Decline of a Philadelphia Music Scene*. Philadelphia: Temple University Press.

Antonio, Robert J. 1981. "Immanent critique as the core of critical theory: Its origins and developments in Hegel, Marx and contemporary thought." *British Journal of Sociology* 330–345.

Barrett, Donald C. and Lance M. Pollack. 2005. "Whose gay community? Social class, sexual expression, and gay community involvement." *The Sociological Quarterly* 46(3):437–456.

Becker, Howard S. 1963. *Outsiders: Studies in the Sociology of Deviance*. New York: The Free Press of Glencoe.

Benjamin, Ruha. 2020. *A Sociology of the Future: Reimagining the Default Settings of Technology and Society*. Eastern Sociological Association Annual Meeting.

——. 2019. *Race After Technology: Abolitionist Tools for the New Jim Code*. Polity Press.

Brekhus, Wayne H. 2003. *Peacocks, Chameleons, Centaurs: Gay Suburbia and the Grammar of Social Identity*. Chicago: University of Chicago Press.

Buckland, Fiona. 2002. *Impossible Dance: Club Culture and Queer World-Making.* Middletown: Wesleyan.
Calhoun, Craig. 2007. *Sociology in America: A History.* Chicago: The University of Chicago Press.
Carter, David. 2010. *Stonewall: The Riots that Sparked the Gay Revolution.* New York: St. Martin's Griffin.
Castells, Manuel. 1983. *The City and the Grassroots: A Cross-cultural Theory of Urban Social Movements.* Berkeley: University of California Press.
Cervini, Eric. 2020. *The Deviant's War: The Homosexual VS the United States of America. Farrar, Straus and Giroux:* New York.
Chasin, Alexandra. 2000. *Selling Out: The Gay & Lesbian Movement Goes to Market.* New York: St. Martin's Press.
Choi, Kyung-Hee, Chong-suk Han, Jay Paul, and George Ayala. 2011. "Strategies for managing racism and homophobia among U.S. ethnic and racial minority men who have sex with men." *AIDS Education and Prevention* 23(2):145–158.
Cohen, Stanley. 1972. *Folk Devils and Moral Panics: The Creation of the Mods and Rockers.* New York: Routledge.
Dawson, Michael C. and Lawrence D. Bobo. 2009. "One year later and the myth of a post-racial society." *Du Bois Review: Social Science Research on Race* 6(2):247–249.
Deener, Andrew. 2012. *Venice: A Contested Bohemia in Los Angeles.* Chicago: University of Chicago Press.
Dickens, David and Andrea Fontana (eds). 1994. *Postmodernism and Social Inquiry.* New York: Taylor and Francis.
Dickson, E.J. 2020. "Virtual sex parties offer escape from isolation if organizers can find a home." *Rolling Stone* 15th April. Accessed 26 April (https://www.rollingstone.com/culture/culture-features/virtual-orgy-sex-party-zoom- nsfw-982785/).
Dunier, Mitchell. 1999. *Sidewalk.* New York: Farrar, Straus and Giroux.
Erickson, Kai T. 1962. "Notes on the Sociology of Deviance." *Social Problems* 9(4):307–314.
Edwards, Harry. 1973. *Sociology of Sport.* Homewood, IL: Dorsey.
Florida, Richard. 2005. *Cities and the Creative Class.* New York: Routledge.
Foster-Gimbel, Olivia and Renee Engeln. 2016. "Fat chance! Experiences and expectations of antifat bias in the gay male community." *Psychology of Sexual Orientation and Gender Diversity* 3(1):63–70.
Fredriksen-Goldsen, Karen I., Taryn Lindhorst, Susan P. Kemp, and Karina L. Walters. 2009. My Ever Dear": Social Work's Lesbian Foremothers A Call for Scholarship. *Affilia* 23:235–336.
Gamson, Joshua. 1995. "Must identity movements self-destruct? A queer dilemma." *Social Problems* 42(3):390–407.
Ghaziani, Amin. 2014. *There Goes the Gayborhood?* Princeton, NJ: Princeton University Press.
Guidotto, Nadia. 2006. "Cashing in on queers: From liberation to commodification." *Online Journal of Queer Studies in Education* 2(1).
Habermas, Jurgen. 1981. "New social movements." *Telos* 49(1):33–37.

Han, Chong-suk. 2008. "No Fats, Femmes, or Asians: The utility of critical race theory in examining the role of gay stock stories in the marginalization of gay Asian men." *Contemporary Justice Review* 11(1):11–12.

Hicklin, Aaron. 2012. "Nate silver: Person of the year." *Out Magazine*. Retrieved on June 21, 2016 (http://www.out.com/news-opinion/2012/12/18/nate-silver-person -year).

Horkheimer, Max and Theodore Adorno. [1944] 1982 *Dialectic of the Enlightenment*. New York: Continuum.

Humphreys, Laud. 1970. *Tearoom Trade: Impersonal Sex in Public Places*. New Brunswick, NJ: Aldine Transaction.

———. 1972. *Out of the Closets: The Sociology of Homosexual Liberation*. New York: Prentice-Hall.

Kahn, Andrew. 2020. "Conravirus diaries: I went to a sex party on zoom." *Slate* March 24. Accessed 26 April (https://slate.com/human-interest/2020/03/sex-party -zoom-coronavirus-quarantine.html).

Kitsuse, John I. 1962. "Societal reaction to deviant behavior: Problems of theory and method." *Social Problems* 9 (Winter):247–256.

Kuhn, Thomas. 1962. *The Structure of Scientific Revolutions*. Chicago, IL: University of Chicago Press.

Lemert, Edwin M. 1951. *Social Pathology*. New York: McGraw-Hill Book Company.

Levine, Martin P. 1998. *Gay Macho: The Life and Death of the Homosexual Clone*. New York: NYU Press.

Lloyd, Richard. 2006. *Neo-Bohemia*. New York: Routledge.

Marcuse, Herbert. 1964. *One Dimensional Man*. New York: Routledge.

———. 1977. *The Aesthetic Dimension: Toward A Critique of Marxist Aesthetics*. Boston, MA: Beacon Press.

Maddux, Stu. 2011. *Gen Silent*. DVD. New York: Frameline.

Mattson, Greggor. 2019. "Are gay bars closing? Using business listings to infer rates of gay bar closure in the United States, 1977-2019." *Socius: Sociological Research for a Dynamic World* 5(1):2378023119894832.

Mattson, Greggor. 2020. "Shuttered by the coronavirus, many gay bars—already struggling—are now on life support." *Conversation* 14 April. Accessed 26 April (https://theconversation.com/shuttered-by-the-coronavirus-many-gay-bars-already -struggling- are-now-on-life-support-135167).

Meyer, Doug. 2012. "An intersectional analysis of lesbian, gay, bisexual, and transgender people's evaluations of anti-queer violence." *Gender & Society* 26(6):849–873.

Mulvey, Laura. 1975. "Visual please and narrative cinema." *Screen* 16(3):6–18.

Piccone, Paul. 1978. "The crisis of one-dimensionality." *Telos* 35(1):43–54.

Pichardo, Nelson A. 1997. "New social movements: A critical review." *Annual Review of Sociology* 23:441–430.

Rabinovitz, Lauren. 2012. *Electric Dreamland: Amusement Parks, Movies, and American Modernity*. New York: Columbia University Press.

Smith, Dusky Lee. 1965. "Sociology and the rise of corporate capitalism." *Science & Society* 29(4):401–418. http://www.jstor.org/stable/40401148.

Smith, Dusky Lee. 1973. "Symbolic interactionism." *Catalyst* (Winter): 62–76.

Tannenbaum, Frank. 1938. *Crime and the Community.* New York: Ginn and Co.

Thornton, Sarah. 1995. *Club Cultures: Music, Media, and Subcultural Capital.* Polity Press.

Valocchi, Steve. 1999. "The class-inflected nature of gay identity." *Social Problems* 46(2):207–224.

Warner, Michael. 1999. *The Trouble with Normal: Sex, Politics, and the Ethics of Queer Life.* Cambridge: Harvard University Press.

Warren, Carol A. B. 1974. *Identity and Community in the Gay World.* New York: Wiley.

Weinberg, Martin S. and Colin J. Williams. 1974. *Male Homosexuals: Their Problems and Adaptations.* New York: Oxford University Press.

Weston, Kath. 1995. "Get thee to a big gay city." *GLQ: A Journal of Lesbian and Gay Studies* 2(3):253–277.

Willis, Paul. 1977. "*Learning to Labor: How Working-Class Kids Get Working Class Jobs.*" New York: Columbia University Press.

Woo, Jamie. 2013. *Meet Grindr.* Toronto, Canada: Jamie Woo.

Wood, Mitchell J. 2004. "The gay male gaze: Body image disturbance and gender oppression among gay men." *Journal of Gay & Lesbian Social Services* 17(2):43–62.

Žižek, Slavoj. 1997. "Multiculturalism, or, the cultural logic of multinational capitalism." *New Left Review* (225):28–51.

Chapter 1

Performative Progressiveness

Accounting for New Forms of Inequality in the Gayborhood

Adriana Brodyn and Amin Ghaziani

Attitudes[1] toward homosexuality have liberalized since the 1990s (Loftus 2001), and the trend has continued into the present (Twenge et al. 2015). This trajectory in public opinion is positive (Saad 2010), but it conceals subtle forms of prejudice. Recent research finds that heterosexuals are willing to extend "formal rights" to same-sex couples, policies like family leave, hospital visitation, inheritance rights, and insurance benefits, but they are unwilling to grant them "informal privileges" (Doan et al. 2014:1172) such as the freedom to express affection in public places by holding hands or sharing a kiss. How does this misalignment between progressive attitudes and actions—this resistance to basic acts of human intimacy and citizenship (Hubbard 2013)—express itself on the shared streets of a city neighborhood?

Social scientists traditionally rely on survey (Westbrook and Saperstein 2015), newspaper (Schilt and Westbrook 2009), experimental (Doan et al. 2014), or other quantitative data (Andersen and Fetner 2008) to assess public opinion about gays and lesbians, including matters related to the decriminalization of consensual sex (Engel 2013), hate crime legislation (Jenness and Grattet 2001), and marriage equality (Brewer 2014; Herek 2006). Humanists make historical (Canaday 2009; Hanhardt 2013) and critical arguments (Duggan 2003; Halberstam 2012; Warner 1991) about inequality and discrimination that are often abstracted from the specific contexts in which straights and sexual minorities interact. These studies nevertheless have produced important conceptual insights, and we build on them with our sensitivity to three features of social life. First, attitudes are an imperfect predictor of behavior (Ajzen and Fishbein 1980; Fishbein and Ajzen 1975). This widely replicated insight from social psychology prompts us to imagine liberal dispositions toward homosexuality as a starting point for new lines of inquiry rather than an outcome that we seek to explain. Second, statistical renderings of public opinion are powerful for the descriptions they offer, but quantitative assessments mask how people perceive one another as neighbors (Rich 2009). To understand how attitudes and actions misalign in the city, we use qualitative data on "cultural practices" (Greene 2014:108) to explain the contradictions between positive public opinions and persistent prejudice. Third and related, scholarly accounts of bias, especially the contact hypothesis (Allport 1954; Herek and Glunt 1993; Sherif 1956), predict that hostility will diminish as members of the majority interact with minority groups (Cullen et al. 2002; Plugge-Foust and Strickland 2000; Raiz 2006). The persistence of prejudice in a shared residential environment, one that offers opportunities for sustained face-to-face interactions, presents a special explanatory challenge: this is precisely the setting where we would expect it to recede (Ihlanfeldt and Scafidi 2002; Putnam 2000).

We hypothesize that the actively unfolding "beyond the closet" (Seidman 2002), "new gay" (Savin-Williams 2005), "post-gay" (Ghaziani 2011), "postmo" (Nash 2013), "postcloseted cultural context" (Dean 2014), or the "post-marriage equality world" (NeJaime 2016), terms that describe in common a climate of greater societal acceptance of homosexuality, will put pressure on heterosexuals to curb explicit displays of prejudice against gays and lesbians. Implicit forms of animus will linger; however, since they represent a safety valve-like "response to problem situations" (Gross 2009:366), such as threats to whether others accurately perceive a person's liberalism and tolerance. To explore sexual prejudice in the contemporary moment, we focus on straight residents who live in demographically integrating gay neighborhoods (Spring 2013). Our objective is to develop the concept of "performative progressiveness" (Ghaziani 2014:255) by describing a set of narrative strategies that these people employ when occupying gay and lesbian urban-cultural spaces. How do heterosexuals navigate the tension between what they believe about homosexuality and how they act toward their gay and lesbian neighbors? By elaborating on the empirical variability of what prior research has assumed to be an undifferentiated theoretical concept, we show how advances toward social equality can be undermined, even in a context of observed improvement in public opinion.

ATTITUDES, ACTIONS, AND PLACEMAKING

Opinion researchers have identified a dramatic liberalization in attitudes toward homosexuality (Andersen and Fetner 2008; Brewer 2007; Werum and Winders 2001; Yang 1997). Such rapid transformations in public perceptions are rare (Page and Shapiro 1992). In this instance, the outcome stems from generational turnover alongside broad shifts in which the entire population has adjusted its outlook toward lesbians and gay men (Flores 2014). These developments have had measurable impacts in presidential elections (Brooks 2000; Brooks and Manza 2006), public policy (Burstein 1998, 1999), media visibility of gays and lesbians (Walters 2001), Supreme Court decisions (Murdoch and Price 2001), civil rights claims (Sherrill and Yang 2000; Wilcox and Wolpert 2000; Wood and Bartkowski 2004), and residential preferences (Ghaziani 2015a).

Underlying this work is an assumption about the effects of contact: Exposure should reduce negative attitudes that members of the majority hold toward a stigmatized minority group (Smith et al. 2009). The sociological antecedents of the contact hypothesis originate in Robert Park's writings on the "progressive and irreversible" course of the race relations cycle, which proceeds from contact to competition, accommodation, and assimilation (Park 1950:150). Early research that applied Park's framework to sexuality found that it applied beyond race: Heterosexuals who knew gays and lesbians reported more positive attitudes than those who lacked such contacts (Herek 1988).

A number of studies since then have documented the effects of contact on lowering negative attitudes toward lesbians and gay men (Costa et al. 2015; Hicks and Lee 2006). Most use survey data to measure "abstract values" (Henry and Reyna 2007:275), or idealizations that influence behavior. However, as Loftus (2001) argues, "how one responds to a survey question concerning attitudes toward a group will not accurately reflect how the respondent will act when encountering an individual from that group" (p. 763). What we *should* do, in other words, is not always what we *actually* do. To evaluate the discomfort that heterosexuals experience in the presence of gays and lesbians, Monto and Supinski (2014) presented their study participants with hypothetical scenarios that described everyday interactions. When placed in scenarios of such "imagined contact" (Miles and Crisp 2014), they found that "subtle and more socially acceptable levels of homonegativity" appeared among heterosexuals (p. 903). Their study draws attention to the limits of contact, and it raises questions about the forms that homonegativity takes when societal acceptance of homosexuality is at historically high levels (Seidman 2002; Ghaziani 2011; Dean 2014).

Homonegativity is a specific form of prejudice against nonheterosexuals (Lottes and Grollman 2010). It is especially difficult to explain among straight residents of gay neighborhoods (Florida 2002; Nash 2013). Some scholars have used the dissimilarity index to show declining rates of sexual segregation in these areas of the city (Spring 2013), while others have documented how interactions between straight and gay people produce tolerance for diversity and difference (Gorman-Murray and Waitt 2009) as well as pro-equality sensibilities (Kanai and Kenttamaa-Squires 2015). Ghaziani (2014) asked straight identified individuals who live in urban gay districts, or "gayborhoods," about their attitudes toward their gay and lesbian neighbors. He found a disjuncture between liberal positions on sexuality and conservative, at times even homonegative behaviors on the ground. To explain the puzzle, he introduces the concept of "performative progressiveness," which he defines as "a blissful but non-malicious ignorance about sexual inequality" (p. 255). Some straights in the study live in a gayborhood and espouse supportive attitudes toward gays and lesbians; yet, they behave in ways that contradict those sentiments.

The Gay and Lesbian Alliance against Defamation (GLAAD) issued an "Accelerating Acceptance Report" in February 2015, which replicated Ghaziani's observations. The nationally representative survey found that "beneath progress lies a layer of uneasiness and discomfort. While the public is increasingly embracing LGBT civil rights and equal protection under the law, many are still uncomfortable with having LGBT people in their families and the communities where they live" (Stokes 2015:2). Fifty-six percent of heterosexual Americans are uncomfortable or very uncomfortable attending a same-sex wedding (34 percent uncomfortable, 22 percent very uncomfortable); 43 percent are uncomfortable bringing a child to a same-sex wedding; and 36 percent are uncomfortable seeing same-sex couples hold hands. The GLAAD report frames the key problem that motivates our study: sexual prejudice remains, despite changing public opinion and legal strides toward gay and lesbian rights—but its forms are subtle and difficult to detect.

The idea of an interactive performance, central to the study of gender and sexuality (Butler 1990a,b; West and Zimmerman 1987) and sociology as a discipline (Goffman 1959), is at the core of these observations. When a straight person "plays a part" of a liberal resident in the "setting" of a gay neighborhood, she hopes that others will "believe the[ir] character" (Goffman 1959:10,13). This is easier to do in theory than it is in practice, which accounts for sentiments like "It's okay to be gay, just don't touch each other" (Hawkins 2015). The concept of performative progressiveness isolates "armchair allies" (Moskowitz 2015) for analysis: straights who say they are open-minded about homosexuality but whose behavior betrays a sexual ethnocentrism, or heterocentrism. These people are not overtly homophobic but neither are they marching in the streets for gay rights.

We use performative progressiveness as a case to describe the spatial expressions of community life (Lefebvre [1974] 1991; Putnam 2000; Sampson 2012) and inequality (Castells 1983; Lauria and Knopp 1985; Wacquant 2008). Research on placemaking points to the "innumerable dramas" (Centner 2008:218) that city living creates for its residents (Gans 1962).

We bridge these insights from urban studies with research on sexuality and public opinion to detail the narrative strategies that straights in the gayborhood deploy to maintain a progressive self-image while sidestepping critical—not to mention self-incriminating—questions about what types of resources minority group members require in order to live and thrive in the safe spaces that their neighborhoods provide (Evans and Boyte 1986; Hanhardt 2013). The concept of performative progressiveness also highlights conflicting visions of place, especially how residents with power and privilege recraft cultural enclaves into "Disneyfied" commodities (Zukin 1995) and strip them of their cultural and political significance (Greene 2014; Orne 2017; Rushbrook 2002) in a neoliberal context of individualism. As more straights view the gayborhood as the "final frontier of diversity" (Florida 2002:13), scholars will need to account for the new forms of inequality that arise within them.

RESEARCH DESIGN AND DATA

Unlike many accounts of public opinion that rely on quantitative methods, we exploit the unique strengths of qualitative approaches—interviews with straight residents of two gay neighborhoods in Chicago, specifically—to describe the divergence between liberal attitudes and homonegative actions on the ground. There are lively debates about our methodological decision. Some scholars argue that interviews capture ex post facto explanations for what people have already done or thought (Vaisey 2008). Others decry an attitudinal fallacy: what people say is a poor predictor of what they do (Jerolmack and Khan 2014). Surveys can capture the prevalence of an attitude (Becker 1954) and snap-judgments (Vaisey 2009)—in a feelings thermometer about integration, for example—but this data exists at an individual level (Swidler 2008) and is abstracted from lived experiences. When ethnographers encounter interview data, they raise questions about the situated nature of social life (Becker and Geer 1957). What does it feel like to be a straight person living next door to a lesbian or gay man? Or to walk down rainbow-lined streets alongside same-sex couples holding hands? We, like others (Monto and Supinski 2014; Miles and Crisp 2014), show the counterintuitive yet innovative inferential possibilities of interview data to capture the interactional tones of social life, provided that researchers ask about groups of people, specific situations, and concrete personal experiences—even if we ourselves were not around when the action occurred.

Chicago is "perhaps the most studied city in the world" (Lloyd 2006:14), one that has inspired its own brand of urban sociology (Park and Burgess 1925). Its history of sexuality, however, is vastly underwritten in comparison to the "vanguard cities" of New York and San Francisco (Stewart-Winter 2016:2). This makes it a compelling site for a case study. The city has two gay neighborhoods: Boystown, a commercial and nightlife district located in the East Lakeview neighborhood, and Andersonville, a historically Swedish section of the Edgewater neighborhood located to the north of Boystown. In 1997, Chicago became the first city in the United States to municipally mark its gay district. Using taxfunded dollars, city officials installed rainbow pylons along North Halsted Street in Boystown. Residents recognize Andersonville as another "queer space" (Betsky 1997). Both areas are "so strongly gay and lesbian identified that even the straight denizens of these 'hoods admit that they live in a gay neighborhood" (Bergquist and McDonald 2006:vii). According to the 2010 American Community Survey, half of Illinois's estimated 25,710 unmarried partner households are in Chicago's Cook County. Of this group, 40 percent reside in the four northernmost lakefront neighborhoods, which includes Lakeview (1,106 households or 12 percent of the city's total) and Edgewater (951, 10.3 percent).[2]

Gender and sexuality scholars have shown that we need to examine dominant groups to understand a system of inequality (Connell 1992). Therefore, the analysis of sexual inequality in the city requires us to ponder the perspectives of heterosexuals who live in a gayborhood. The data for our study comprise fifty-three snowball-sampled interviews that the second author conducted with straight residents of Andersonville and Boystown. Respondents come from diverse backgrounds, and their occupations span from students and waiters to attorneys, physicians, professors, social workers, flight attendants, bartenders, dog walkers, and the unemployed. Interviews averaged fifty-one minutes and ranged from twenty-five to eighty minutes. The second author transcribed each interview, which produced 1,573 pages of textual data. Table 1.1 describes the demographic characteristics of the sample, especially those features that scholars who study sexual geographies commonly emphasize (Anacker and Morrow-Jones 2005; Gates and Ost 2004). Compared to Andersonville, the Boystown sample is younger, less partnered, and less established in the neighborhood—yet, with more owners, women, and more racially diverse.

The second author organized a portion of the interview protocol around newspaper articles that captured a range of interactional dynamics in contemporary gayborhoods. One story from the *San Francisco Chronicle* was titled "SF's Castro District Faces an Identity Crisis: As Straights Move In, Some Fear Loss of the Area's Character." The article includes a photograph of a woman, whom the reader is to assume is straight, pushing a baby carriage on Castro Street, a rainbow flag visible behind her. The second author read out loud the following passage:

Table 1.1 Interview Profiles

	Boystown Residents	Andersonville Residents	Public Officials
Age	Average: 34 years	Average: 38 years	Average: 41 years
	Range: 24–59 years	Range: 30–54 years	Range: 39–45 years
Sex	9 men (36%)	11 men (44%)	3 women (100%)
	16 women (64%)	14 women (56%)	
Race/Ethnicity	21 Whites (84%)	22 Whites (88%)	3 Whites (100%)
	1 Hispanic/Latino (4%)	3 multiracial (12%)	
	3 Multiracial (12%)		
Relationship Status	6 singles (24%)	7 singles (28%)	1 single (33%)
	19 partnered (76%)	18 partnered (72%)	2 partnered (67%)
	6 with kids (24%)	10 with kids (40%)	2 with kids (67%)
Residential Status	10 renters (40%)	12 renters (48%)	3 owners (100%)
	15 owners (60%)	13 owners (52%)	
Residential Duration	Average: 5.8 years	Average: 5.9 years	Average: 11.7 years
	Range: 1–13 years	Range: 0.25–20 years	Range: 10–15 years
N	25	25	3

To walk down San Francisco's Castro street—where men casually embrace on sidewalks in the shadow of an enormous rainbow flag—the neighborhood's status as a "gay Mecca" seems obvious. But up and down the enclave that has been a symbol of gay culture for more than three decades, heterosexuals are moving in. They have come to enjoy some of the same amenities that have attracted the neighborhood's many gay and lesbian residents: charming houses, convenient public transportation, safe streets and nice weather.

Drawing on the principle of triangulation, the second author followed the same procedure with a second story that was published in the *New York Times* and entitled "TURF: Edged Out by the Stroller Set." The piece also includes a photograph of a woman with a baby stroller with two presumably gay men on either side of her who have been wedged apart. The second author read out loud the following excerpt:

It was supposed to be a kind of homecoming. Last year, Chris Skroupa and John Wilson sold their apartment in Hudson Heights, in northern Manhattan, and moved to Chelsea, where, as a gay couple, they already spent most of their time socializing. But they soon discovered that the neighborhood was changing faster than they expected. Home prices were rising, and many of their friends were moving to Hell's Kitchen, a few blocks west of Times Square. In restaurants that used to be almost exclusively gay, they noticed an influx of straight customers, often with children in strollers. On a recent Saturday, Mr. Skroupa and Mr. Wilson went out for brunch and "literally less than one-third of the restaurant was gay," Mr. Skroupa said last week, pausing between bench presses at a New York Sports Club on Eighth Avenue.

The final story comes from *The Huffington Post*, and it describes a local controversy in Chicago. The piece was titled "Boystown Gay Bar Bans Bachelorette Parties":

Bar owner Geno Zaharakis sat one busy evening at the window of his gay night-club, watching as groups of straight women celebrating bachelorette parties made their way along a strip of bars in Chicago's gay-friendly "Boystown" neighbor-hood. That's when he made a decision now posted for all to see: "No Bachelorette Parties." Though the small sign has been there for years, it's suddenly making a big statement amid the national debate over gay marriage. While most gay bars continue to welcome the raucous brides to be, Zaharakis's bar Cocktail is fighting for what he sees as a fundamental right, and his patrons - along with some peeved bachelorettes - are taking notice. "I'm totally losing money because of it, but I don't want the money," Zaharakis said. "I would rather not have the money than host an event I didn't believe in." Gay bars are popular with bachelorettes, both for the over-the-top drag shows that some offer and for the ability to let loose in a place where women are unlikely to be groped or ogled.

This innovative interviewing strategy has several advantages. First, each scenario describes groups of people, specific situations, and concrete personal experiences, including men embracing on sidewalks, straight couples pushing strollers, bodies brunching, and bachelorette parties. Crafting questions in this manner enabled the second author to use interview data to make inferences about imagined contact (Miles and Crisp 2014) and quotidian interactions (Monto and Supinski 2014). Using media headlines, photos, and texts as an "indirect questioning technique" to measure "truthful responses to sensitive questions" also reduces social desirability bias (Rosenfeld et al. 2016:783) since respondents can offer comments about the characters and scenarios in a story without implicating themselves personally.

Like Goffman (1959), we try "to see through the act" (p. 10) of a progressive sensibility. Our analytic goal was to create a typology of the conditions under which a progressive performance fails, along with a corresponding conception of queer space that each respective condition implies. To accomplish this, we followed five steps. First, we used NVivo to read our interview transcripts line by line and asked: What is this statement or expression an example of? We applied conceptual labels, or codes, to attitudinal claims (what people say) and behavioral expressions (what people do) of acceptance and homonegativity. Data reduction was our goal in this initial stage of analysis. Second, we followed a "loop-like pattern of multiple rounds of revisiting the data" (Frechtling and Sharp 1997) to identify emerging patterns. This stage involved a focus on the "recurring regularities" (Miles and Huberman 1994:246) of our codes, including narrative consistencies, metaphors and analogies, symbols, and topics that our respondents avoided (Ryan and Bernard 2003). It was here that we began to create a typology of performative progressiveness and their implications for urban placemaking. In the third stage of analysis, we linked our theoretical concepts (contact, acceptance, performance, homonegativity, and place) with empirical themes using visualization techniques like data tables and thematic networks (Attride-Stirling 2001). These pattern-making exercises are qualitative versions of factor analysis; they assist researchers in grouping a large number of observed measurements into fewer unobserved conceptual categories (Miles and Huberman 1994:256). Once we identified our major themes, we asked in a penultimate step how those themes were related to theoretical debates (Zhang and Wildemuth 2009). Finally, we interpreted our findings vis-a-vis our research questions.

We now turn to the results. We begin by demonstrating our sample's positive attitudes about gays and lesbians. From here, we provide evidence for four narrative strategies that heterosexuals use as they navigate queer urban-cultural spaces.

RESULTS

Attitudes toward Homosexuality

The majority of straight residents in our sample say that they support gay people. Their advocacy takes several forms: acknowledging a common humanity with gays and lesbians, backing their rights, endorsing urban spaces that are culturally associated with them, and supporting integration. Next, we discuss each in turn.

Many straight residents felt a common humanity with gay men and lesbians. One thirty-year-old female resident of Andersonville remarked, "I think people make too big a deal about people being gay . . . Gay people are people." With this tautology—gay people are people—she signaled a cultural sameness that she feels with gays and lesbians. A fifty-two-year-old male respondent in the same area described gay relationships as emblematic of "sexual diversity, rather than something being wrong [with them]." Like the first respondent, he too concluded universally that "we're all just people." A third, younger man of age thirty-nine years mused on a milieu of acceptance and asked in disbelief, "Is there anybody left in this country who actually has a problem with this? . . . I can't believe that anybody would get upset about homosexuality in this day and age."

Identifying with their gay and lesbian neighbors as "just people" prompted straights to support their rights as well, especially marriage equality (which was not yet legal at the time of the interviews). "My take on gay marriage," one female resident of Andersonville began, "is that all the ridiculousness around saying that marriage is for a man and a woman . . . at some point we're going to look back and be like, 'oh, my God! How stupid were we that it took us so long to do that?'" A straight man in Boystown echoed, "The idea of straight people saying that if two gay people get married, it's a threat to the institution, it's the most ludicrous thing. I mean, fifty-two percent of all straight marriages end in divorce. What kind of sacred thing is going on here?"

Straight residents also agreed with the city of Chicago's decision to mark Boystown as a formal gayborhood. "It did strike me that this was an official kind of thing that someone had to sponsor or approve," said a woman in Andersonville, "and it seemed impressive to me that the city had either sponsored or gone along with something to recognize that this was a gay area and promote gay pride." Another woman in the same neighborhood agreed, "As far as marking the neighborhood and marking this as a place where a lot of gay Chicago residents live, I think it's great."

Finally, straights expressed positive attitudes about integration. A female resident of Andersonville described gayborhoods as places where people can "thrive together." She explained, "I think Andersonville . . . [is] a very successful neighborhood . . . There are a lot of gay and lesbian families and single people, and there are gay businesses, and there are children—child-friendly places and gay bars—and they're all there together. I think it's the future." Sexual integration creates a "welcoming," "inclusive," and "open" environment, other residents remarked. Many straights defined this as progress. A man in Andersonville said, "I remember walking down Halsted and feeling like I am not in Kansas anymore. I'm in a real city now where you'll see stuff like this and where you have this level of diversity and openness and progressive liberal thought."

Attitudinal claims like these show rhetorical support for gay people, their legal rights, geographic spaces, and demographic trends of integration. But these liberal stances often lack behavioral backing. Scholars call this bifurcated outcome "performative progressiveness" (Ghaziani 2014), and our data document its empirical variations.

Performative Progressiveness

Our analysis shows four ways in which liberal straight residents of gay neighborhoods manage the dilemmas that arise for them when they enter minority spaces: spatial entitlement, rhetorical moves, political absolution, and affect.

Spatial Entitlements

Spatial entitlements are ways of enacting dominant social position in specific places (Bourdieu 1984). Especially apparent in this mode is a belief among some heterosexual residents that they should have unrestricted access to gayborhoods, along with the "cool" commodities (Rushbrook 2002) and "chic" (Collins 2004) social spaces within them, while denying their own sense of entitlement. Consider a personal story that one male interviewee in his late thirties relayed: "Right after our daughter was born, we needed to get out of the house for a nice, really long walk. And we ended up over in Boystown. We were starting to get hungry, and so we were going to stop for dinner. Went to this restaurant, but we walked in with a stroller, and it was like, you know how you have that proverbial scratching of the music when somebody walks in the door? It was literally like all the heads turned, and we were like, maybe we shouldn't be here." Straight couples like this are aware of their outsider status in a culturally queer space, yet, many ignore it. The man decided, "This place looks nice. There's not really that much around here [that interests us]. Let's just stay." But their baby stroller marked them as heterosexual. "They didn't have a child seat, high chair," he complained. "They wanted us to put the stroller outside on the sidewalk. I mean, it was just like all these things," he sighed. "We're just kind of like, all right, fine. We're not going to stay here. We're going to get out. So, it was almost like they went out of their way to make us feel not welcome." Expectations of open access are key characteristics of spatial entitlements. These assumptions are violated in the aforementioned incident, as conflict unfolds around the stroller, which is a symbol of heterosexual presence in gayborhoods. Underlying the restlessness is a conception of gayborhoods as apolitical, neoliberal, commodity spaces (Binnie and Skeggs 2004) that the "noveau cosmopolitan citizen" (Nash and Gorman-Murray 2014:759) should be able to freely access and enjoy.

Because spatial entitlements conceal the political dimensions of queer spaces, they are characterized by another assumption: straights have the power to shape the tone of an area. A thirty-six-year-old male interviewee noted, "I don't want to be *that* guy or *that* family . . . [who] came in and wield[ed] our power in the neighborhood." Unlike the overtly bigoted, those who perform progressiveness are quick to highlight how they do not exert power in the same way as an imagined, generalized other (Mead 1934). The straights who enter queer spaces and exert their privilege are defined as culturally insensitive outsiders, as the following thirty-two-year-old female interviewee described: "It's not so much [all] families; it's privileged, upper middle-class families moving in because these neighborhoods are cool or interesting but then trying to strong-arm [them]: we want this type of restaurant, we want baby stores, and we want, you know, lots of lots of things, we want sports bars, we want these sorts of businesses."

Straights who express a liberal sensibility use spatial entitlements to distinguish themselves from other "strong-arm" straight people, yet both groups assume that they have the power to shape the character, composition, complexion, or tone of the area. Our respondents think of themselves as benevolent individuals who would never "wield" their power, but research shows that they transform gay neighborhoods into "visible niche markets for retail commerce and realty speculation" (Hanhardt 2008:65). The mechanism of change is a difference in tastes about the built environment: straight residents prefer large chain stores, which threaten "the cultural icons of queer neighborhoods" (Doan and Higgins 2011:16).

Lastly, spatial entitlements describe how straights consume gay neighborhoods in a "cosmopolitan buffet" (Rushbrook 2002:188). Gay people enter an area, "make it nice," and then straight individuals and families benefit from their efforts. This is a familiar and wide-reaching narrative on the streets. One female interviewee in her mid-twenties stated, "This is going to be a horrible example, but the [Boystown] neighborhood was 'Queer Eye for a Straight Guy'd' and now everyone's like, 'Great, let's move in because it's ready' type of a thing." Her phrase "let's move in because it's ready" suggests that many straights shift the burden of urban revitalization onto gay people. Only after they have done the groundwork do straights come in and reap the rewards. One white Andersonville resident, a male in his late forties, noted, "When a neighborhood becomes more gay, there seems to be a cleaning up of the neighborhood. There seems to be a beautification of the neighborhood. And that's a draw." Consider another example: "There's a trope," began a thirty-two-year-old female interviewee. "I've heard it over and over—of gay people moving into a neighborhood and making it really cool and a really great place to live, and then straight people coming in and messing it up, and then gay people needing to move somewhere else." Another white female in her early forties added that the presence of gays also creates safer neighborhoods, which is appealing: "Gays have done a nice job of gentrifying certain neighborhoods, and that makes it feel safe for straight couples, especially with kids." All these statements are consistent with scholarly accounts about the social relations that transpire in gentrifying neighborhoods (Brown-Saracino 2009; Knopp 1990). Some heterosexuals are aware that gay neighborhoods provide safe spaces to sexual minorities, but this recognition does little to influence their occupation of the area. One female respondent reflected, "I don't know if it's an irony or a paradox, but people who had gone there to try and create their own space, in some ways separate, deliberately so, or at least a place that they could define and create, then gets invaded by families who say, 'Oh, they made it all nice. Oh, it's pretty. Oh, there are some cute stores here.'"

In summary, spatial entitlements describe beliefs about access to space, feelings of ownership, assumptions about power and privilege, and acts of consumerism that enable straights to occupy spaces that are designated as culturally queer in a way that feels inclusive but noninvasive and nonexploitative. The belief that gay people may have a reason to create and then protect their own spaces arises in some occasions, but even when it does, this supportive attitude among straight residents seldom translates into critical self-reflection, let alone pause, about their presence in those very same spaces.

Rhetorical Moves

The second narrative device, rhetorical moves, builds on a principle of linguistic relativity (Sapir 1929; Whorf and Carroll 1956; Whorf 1940) to highlight the conditional nature of acceptance. Our analysis shows several variants: First, some straights restrict their acceptance of homosexuality toward a heteronormative subset of gays and lesbians (Duggan 2003). Second, rhetorical moves urge gays and lesbians to abdicate what makes them culturally distinct. A third component is the strategic use of diversity to define homosexuality as a desirable expression of urban difference, in contrast to racial and ethnic minorities. Finally, straights also use the language of diversity to reframe the meaning of inclusion and allow charges of reverse discrimination. In this section, we consider each subtype of rhetorical moves.

Although some straights claim a progressive stance on matters related to gay and lesbian rights, they qualify their acceptance by admitting that they are uncomfortable with "those" people who are "in your face," as a male respondent in his early thirties said, "I don't like it when people are putting on too much of a show all the time. I just want to go to a place where people are relaxed and they're not trying to prove something . . . That 'in your face' stuff, it makes me feel a little bit uncomfortable." In this example, "in your face" is a rhetorical move that stigmatizes gay and lesbians who fall outside the charmed circle (Rubin 1993) of sexual restraint. The respondent and his female partner were pleased when a sexually explicit gay nightclub in Boystown—called "The Manhole"—closed while a "less obvious" business—named "Hydrate"—opened in its place: "The sexuality has diminished. I would say it's much less obvious, like, the leather-wearing and that kind of [stuff]." Implied in their pleasure is an understanding of Boystown as a sanitized place, rather than one that celebrates queer cultural communities that form around sex (Orne 2017).

Rhetorical moves celebrate gains for equality—but with a caveat. Gays and lesbians should adopt heteronormative ideals and embrace monogamy, marriage, and children. "This is what you wanted," a male respondent argued while aggressively waving his index finger in the second author's face during the interview. "*You* wanted equality. *You* wanted your rights. *You* wanted to get married. This is it!" The respondent wanted gays to soften their differences. "If my gay neighbors upstairs decided to adopt, I would hope that they would come to me to learn how to change a diaper. Why not? I mean, I have the experience. This is what you want. This is what I would want." An emphasis on mainstream values like marriage and childrearing exclude radical and sexualized aspects of queer cultures. Not a single heterosexual resident remarked on kinship structures, bathhouses, or the connective and communal powers of sex.

In a third variation, straights deploy diversity discourse to allow themselves to celebrate tolerance, a notion that overgeneralizes support based on attitudes toward a narrow segment of gay people (Walters 2014). A male interviewee drew a comparison with race to reflect on the meaning of urban diversity: "In terms of ethnicity, it's a way of white people being able to say that they live in a diverse neighborhood without it being racially diverse. . . . I think it's part of the appeal because they can say, 'Look how diverse it is,' and yet it's not necessarily ethnically diverse." The logic is the same for sexuality and race. He continued, "I think that that's part of the appeal of both [gay] neighborhoods . . . It's a way of saying we live in a very diverse neighborhood . . . White liberals can make a claim to diversity without having to actually live around ethnic minorities." Consider another brief example from a male interviewee in his late thirties who said directly, "The reason that straight people want to live in these neighborhoods is that they're white liberals who want to make a claim to diversity without having to live around ethnic minorities." Data from the 2014 ACS support this intuition: 79.7 percent of residents in Lakeview (the neighborhood that houses Boystown) identified as white, 7.3 percent as Hispanic or Latino, 3.5 percent as black, and 6.8 percent as Asian, and 2.7 percent as other.[3]

Many straight residents of gay neighborhoods use diversity to reframe the meaning of inclusion in a way that enables a charge of reverse discrimination. For example, when a local gay-owned bakery instituted a no-child policy for their business, some straights felt discriminated against, and they criticized the business for creating an exclusive space. One female resident with children explained how she felt attacked by the policy: "I'd really love a scone because it's half-price scone day. But it's impossible to get your stroller in there, with the two doors the way they are, and also with the small size. So, you don't even bother to go in there. It makes me feel sad. I do feel discriminated against." Another couple with a child described how several straight friends of theirs perceived the policy: "We know a lot of families, [and] we felt like it [the no-child policy] was excluding us in a neighborhood where nobody's [supposed to be] excluded."

Straights who perform progressiveness imagine gay neighborhoods and their businesses as spaces where everyone is welcome, rather than specific sites of queer cultures and communities. In response to experiencing spaces as closed off to them, some straights felt that they were targets of discrimination. They accused gays and lesbians who advocated for queer spaces as "segregationist," "separatist," and "heterophobic." Each rhetorical move positions the straight "victim" as a member of marginalized group. A thirty-three-year-old female interviewee argued, "To me, that gets a bit segregationist. It's like—is 'heterophobic' a word?—I've definitely felt the 'oh, I'm a breeder,' . . . 'oh, breeders are moving in' mentality [and] that . . . piss[es] me off because I've been called 'breeder' one too many times." Another respondent linked this strategy to diversity, "We talk about diversity, and we talk about black people versus white people, like, racially getting along, and people really want that. It seems to me that by calling this out, it's like, 'No, don't come into our space. We just want our own space,' which feels like a little bit of a diversity issue or, for lack of a better word, being racist for straight people." Drawing on racialized discourses, rhetorical moves allow straights to think of themselves as targets of "racism for straight people."

Accusations of reverse discrimination are unconvincing because there is no structural system that supports anti-heterosexuality. Heterosexism and homophobia are institutional logics that heterosexuals have designed and that they control. They are unidirectional. Sexual minorities are responding to this system when they react against straights who move into gay neighborhoods and make claims on the area and its businesses. Cries of "straight racism" are illogical because gay people cannot institutionalize "homosexism" and "heterophobia," while cries of reverse discrimination disavow the cultural autonomy of queer spaces. More broadly, our findings about rhetorical moves suggest that straight residents see the gayborhood as a marker of cosmopolitanism, diversity, and economic competitiveness—but they are bereft to see gay people as targets of exploitation.

Political Absolution

The third expression of performative progressiveness, political absolution, emphasizes inaction, a phenomenon that is part of a larger American culture of political avoidance and apathy (Eliasoph 1998). In this section, we specify three findings that show how straights absolve themselves from political solidarity with the gay community, despite coming into contact with its members in a shared residential context: a "gay-blindness" toward inequality, solidarity exemptions, and redefining solidarity as place-based mere presence.

The first instance showcases a nonchalant attitude about social inequality. A male Boystown resident who was in his mid-forties explained the parallels between being "gay-blind" and colorblind: "[My friend is] totally 'gay-blind,' you know—a non-factor . . . . It's [like being] color-blind." Those who turn a blind eye to intergroup differences believe that society has surpassed a certain threshold of equality and that gays and lesbians experience less societal disapproval (Jewell and Morrison 2012). These views imply that political activism is no longer needed, an assumption that makes straight residents feel exempt from being an active ally. Gayborhoods become social sites where gays and straights casually interact, rather than crucibles of politics and queer empowerment.

In another example, a female respondent in her early thirties reflected on how acceptance of homosexuality has contributed to the sexual integration of gay neighborhoods: "It [being gay] doesn't have the stigma that it used to, even in areas that certainly are very far away from Boystown. So, I view this as maybe just another step . . . Maybe they don't need—it's not necessary to have a separate area, you know, safety in numbers, strength in numbers now." Many residents stated that liberal ideals had not only been realized but that experiences of discrimination were relics of the past. A female Andersonville resident in her early forties remarked, "By the time the '90s rolled around, it was sort of like, 'OK, do we really need this anymore?' Can't we just accept that gay people live everywhere, and they don't need their own separate neighborhood?" When straights express knowledge of a civil rights violation and express verbal solidarity—even outrage with it—there is a surprising level of political disengagement. "I'm just so angry about the gay marriage thing," began a forty-five-year-old male respondent living in Boystown. But when the second author asked follow-up questions about whether he had engaged in any concrete actions on behalf of gay rights, the man admitted to his apathy and inaction. "Well, if I really was angry enough, I'd be going out and trying to do something politically about it. So, for all my words, I haven't gone out and tried to really effect change in terms of writing letters to the editor, things like that."

Some straights redefine solidarity by excluding requirements for political engagement. One resident of Andersonville described how he felt solidarity with his gay and lesbian neighbors. When the interviewer probed about whether his solidarity translated to specific actions, he freely reported that it did not and compared his political absolution with the Swedish heritage of the neighborhood:

Respondent: "I'm not Swedish, but I feel solidarity with the Swedish markers in Andersonville.
Interviewer: You do? *[Logic: a soft inquiry about identity and solidarity]*
Respondent: Yes. It's become my home.
Interviewer: If you feel solidarity with Swedes, do you do things on behalf of the Swedish community to show your support? *[Logic: a direct inquiry about the relationship between solidarity and social action]*

Respondent: No. It has nothing to do with being Swedish.

Interviewer: Are actions in support of the community not related to solidarity? *[Logic: specification of relationships among variables]*

Respondent: When I see those symbols [a water tower painted in the colors of the Swedish flag, bakeries and delis, and a Swedish American Museum, all of which are based in the neighborhood], it makes me feel like I'm home. It doesn't have anything to do with it being Swedish or not."

For this respondent, solidarity is a place-based personal experience, not something that emerges from interpersonal networks and alliances. "It's a differentiation of a place," he continued. "So what defines my neighborhood? Well, part of it is that there are these symbols, [and] there is something to rally behind, like the Swedish flag. I can see that [the water tower] from my living room window. So, I feel like I'm home." Notice the absence of sexuality as a defining characteristic of the neighborhood. Straight residents like this identify with impersonal markers, rather than the people who live in an area. In doing so, they redefine solidarity as their mere presence, a notion that eliminates expectations for actual political engagement.

The theme of feeling progressive by virtue of living in a minority neighborhood—but not doing anything on behalf of the group—emerged repeatedly in the data. A male interviewee in his late twenties stated, "I guess living here makes me feel good as an overall accepting person, and I would hate to lose that." His partner, also in her late twenties, echoed the sentiment: "I have taken some pride in the fact that I live in a gay neighborhood. Like I said, it makes me feel better about myself, [that I'm] more accepting." Some residents were aware of this potentially hypocritical stance, which one individual described as "talk[ing] out of both sides of your mouth": "You see that with people [who] move into the neighborhood, and they go, 'Oh, it's really cute to be gay,'" began a forty-eight-year-old male Andersonville resident, "and then on the other hand, they're complaining, saying, 'Oh, we've got to shut that bar down,' or 'we've got to do this,' or saying 'we don't like it,' you know what I mean—where you talk out of both sides of your mouth." As a narrative device, political absolution involves denying inequality and redefining solidarity as unrelated to material support.

Affect

The final expression of performative progressiveness that emerged in our data pertains to the emotional expectations that straights have for their gay and lesbian neighbors. Scholars have documented emotion work in family contexts (Hochschild 1979); we extend the finding to urban settings. Our analysis identifies a belief that gays and lesbians should "be happy" about the presence of straight people in gay neighborhoods. An Andersonville resident asked, "Isn't that what *they* wanted?" To clarify, he compared sexuality with race, as many others had done as well: "If we just stopped talking about racism and just got along, or homophobia, isn't that what *you* want? What would happen to these people [gays and lesbians] once they got what they wanted? . . . If everybody got along, and let's say there was no sexuality, what would these people have to be mad about then? And if you really are striving for utopia, you have to keep that in the back of your mind that once you get what you want, you have to be happy with that." This resident seems unaware that the legislative landscape is far from a "utopia." Later in the conversation, he conflates equality with cultural loss, assuming the former requires the latter: "This is what you wanted. Maybe it wasn't the consequences that they wanted, and if it's not the consequence that they wanted—that they did want to have their own neighborhood with no straight people living in it—then that's just not a good person, whether you're gay or straight. That makes you a racist or a bad person." The interviewee concluded that those gays and lesbians who wish to maintain their own culturally designated neighborhood are "bad people" because they violate an expectation of happily including straight newcomers. Another interviewee similarly struggled to understand why gays and lesbians were unhappy with the demographic changes in gay neighborhoods: "While I can understand that they might want their quote-unquote 'space,' I'm like, well, if you want equality, why aren't you happy that it's people just wanting to live together in harmony and one big neighborhood?"

Arguments about affect locate the cause of conflict in gay individuals, rather than a structural context of disadvantage and discrimination that creates a need for gay neighborhoods in the first place. According to this narrative device, discontent with the straightening of urban gay districts is an individual problem that gay people need to "just get over." One interviewee said, "If people are really upset about straight couples moving in and having families and pushing strollers and having kids running around, just get over yourselves. I consider that more of an individual—it's that person's problem, not my problem." Said another, "Anybody that is upset about a straight man or a family moving into a gay neighborhood because they're comfortable in it, I would think that your ultimate goal is for people to be comfortable with who you are and what you are and how you live your life. So, why would you be upset about that?"

All these examples highlight a disbelief among straights that some gays and lesbians might desire their own spaces and to be around others who are like them. Gay people should be "happy," they say, and "welcoming" to straights who want to live next to them. When straights encounter gay and lesbian residents who express displeasure or resistance, they become angry and confused, as was the case with a thirty-six-year-old male interviewee: "When I see those rants and raves [against straight people moving into gay neighborhoods], it makes me mad because isn't that what you want? I don't understand. You want equality, but when it's there and we're all comfortable together, and we all can live together, why would you look down on us? Why would you fight that?" These respondents misattribute a desire to maintain queer spaces as a rejection of the ideal of equality. "If they really thought about it, and they really wanted to have equality, then that [sexual integration] is what that means," one man asserted. "We should all live in the same neighborhood. It's one big neighborhood, whether you're black, Puerto Rican, gay, lesbian, straight." According to their view, gays are obliged to repay the acceptance that society has shown to them by welcoming straights into the gayborhood. Anger is an individual problem, they say, thereby concealing the institutional nature of inequality.

CONCLUSIONS: INEQUALITY IN THE GAYBORHOOD

An emerging trend in sexualities research is to identify the pathways through which inequality remains central to the social construction of sexuality and the sexual construction of social life (Moon 2008; Teunis and Herdt 2007). We began with a puzzle that is made murky by statistics that show a liberalization of attitudes toward homosexuality: Acceptance does not displace prejudice; it recrafts it into subtler forms (Doan et al. 2014). In an era of public support (Dean 2014; Nash 2013; Savin-Williams 2005; Seidman 2002; Sullivan 1996) and favorable opinion (Flores 2014; Loftus 2001; Twenge et al. 2015), how exactly does the disjuncture between progressive attitudes toward gays and lesbians and inaction toward addressing the inequalities that are directed at them manifest on the shared streets of a gayborhood? Based on an innovative use of interview data, we developed four aspects of "performative progressiveness" (Ghaziani 2014): spatial entitlements, rhetorical moves, political absolution, and affect (table 1.2).

The narrative devices, cognitive frames, and styles of reasoning listed in the table provide different ways that liberal-minded straights decouple their attitudes toward gays and lesbians from their resistant behavioral responses to the unique "sex cultures" (Ghaziani 2017) that gayborhoods promote for their residents and the "vicarious citizens" (Greene 2014) who maintain ties with the area.

Our findings advance theoretical conversations about the contact hypothesis. Those who champion it suggest that only sustained contact, rather than incidental exposure, is necessary to change attitudes (e.g., Henry and Hardin 2006). We have shown that even this is not enough. The fact that performative progressiveness appears in gayborhoods—urban districts that provide ample opportunities for extended face-to-face contact—offers a striking

Table 1.2   Performative Progressiveness, Inequality, and Placemaking

Mode	Key Feature	Expressions of Inequality	Conflicting Views of Place
Spatial Entitlements	Relationship with space	Open access to queer spaces Assumptions of power within queer spaces Consumption of queer spaces	The surprise that comes from "feeling not welcome" implies a view of gayborhoods as trendy commodities, rather than safe spaces for sexual minorities.
Rhetorical Moves	Linguistic relativity	Acceptance contingent on heteronormativity Equality contingent on the loss of cultural identity Diversity discourse justifies racial homogeneity Diversity discourse allows reverse discrimination	The discomfort from meeting someone who is "in your face" implies a heteronormative view of gayborhoods, rather than places that celebrate queer sex and cultural communities.
Political Absolution	Ignorance about sexual inequality	"Gay blindness" Solidarity exemptions Redefining solidarity as place-based	To say that being gay is a "nonfactor" implies a view of gayborhoods as places of casual social interactions, rather than crucibles of political engagement and material support.
Affect	Emotion work	Be happy and welcoming to straights "This is what you wanted" Individual versus structural context of disadvantage	The desire "to just get along" implies that gayborhoods are utopias where everyone can live, rather than places where minorities find relief from structural discrimination and social isolation.

challenge to such scholarly predictions: exposure to sexual diversity does not change minds fully, at least not in a way that enables the straight residents of gayborhoods like Boystown and Andersonville to recognize and respect the culturally specific uses of those spaces. At the core of our observations is a consistent demand by heterosexuals to experience the gayborhood on *their* terms, a move that allows them to infuse their privilege into the interactional dynamics of urban space and thus to dispute its queer ethos. This explains why contact can produce discomfort and homonegativity, even after twenty years of sharing the same streets. The performance of progressiveness brings into focus the limits of acceptance, rather than its positive trajectory as revealed by public opinion polls, and the fuzzier ways in which power operates on the ground.

We can also position our research in the literature on the consumption of diversity among urban cosmopolitans—also known as members of the creative class (Florida 2002)—who seek out certain communities in postindustrial cities to indicate their "hip" and "tolerant" cultural capital (Bourdieu 1986). Rather than emphasizing the role of economics (Black et al. 2002; Ruting 2008), assimilation (Ghaziani 2015a), voluntarily shared tastes (Brown-Saracino 2011), sex (Orne 2017), or mutual respect between gays and straights (Nash and Gorman-Murray 2014), we elevate the roles of contact and conflict. The range of dynamics within performative progressiveness challenges the assumptions that scholars make about the contexts in which people relate to one another spatially, especially those moments that create opportunities for interactions across categories of sexual orientation. Our findings suggest that living in a diverse urban area, whether defined by its racial, economic, or sexual composition, can flare unease (Dixon et al. 2005; Lee 2000; Stein et al. 2000)—even if interactions have a positive tone (Barlow et al. 2012)—because attitudes that are directed toward individuals do not always scale up to the group level (Lee et al. 2004; Matejskova and Leitner 2011).

The empirical variations of performative progressiveness that we found in our data also challenge arguments about the integration of gayborhoods as evidence of the declining significance of compulsory heterosexuality (Brown 2014; Dean 2014) and homophobia (McCormack 2012). Had we restricted our analysis to trends in public opinion (Saad 2010) or the media's declaration of gayborhoods as passe (James 2017; Leigh Brown 2007), we would have mistakenly concluded that integration is an always desirable outcome, one that signals a change in how sexuality structures our lives, relationships, and cities. We would have overlooked the subtle interactional dynamics through which straight people continue to exert their perspectives and preferences in queer spaces—and thus the protean quality of prejudice. In addition, celebrating the arrival of straight people into gayborhoods as evidence of equality valorizes heterosexuality as a symbol for what is normal, moral, and desirable. Implied in such an assessment is an unstated "problem" of homosexuality and queer spaces. This is a beguiling misdirection. Integration may be a means for achieving equality, but it cannot be the substance of equality, which must include advancements like employment nondiscrimination, closing the sexual orientation wage gap, addressing antigay hate crimes, and redressing housing discrimination (Ghaziani 2015b). We encourage future researchers to measure tolerance as a variable property of social life, and to conceptualize urban cultures and diversity not as epiphenomenal to economics (Florida 2002) or a mere residual but as a core set of textured experiences (Suttles 1984).

Qualitative analysis is less interested in generalizing to a larger population than it is in the "generalization of ideas" (Suter 2012:353). In this spirit, we offer one final thought about the portability of our findings. Similar to Goffman's (1959) writings on performance, our concept of performative progressiveness applies to race as well as sexuality, and its explanatory potential reaches well beyond the gayborhood. Consider California, a state whose population is 39 percent white, 38 percent Latino, 14 percent Asian, 7 percent black, and 2 percent Native American. Dan Schnur, executive director of the Unruh Institute of Politics, described the state as "the most demographically diverse community in the history of the planet Earth."[4] In an April 2015 poll of 1,504 Californians, nearly two-thirds of voters say race relations are better in their home state than they are in other areas of the country—and that diversity plays a positive role in their daily interactions.[5] The pollsters followed-up and asked if "diversity creates a racism-free utopia." They, like scholars (Ayers et al. 2009; Stein et al. 2000), found that the highest levels of hostility occur in the most racially diverse areas where contact between groups is common. The lesson? "Diversity" says more about *perceptions* of improved race relations than it does the *material conditions* of racial discrimination. It is a "feel good" word that "lets white people off the hook from doing something" and allows them to "sidestep persistent, alarming racial inequalities" (Berrey 2015). Some scholars call this "racism without racists" (Bonilla-Silva 2013). We similarly found homonegativity without homophobes. Writing for *Vox* and creating a powerful bridge with our findings about performative progressiveness as a new form of inequality, Jenee Desmond-Harris (2015) warns, "It is a sobering reminder not´ to assume that melting pots automatically create equality."

NOTES

1. This chapter was originally published as Brodyn, A. and Ghaziani, A. (2018), Performative Progressiveness: Accounting for New Forms of Inequality in the Gayborhood. City & Community, 17: 307–329. https://doi.org/10.1111/cico.12298

2. For ACS data, see www.windycitymediagroup.com/gay/lesbian/news/article.php?AID=31459. While Boystown is a municipally recognized gay neighborhood, Andersonville's reputation is more layered and "textured" (Suttles, 1984). Some residents are drawn to it as an historic ethnic enclave (a Swedish neighborhood), while others are attracted to its gendered residential and social composition as "Girlstown" (Ghaziani, 2014). Research shows that local place characteristics can affect "orientations to sexual identity" (Brown-Saracino, 2015). We did not find similar variation in our data (e.g., expressions of performative progressiveness as a function of neighborhood). Whereas Brown-Saracino asks how place affects identity, we show how

acceptance affects inequality. The implications of our differences are provocative: Place may shape identity more readily than inequality.

3. http://www.cmap.illinois.gov/documents/10180/126764/Lake+View.pdf
4. http://www.vox.com/2015/4/20/8445003/race-relations-diversity-racism
5. https://www.latimes.com/local/politics/la-me-pol-race-poll-20150413-story.html

REFERENCES

Ajzen, Icek, and Martin Fishbein. 1980. *Understanding Attitudes and Predicting Social Behavior.* Englewood Cliffs, NJ: Prentice-Hall.

Allport, Gordon W. 1954. *The Nature of Prejudice.* Cambridge, MA: Addison-Wesley.

Anacker, Katrin B., and Hazel A. Morrow-Jones. 2005. "Neighborhood Factors Associated with Same-Sex Households in U.S. Cities." *Urban Geography* 26(5):385–409.

Andersen, Robert, and Tina Fetner. 2008. "Cohort Differences in Tolerance of Homosexuality: Attitudinal Change in Canada and the United States, 1981–2000." *Public Opinion Quarterly* 72(2):311–330.

Attride-Stirling, Jennifer. 2001. "Thematic Networks: An Analytic Tool for Qualitative Research." *Qualitative Research* 1(3):385–405.

Ayers, John W., C. Richard Hofstetter, Keith Schnakenberg, and Bohdan Kolody. 2009. "Is Immigration a Racial Issue? Anglo Attitudes on Immigration Policies in a Border County." *Social Science Quarterly* 90:593–610.

Barlow, Fiona Kate, Stefania Paolini, Anne Pedersen, Matthew J. Hornsey, Helena R. M. Radke, Jake Harwood, Mark Rubin, and Chris G. Sibley. 2012. "The Contact Caveat: Negative Contact Predicts Increased Prejudice More Than Positive Contact Predicts Reduced Prejudice." *Personality and Social Psychology Bulletin* 38(12):1629–1643.

Becker, Howard S. 1954. "Field Methods and Techniques: A Note on Interviewing Tactics." *Human Organization* 12(4):31–32.

Becker, Howard S., and Blanche Geer. 1957. "Participant Observation and Interviewing: A Comparison." *Human Organization* 16(3):28–32.

Bergquist, Kathie, and Robert McDonald. 2006. *A Field Guide to Gay and Lesbian Chicago.* Chicago, IL: Lake Claremont Press.

Berrey, Ellen. 2015. "Diversity Is for White People: The Big Lie behind a Well-Intended Word." *Salon* (October 26) (http://www.salon.com/2015/10/26/diversity is for white people the big lie behind a well intended word/). Accessed May 1, 2016.

Betsky, Aaron. 1997. *Queer Space: Architecture and Same-Sex Desire.* New York: William Morrow and Company, Inc.

Binnie, Jon, and Beverley Skeggs. 2004. "Cosmopolitan Knowledge and the Production and Consumption of Sexualized Space: Manchester's Gay Village." *Sociological Review* 52(1):39–61.

Black, Dan, Gary Gates, Seth Sanders, and Lowell Taylor. 2002. "Why Do Gay Men Live in San Francisco?" *Journal of Urban Economics* 51(1):54–76.

Bonilla-Silva, Eduardo. 2013. *Racism without Racists: Color-Blind Racism and the Persistence of Racial Inequality in America*. Lanham, MD: Rowman & Littlefield Publishers.

Bourdieu, Pierre. 1984. *Distinction: A Social Critique of the Judgement of Taste*. Cambridge, MA: Harvard University Press.

———. 1986. "The Forms of Capital." in *Handbook of Theory and Research for the Sociology of Education*, edited by John Richardson (pp. 46–58). New York: Greenwood.

Brewer, Paul R. 2007. *Value War: Public Opinion and the Politics of Gay Rights*. Lanham, MD: Rowman & Littlefield Publishers, Inc.

———. 2014. "Public Opinion about Gay Rights and Gay Marriage." *International Journal of Public Opinion Research* 26(3):279–282.

Brooks, Clem. 2000. "Civil Liberalism and the Suppression of a Republican Political Realignment in the United States, 1972 to 1996." *American Sociological Review* 65:483–505.

———, and Jeff Manza. 2006. "Social Policy Responsiveness in Developed Democracies." *American Sociological Review* 71(3):474–494.

Brown, Michael. 2014. "Gender and Sexuality II: There Goes the Gayborhood?" *Progress in Human Geography* 38(3):457–465.

Brown-Saracino, Japonica. 2009. *A Neighborhood That Never Changes: Gentrification, Social Preservation, and the Search for Authenticity*. Chicago, IL: University of Chicago Press.

———. 2011. "From the Lesbian Ghetto to Ambient Community: The Perceived Costs and Benefits of Integration for Community." *Social Problems* 58(3):361–388.

———. 2015. "How Place Shapes Identity: The Origins of Distinctive LBQ Identities in Four Small U.S. Cities." *American Journal of Sociology* 121(1):1–63.

Burstein, Paul. 1998. "Bringing the Public Back In: Should Sociologists Consider the Impact of Public Opinion on Public Policy?" *Social Forces* 77:27–62.

———. 1999. "Social Movements and Public Policy." in *How Social Movements Matter*, edited by Marco G. Giugni, Doug McAdam, and Charles Tilly (pp. 3–21). Minneapolis, MN: University of Minnesota Press.

Butler, Judith. 1990a. *Gender Trouble*. New York: Routledge.

———. 1990b. "Performative Acts and Gender Constitution." in *Performing Feminisms*, edited by Sue-Ellen Case (pp. 270–282). Baltimore, MD: Johns Hopkins University Press.

Canaday, Margot. 2009. *The Straight State: Sexuality and Citizenship in Twentieth-Century America*. Princeton, NJ: Princeton University Press.

Castells, Manuel. 1983. *The City and the Grassroots: A Cross-Cultural Theory of Urban Social Movements*. Berkeley, CA: University of California Press.

Centner, Ryan. 2008. "Places of Privileged Consumption Practices: Spatial Capital, the Dot-Com Habitus, and San Francisco's Internet Boom." *City & Community* 7(3):193–223.

Collins, Alan. 2004. "Sexual Dissidence, Enterprise and Assimilation: Bedfellows in Urban Regeneration." *Urban Studies* 41(9):1789–1806.

Connell, Raewyn W. 1992. "A Very Straight Gay: Masculinity, Homosexual Experience, and the Dynamics of Gender." *American Sociological Review* 57(6):735–751.

Costa, Pedro Alexandre, Henrique Pereira, and Isabel Leal. 2015. "'The Contact Hypothesis' and Attitudes toward Same-Sex Parenting." *Sexuality Research and Social Policy* 12(2):125–136.

Cullen, Jennifer M., Lester W. Wright Jr., and Michael Alessandri. 2002. "The Personality Variable Openness to Experience as It Relates to Homophobia." *Journal of Homosexuality* 42(4):119–134.

Dean, James Joseph. 2014. *Straights: Heterosexuality in a Post-Closeted Culture.* New York: New York University Press.

Desmond-Harris, Jenee. 2015. "Think Diversity Creates a Racism-Free Utopia? Check Out This California Poll." *Vox*, April 20, 2015. http://www.vox.com/2025/4/20/844503/race-relations-diversity-racism

Dixon, John, Kevin Durrheim, and Colin Tredoux. 2005. "Beyond the Optimal Contact Strategy: A Reality Check for the Contact Hypothesis." *American Psychologist* 60(7):697–711.

Doan, Long, Annalise Loehr, and Lisa R. Miller. 2014. "Formal Rights and Informal Privileges for Same-Sex Couples: Evidence from a National Survey Experiment." *American Sociological Review* 79(6):1172–1195.

Doan, Petra L., and Harrison Higgins. 2011. "The Demise of Queer Space? Resurgent Gentrification and the Assimilation of LGBT Neighborhoods." *Journal of Planning Education and Research* 31(1):6–25.

Duggan, Lisa. 2003. *The Twilight of Equality? Neoliberalism, Cultural Politics, and the Attack on Democracy.* Boston, MA: Beacon.

Eliasoph, Nina. 1998. *Avoiding Politics: How Americans Produce Apathy in Everyday Life.* Cambridge, UK: Cambridge University Press.

Engel, Stephen M. 2013. "Frame Spillover: Media Framing and Public Opinion of a Multifaceted LGBT Rights Agenda." *Law & Social Inquiry* 38(2):403–441.

Evans, Sara M., and Harry C. Boyte. 1986. *Free Spaces: The Sources of Democratic Change in America.* Chicago, IL: University of Chicago Press.

Fishbein, Martin, and Icek Ajzen. 1975. *Belief, Attitude, Intention and Behavior: An Introduction to Theory and Research.* Reading, MA: Addison-Wesley.

Flores, Andrew R. 2014. *National Trends in Public Opinion on LGBT Rights in the United States.* Los Angeles: Williams Institute.

Florida, Richard. 2002. *The Rise of the Creative Class.* New York: Basic Books.

Frechtling, Joy and Laure Sharp, eds. 1997. *User-Friendly Handbook for Mixed Method Evaluations.* WWW Document:National Science Foundation: Division of Research, Evaluation, and Communication. http://www.nsf.gov/pubs/1997/nsf971 53/start.htm. Accessed May 1, 2016.

Gans, Herbert J. 1962. *The Urban Villagers: Group and Class in the Life of Italian Americans.* New York: Free Press.

Gates, Gary J., and Jason Ost. 2004. *The Gay and Lesbian Atlas*. Washington, DC: Urban Institute.

Ghaziani, Amin. 2011. "Post-Gay Collective Identity Construction." *Social Problems* 58(1):99–125.

———. 2014. *There Goes the Gayborhood?* Princeton, NJ: Princeton University Press.

———. 2015a. "'Gay Enclaves Face Prospect of Being Passe': How Assimilation Affects the Spatial Expressions´ of Sexuality in the United States." *International Journal of Urban and Regional Research* 39(4):756–771.

———. 2015b. "The Radical Potential of Post-Gay Politics in the City." *Environment and Planning A* 47:2409–2426.

———. 2017. *Sex Cultures*. Boston, MA: Polity Press.

Goffman, Erving. 1959. *The Presentation of Self in Everyday Life*. New York: Random House.

Gorman-Murray, Andrew, and Gordon Waitt. 2009. "Queer-Friendly Neighbourhoods: Interrogating Social Cohesion across Sexual Difference in Two Australian Neighbourhoods." *Environment and Planning A* 41(12):2855–2873.

Greene, Theodore. 2014. "Gay Neighborhoods and the Rights of the Vicarious Citizen." *City & Community* 13(2):99–118.

Gross, Neil. 2009. "A Pragmatist Theory of Social Mechanisms." *American Sociological Review* 74(3):358–379.

Halberstam, J. Jack. 2012. *Gaga Feminism: Sex, Gender, and the End of Normal*. Boston, MA: Beacon Press.

Hanhardt, Christina B. 2008. "Butterflies, Whistles, and Fists: Gay Safe Street Patrols and the New Gay Ghetto, 1976–1981." *Radical History Review* Winter (100):60–85.

———. 2013. *Safe Space: Gay Neighborhood History and the Politics of Violence*. Durham, NC: Duke University Press.

Hawkins, Rich. 2015. "It's Okay to Be Gay, Just Don't Touch Each Other." *Huffington Post*. June 23. http:// www.huffingtonpost.com/rich-hawkins/its-okay-to-be-gay-just-d b 7637046.html. Accessed May 1, 2016.

Henry, P.J., and Curtis D. Hardin. 2006. "The Contact Hypothesis Revisited." *Psychological Science* 17(10):862–868.

———, and Christine Reyna. 2007. "Value Judgments: The Impact of Perceived Value Violations on American Political Attitudes." *Political Psychology* 28(3):273–298.

Herek, Gregory M. 1988. "Heterosexuals' Attitudes toward Lesbians and Gay Men: Correlates and Gender Differences." *Journal of Sex Research* 25:451–477.

———. 2006. "Legal Recognition of Same-Sex Relationships in the United States: A Social Science Perspective." *American Psychologist* 61(6):607–621.

———, and Eric K. Glunt. 1993. "Interpersonal Contact and Heterosexuals' Attitudes toward Gay Men: Results from a National Survey." *Journal of Sex Research* 30:239–244.

Hicks, Gary R., and Tien-Tsung Lee. 2006. "Public Attitudes toward Gays and Lesbians: Trends and Predictors." *Journal of Homosexuality* 51(2):57–77.

Hochschild, Arlie. 1979. "Emotion Work, Feeling Rules, and Social Structure." *American Journal of Sociology* 85(3):551–575.

Hubbard, Phil. 2013. "Kissing Is Not a Universal Right: Sexuality, Law, and the Scales of Citizenship." *Geoforum* 49:224–232.

Ihlanfeldt, Keith R., and Benjamin P. Scafidi. 2002. "The Neighbourhood Contact Hypothesis: Evidence from the Multicity Study of Urban Inequality." *Urban Studies* 39(4):619–641.

James, Scott. 2017. "There Goes the Gayborhood." *New York Times* June 21.

Jenness, Valerie, and Ryken Grattet. 2001. *Making Hate a Crime: From Social Movement to Law Enforcement.* New York: Russell Sage Foundation.

Jerolmack, Colin, and Shamus Khan. 2014. "Talk Is Cheap: Ethnography and the Attitudinal Fallacy." *Sociological Methods and Research* 43(2):178–209.

Jewell, Lisa Margaret, and Melanie Ann Morrison. 2012. "Making Sense of Homonegativity: Heterosexual Men and Women's Understanding of Their Own Prejudice and Discrimination toward Gay Men." *Qualitative Research in Psychology* 9(4):351–370.

Kanai, Juan Miguel, and Kai Kenttamaa-Squires. 2015. "Remaking South Beach: Metropolitan Gayborhood Rrajectories under Homonormative Entrepreneurialism." *Urban Geography* 36(3):385–402.

Knopp, Lawrence. 1990. "Some Theoretical Implications of Gay Involvement in an Urban Land Market." *Political Geography Quarterly* 9(4):337–352.

Lauria, Mickey, and Lawrence Knopp. 1985. "Toward an Analysis of the Role of Gay Communities in the Urban Renaissance." *Urban Geography* 6(2):152–169.

Lee, Barrett A., Chad R. Farrell, and Bruce G. Link. 2004. "Revisiting the Contact Hypothesis: The Case of Public Exposure to Homelessness." *American Sociological Review* 69(1):40–63.

Lee, Jennifer. 2000. "The Salience of Race in Everyday Life: Black Customers' Shopping Experiences in Black and White Neighborhoods." *Work and Occupations* 27(3):353–376.

Lefebvre, Henri. 1991 [1974].*The Production of Space.* Cambridge, MA: Blackwell.

Leigh Brown, Patricia. 2007. "Gay Enclaves Face Prospect of Being Passe"*New York Times* October 24. Retrieved 7 December, 2011. http://www.nytimes.com/20 07/10/30/us/30gay.html.

Lloyd, Richard. 2006. *Neo-Bohemia: Art and Commerce in the Postindustrial City.* New York: Routledge.

Loftus, Jeni. 2001. "America's Liberalization in Attitudes toward Homosexuality, 1973–1998." *American Sociological Review* 66:762–782.

Lottes, Ilsa L., and Eric Anthony Grollman. 2010. "Conceptualization and Assessment of Homonegativity." *International Journal of Sexual Health* 22(4):219–233.

Matejskova, Tatiana, and Helga Leitner. 2011. "Urban Encounters with Difference: The Contact Hypothesis and Immigrant Integration Projects in Eastern Berlin." *Social and Cultural Geography* 12(7):717–741.

McCormack, Mark. 2012. *The Declining Significance of Homophobia.* New York: Oxford University Press.

Mead, George Herbert. 1934. *Mind, Self, and Society from the Standpoint of a Social Behaviorist.* Chicago, IL: University of Chicago Press.

Miles, Eleanor, and Richard J. Crisp. 2014. "A Meta-Analytic Test of the Imagined Contact Hypothesis." *Group Processes & Intergroup Relations* 17(1):3–26.

Miles, Matthew B., and A. Michael Huberman. 1994. *Qualitative Data Analysis.* Thousand Oaks, CA: Sage.

Monto, Martin A., and Jessica Supinski. 2014. "Discomfort with Homosexuality: A New Measure Captures Differences in Attitudes toward Gay Men and Lesbians." *Journal of Homosexuality* 61(6):899–916.

Moon, Dawne. 2008. "Culture and the Sociology of Sexuality: It's Only Natural?" *Annual Review of Sociology* 619:183–205.

Moskowitz, Peter. 2015. "Why You Should Stop Waving the Rainbow Flag on Facebook." *Washington Post*, July 2. http://www.washingtonpost.com/posteveryt hing/wp/2015/07/02/why-you-should-stopwaving-the-rainbow-flag-on-facebook/. Accessed May 1, 2016.

Murdoch, Joyce, and Deb Price. 2001. *Courting Justice: Gay Men and Lesbians V. The Supreme Court.* New York: Basic Books.

Nash, Catherine J. 2013. "The Age of the 'Post-Mo'? Toronto's Gay Village and a New Generation." *Geoforum* 49:243–52.

———, and Andrew Gorman-Murray. 2014. "LGBT Neighbourhoods and 'New Mobilities': Towards Understanding Transformations in Sexual and Gendered Landscapes." *International Journal of Urban and Regional Research* 38(3):756–772.

NeJaime, Douglas. 2016. "Marriage Equality and the New Parenthood." *Harvard Law Review* 129(5):1185–1266.

Orne, Jason. 2017. *Boystown: Sex and Community in Chicago.* Chicago, IL: University of Chicago Press.

Page, Benjamin I., and Robert Y. Shapiro. 1992. *The Rational Public: Fifty Years of Trends in Americans' Policy Preferences.* Chicago, IL: University of Chicago Press.

Park, Robert E. 1950. *Race and Culture (Collected Writings).* New York: Free Press.

———, and Ernest W. Burgess, eds. 1925. *The City: Suggestions for Investigation of Human Behavior in the Urban Environment.* Chicago, IL: University of Chicago Press.

Plugge-Foust, Carol, and George Strickland. 2000. "Homophobia, Irrationality, and Christian Ideology: Does a Relationship Exist?" *Journal of Sex Education and Therapy* 25(4):240–244.

Putnam, Robert D. 2000. *Bowling Alone: The Collapse and Revival of American Community.* New York: Simon and Schuster.

Raiz, Lisa. 2006. "College Students' Support of Rights for Members of the Gay Community." *Journal of Poverty* 10(2):53–76.

Rich, Meghan Ashlin. 2009. "'It Depends on How You Define Integrated': Neighborhood Boundaries and Racial Integration in a Baltimore Neighborhood." *Sociological Forum* 24(4):828–853.

Rosenfeld, Bryn, Kosuke Imai, and Jacob N. Shapiro. 2016. "An Empirical Validation Study of Popular Survey Methodologies for Sensitive Questions." *American Journal of Political Science* 60(3):783–802.

Rubin, Gayle S. 1993. "Thinking Sex: Notes for a Radical Theory of the Politics of Sexuality." in *The Lesbian and Gay Studies Reader*, edited by Henry Abelove, Michele Aina Barale, and David M. Halperin (pp. 3–44). New York: Routledge.

Rushbrook, Dereka. 2002. "Cities, Queer Space, and the Cosmopolitan Tourist." *GLQ: A Journal of Lesbian and Gay Studies* 8(1–2):183–206.

Ruting, Brad. 2008. "Economic Transformations of Gay Urban Spaces: Revisiting Collins' Evolutionary Gay District Model." *Australian Geographer* 39(3):259–269.

Ryan, Gery W., and H. Russell Bernard. 2003. "Techniques to Identify Themes." *Field Methods* 15(1):85–109.

Saad, Lydia. 2010. "Americans' Acceptance of Gay Relations Crosses 50% Threshold." http://www.gallup.com/poll/135764/americans-acceptance-gay-relati ons-crosses-threshold.aspx. Accessed May 1, 2016.

Sampson, Robert J. 2012. *Great American City: Chicago and the Enduring Neighborhood Effect*. Chicago, IL: University of Chicago Press.

Sapir, Edward. 1929. "The Status of Linguistics as a Science." *Language* 5(4):207–214.

Savin-Williams, Ritch C. 2005. *The New Gay Teenager*. Cambridge, MA: Harvard University Press.

Schilt, Kristen, and Laurel Westbrook. 2009. "Doing Gender, Doing Heteronormativity: 'Gender Normals,' Transgender People, and the Social Maintenance of Heterosexuality." *Gender & Society* 23(4):440–464.

Seidman, Steven. 2002. *Beyond the Closet: The Transformation of Gay and Lesbian Life*. New York: Routledge.

Sherif, Muzafer. 1956. "Experiments in Group Conflict." *Scientific American* 193:420–429.

Sherrill, Kenneth, and Alan S. Yang. 2000. "From Outlaws to in-Laws: Anti-Gay Attitudes Thaw." *Public Perspective* 11(1):20–31.

Smith, Sara J., Amber M. Axelton, and Donald A. Saucier. 2009. "The Effects of Contact on Sexual Prejudice: A Meta-Analysis." *Sex Roles* 61(3):178–191.

Spring, Amy L. 2013. "Declining Segregation of Same-Sex Partners: Evidence from Census 2000 and 2010." *Population Research and Policy Review* 32(5):687–716.

Stein, Robert M., Stephanie Shirley Post, and Allison L. Rinden. 2000. "Reconciling Context and Contact Effects on Racial Attitudes." *Political Research Quarterly* 53(2):285–303.

Stewart-Winter, Timothy. 2016. *Queer Clout: Chicago and the Rise of Gay Politics*. Philadelphia, PA: University of Pennsylvania Press.

Stokes, Zeke. 2015. *Accelerating Acceptance*. New York: GLAAD.

Sullivan, Andrew. 1996. *Virtually Normal: An Argument about Homosexuality*. New York: Vintage.

Suter, W. Newton. 2012. *Introduction to Educational Research*. New York: Sage.

Suttles, Gerald D. 1984. "The Cumulative Texture of Local Urban Culture." *American Journal of Sociology* 90(2):283–304.

Swidler, Ann. 2008. "Comment on Stephen Vaisey's 'Socrates, Skinner and Aristotle: Three Ways of Thinking about Culture in Action'." *Sociological Forum* 23(3):614–618.

Teunis, Niels, and Gilbert H. Herdt, eds. 2007. *Sexual Inequalities and Social Justice.* Berkeley/Los Angeles: University of California Press.

Twenge, Jean M., Nathan T. Carter, and W. Keith Campbell. 2015. "Time Period, Generational, and Age Differences in Tolerance for Controversial Beliefs and Lifestyles in the United States." *Social Forces* 94(1):379–399.

Vaisey, Steven. 2008. "Socrates, Skinner, and Aristotle: Three Ways of Thinking about Culture in Action." *Sociological Forum* 23(3):603–613.

———. 2009. "Motivation and Justification: A Dual-Process Model of Culture in Action." *American Journal of Sociology* 114(6):1675–1715.

Wacquant, Loic. 2008. "Ghettos and Anti-Ghettos: An Anatomy of the New Urban Poverty." *Thesis Eleven* 94(1):113–118.

Walters, Suzanna Danuta. 2001. *All the Rage: The Story of Gay Visibility in America.* Chicago, IL: University of Chicago Press.

———. 2014. *The Tolerance Trap.* New York: New York University Press.

Warner, Michael. 1991. "Introduction: Fear of a Queer Planet." *Social Text* 29(4):3–17.

Werum, Regina, and Bill Winders. 2001. "Who's 'In' and Who's 'Out': State Fragmentation and the Struggle over Gay Rights, 1974–1999." *Social Problems* 48(3):386–410.

West, Candace, and Don H. Zimmerman. 1987. "Doing Gender." *Gender & Society* 1(2):125–151.

Westbrook, Laurel, and Aliya Saperstein. 2015. "New Categories Are Not Enough: Rethinking the Measurement of Sex and Gender in Social Surveys." *Gender & Society* 29(4):534–560.

Whorf, Benjamin, and John B. Carroll, eds. 1956. *Language, Thought, and Reality: Selected Writings of Benjamin Lee Whorf.* Cambridge, MA: MIT Press.

Whorf, Benjamin Lee. 1940. "Science and Linguistics." *Technology Review* 42(6):229–231.

Wilcox, Clyde, and Robin Wolpert. 2000. "Gay Rights in the Public Sphere: Public Opinion on Gay and Lesbian Equality." in *The Politics of Gay Rights*, edited by Craig A. Rimmerman, Kenneth Wald, and Clyde Wilcox (pp. 409–432). Chicago, IL: University of Chicago Press.

Wood, Peter B., and John P. Bartkowski. 2004. "Attribution Style and Public Policy Attitudes toward Gay Rights." *Social Science Quarterly* 85(1):58–74.

Yang, Alan S. 1997. "Trends: Attitudes toward Homosexuality." *Public Opinion Quarterly* 61(3):477–507.

Zhang, Yan, and Barbara M. Wildemuth. 2009. "Qualitative Analysis of Content." in *Applications of Social Research Methods to Questions in Information and Library Science*, edited by Barbara M. Wildemuth (pp. 308–319). Westport, CT: Libraries Unlimited.

Zukin, Sharon. 1995. *The Cultures of Cities.* Oxford, UK: Blackwell.

Chapter 2

Style and the Value of Gay Nightlife

Homonormative Placemaking in San Francisco

Greggor Mattson

WHAT IS THE VALUE OF GAY NIGHTLIFE?

Gay[1] bars and the neighborhoods they anchor are in trouble (Brown, 2014; Ghaziani, 2014; Kelly et al., 2014; Podmore, 2013). Entertainment blogs on both coasts mourn waves of gay bar closures (Kane, 2013; e.g., Musto, 2010), while even in Milwaukee Wisconsin "tolerant times bring change to gay bars" (Flanigan, 2012). Yet, only years earlier, urbanists celebrated gays as bellwethers of tolerant, diverse urban economies (e.g., Clark, 2003; Florida, 2003), heralding their nightlife for its promise of cosmopolitan, self-policing, twenty-four-hour neighborhoods (Roberts et al., 2006; Shaw, 2013; Yeo and Heng, 2014). Critics documented the costs of these policies, however, including racial segregation (Talbot, 2004), the homogenization of nightlife opportunities (Chatterton and Hollands, 2002; Hubbard et al., 2008; Zukin, 1998), and conflicts between nightlife goers and new residents attracted by the scene in the first place (Gotham, 2005; Hae, 2011).

Bar districts are important indicators of the vitality of gay neighborhoods as "anchor institutions" of gay community (Ghaziani, 2014); socializing with other gays, not only gay enclave residence, is associated with stronger community perceptions and attachments (Kelly et al., 2014). Gay bars are the public front to gay social "scenes" that spill onto the streets and into private residences (see Valentine and Skelton, 2003). For twentieth-century gay men, bars were the most important cultural institution where newly "out" men were socialized; interpersonal contacts were made; social isolation was alleviated; and community art exhibitions, charity auctions, and political meetings were held (e.g., Armstrong, 2002). From the 1960s through the 1970s, "gay politics in San Francisco, as in L.A. and New York, had been formed almost entirely in reaction to the continuing crackdown by authorities on gay bars and gay male sexuality" (Clendinen and Nagourney, 1999: 150). Today bars still serve as sites of "identity pilgrimage" (Howe, 2001) for "lifestyle commuters" (Brekhus, 2003) who may not be openly gay or live suburban lives among heterosexual families but can travel to "mitigate the effects of social and spatial isolation" (Hunter, 2010: 165).

Yet, the relationships among economic development, gay nightlife, and the neighborhoods they anchor are unclear (see Brown, 2014). Some researchers find declarations of gay neighborhood decline alarmist (Ghaziani, 2010), while others find younger LGBTs prefer mixed socializing over gay places (Nash, 2013). Studies document developer pressure to remove gay bars from gentrifying neighborhoods (Boyd, 2005; Doan and Higgins, 2011), yet elsewhere, urban planners create "gay villages" through strategic zoning and alcohol licensing (e.g., Lewis, 2013). Still others note the displacement of gay residents by tourists drawn to gay enclaves (Collins, 2004). Researchers agree, however, that urban development means gay men, who overwhelmingly dominate erstwhile "gay" or "queer" public space (e.g., Armstrong, 2002).

Descriptions of gay bars and neighborhoods—from creative cities' promoters but also in their nostalgic eulogies—are pervaded by assumptions that they are the same, cause gentrification, and are recipes for urban revitalization (e.g., Florida, 2003). Even critical accounts overgeneralize from single cases, inadvertently positing universal trajectories (Brown, 2009; Podmore, 2013). These reductionist understandings of gay scenes have obscured their different stylistic practices, the cultural and economic competition underpinning them, and their differential appeals to "potential gentrifiers" (Beauregard, 1986). As this study demonstrates, only those gay neighborhoods that confer valued qualities upon cosmopolitans gentrify from within, annexing adjacent areas and prompting concerns about preserving their gay character (Brown-Saracino, 2010). Streetscapes anchored by gay bar districts patronized primarily by sex workers, poor gays, and men of color are vulnerable to gentrification from without and its attendant displacement. Despite calls to protect "nocturnal rights to the city" for sexual nonconformists (Prior et al., 2012), only streetscapes that present low-friction consumption opportunities for cosmopolitans are valued on the market—even at the expense of their nonconformity.

This study presents the divergent trajectories of San Francisco's (SF) three gay bar districts between 1999 and 2012 to demonstrate how the practices of gay style help explain the vitality or displacement of gay nightlife and the neighborhoods they anchor. Though San Francisco is a unique case as a paradigmatic gay metropolis (Armstrong, 2002; Howe, 2001; Sides, 2009),

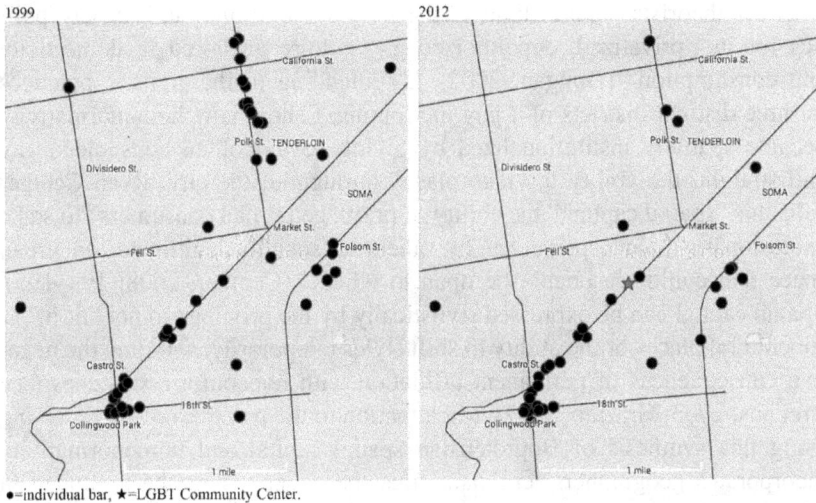

•=individual bar, ★=LGBT Community Center.

Figure 2.1   San Francisco Gay Bars, 1999 and 2012. See http://goo.gl/yVkpPR. Map data ©2014 Google.

it is precisely its internal variation that permits an analysis of multiple gay neighborhoods (Polk, Soma, and the Castro) under similar regional economic and social pressures. The nonconformist Polk district succumbed to gentrification from without (see figure 2.1), unable to attract new nonconformists or adapt to changing gay tastes, while the district south of Market Street (Soma) completed its adaptation from a hypermasculine fetish neighborhood to a mixed-orientation nightlife district.

The Castro's appeal to cosmopolitans, gay and straight, was reflected in its geographical expansion and increasing stylistic homogeneity.

By focusing on nightlife districts and not individual bars or events, this study focuses on the importance of durable streetscapes, the sites of institutionalized placemaking for the possibilities and potentials of gay sociality. That such diversity decreased in an iconic gay metropolis is important for understandings of gay neighborhoods, nightlife economies, and urban cosmopolitanism.

HOMONORMATIVITY TAKING PLACE

Respectable gays like to think that they owe nothing to the sexual subculture they think of as sleazy. But their success, their way of living, their political rights, and their very identities would not have been possible but for the existence of the public sexual culture they now despise (Berlant and Warner, 1998: 563).

Queer theorists have critiqued "the new homonormativity" in gay politics for its "privatized, depoliticized gay culture anchored in domesticity and consumption" (Duggan, 2002). By attending to the stylistic practices in three distinct districts of a gay metropolis, I show how homonormativity became spatially institutionalized by giving cosmopolitan consumers, gay and straight, the ability to "take place" throughout the city. Ryan Centner calls this "spatial capital," the ability of privileged urban consumers "to stake exclusionary claims, perceived by others as socially legitimate, on urban space that could reasonably be open to others" (Centner, 2008: 194–195). Spatial capital can be expressed stylistically by the privilege to not "fit in" to subcultural places or the ability to shift styles temporarily, avoiding the negative consequences of permanent affiliation with nonconformist scenes (see Brekhus, 2003; Grazian, 2007). My attention to the practices of placemaking using this synthesis of Bourdieusian spatial capital and homonormativity incorporates geographers' criticisms that the concept must be grounded in local historical conditions and practices (Brown, 2009; Podmore, 2013).

Centner's spatial capital emerged from a study of San Francisco's dot-com workers who presided over the region's boom-and-bust economy. These educated young workers flooded into the region in the 1990s, following venture capital-financed technology companies that celebrated a culture of entrepreneurism, free-market libertarianism, and flexibility that blended workplace and leisure with corporate amenities like foosball tables and on-site masseurs and laundry services (see review in Walker, 2006). They took this workplace with them into places where they met like-minded others: as one nightlife impresario explained, "working and socializing are connected here—people don't come to San Francisco just to settle down and have a quiet existence" (Borden, 2000: 224). Such workers flooded the bars of the Latino Mission district and flocked to brunch in the homonormative Castro, while poor and black San Franciscans were increasingly displaced (Centner, 2008; Walker, 2006). Newcomers largely eschewed the nonconformist gay bars, with their subcultural barriers to entry and queer focus on participation over consumption, as I show further.

The homonormative critique rejects the gay movement's abandonment of sexual radicalism and solidarities across and race and social class in favor of bourgeois marriage and military service. This mainstreaming of gay politics paralleled the acceptance of gay marriage by Americans and the new economy workers' embrace of gay bars for their leisure. This neoliberal flexibility was reflected spatially in the de-concentration of gay neighborhoods (Ghaziani, 2014), a shift from durable, 24/7 places to scenes that are "networked and online, located in nebulous, diffuse, often suburban spaces . . . less territorially defined" (Weiss, 2011: 37). The Castro, like other gentrified neighborhoods, engaged in a "sanitation process" to remove unwanted gays from public space, conflating safety with homogeneity (Brown-Saracino, 2010), provoking controversies that revealed a particular community vision that legitimized exclusionary practices against the young, the poor, the homeless, and gay men of color.

The homonormative homogenization of San Francisco's gay places was not inevitable. Both Polk and Soma's 1999 configurations had survived the AIDS crisis and decades of intense municipal development pressures (e.g., Hartman, 2002; Plaster, 2009; Rubin, 1998). Gay cooperative businesses and nonprofits still espouse radical politics (Brown, 2009), and London's Vauxhall is analyzed as an exception to "assumptions about the desexualization and sanitization of contemporary gay culture" (Andersson, 2011: 85). Yet these alternatives are framed as such, and the nonconformist scenes that were uprooted in San Francisco did not find permanent resettlement elsewhere through 2012.

Sarah Schulman (2012) argues that gay neighborhoods gentrified when "conservative," "consumerist" settlers replaced the "rebellious," "queer" pioneers killed by AIDS, a political shift she calls *The Gentrification of the Mind*. Though not yet empirically verified, it joins other challenges to gay historical memory like reminders of Polk's "forgotten AIDS crisis" (Sides, 2009: 182), past celebrations of promiscuity in the Castro (Murray, 1996), and Soma's disintegration—not from higher rates of AIDS than the other neighborhoods, but from more concentrated urban redevelopment (Rubin, 1998). Though Schulman does not use the term, homonormativity captures this "gentrification" of gay historical memory, reflected by the mainstream's conflation of homonormativity with homosexuality reflected in creative cities' urbanism and nostalgic eulogies of gay bars alike.

OBSERVING THE EROTICS OF STYLISTIC PRACTICES

Baseline data to document gay streetscapes come from a team ethnography of bargoing from 1999 to 2002. We did not know it at the time, but we were observing the last moments of a viable gay Polk streetscape, a time before the Castro was hegemonic of regional gay nightlife, and the widest range of gay stylistic practices. In pairs, we visited each bar in the San Francisco bay area identified as a sexual marketplace (Cavan, 1966) by focus groups (N=147), including all bars for gay men (N=51). We made multiple visits to each gay nightlife district, observing from 9 p.m. until lingering patrons outside dispersed after the 2 a.m. closing time. Subsequent data come from independent ethnographic visits three to four times yearly until 2007 and subsequent annual visits until 2012. I observed not only specific venues but also pedestrian flows among bars in nightlife districts.

These are supplemented with analysis of newspaper articles, nightlife fliers, online nightlife reports, and the archives of the GLBT Historical Society of Northern California and the California Department of Alcoholic Beverage Control (ABC).

I was hired as a native informant for the initial project—a white gay bargoing man in his mid-twenties, among young men and women of diverse racial backgrounds that also included non-drinkers and non-bargoers. My regular patronage of gay bars in several American and European cities familiarized me with a broader range of stylistic practices than we observed in San Francisco, while my residence in a low-rent neighborhood in Oakland made me one of Brekhus' "gay chameleon" "identity commuters" to gay districts (2003). My youth, height, swimmer's physique, and light hair and eyes gave me relatively high status, experiences tempered by the experiences of coworkers and my loss in status from weight gain in 2005.

Tasked with providing estimates of the social class mix of bar patrons, my colleagues and I were confronted with the fact that the social class presentation (Goffman, 1951) of many gay men did not match biographic details revealed in conversation. Stylishly groomed young men in designer fashions frequently revealed themselves as holding multiple low-wage service jobs. Similarly, gay men in nonconformist bars wearing work coveralls or leather fetish gear were actually bankers and managers.

These experiences highlighted the importance of attending to the erotics of social class in cosmopolitan placemaking. These are aspirational, upward to appear upper-middle class but also *downward* to signal nonconformist or radical sexuality. Style is not mere surface, but a set of social relations and practices organized in space, the embodiment of subcultural affiliation (Hebdige, 1981; Zukin, 1998) through the (re)creation of symbolic boundaries (Bourdieu, 1984). I describe as "homonormative" the stylistic practices of décor or comportment that reflected middle-class privacy and propriety, and nonconformist those that celebrated sexual contact or socializing across social cleavages. As I document further, nonconformist streetscapes and bars were replaced by a homonormativity in the brief five-year period of 1999–2004, reflected in the decline of nonconformism throughout the City and the Castro's continuing dominance of its gay nightlife.

THE DECLINE OF STYLISTIC DIVERSITY IN
SAN FRANCISCO'S GAY NIGHTLIFE DISTRICTS

In the temperate climate of San Francisco a thousand separate and unique species of queer animal have evolved, each inhabiting his or her own bar or club. (*San Francisco Chronicle*, 2000)[2]

Although the Castro as "gay capital" is well known, its status as the youngest of San Francisco's three gay bar districts is not. It was settled only in the 1970s, joining the late-1950s-era Polk Gulch, and 1960s Soma (Boyd, 2005). In 1999, each neighborhood had eight to nineteen gay bars, with thirteen others scattered singly around the city, including both lesbian bars. In 2004, Polk had lost more than half its bars and the Castro's share had increased from 36 percent to 52 percent despite a citywide loss of seven bars (see figure 2.1). These changes were durable; by 2012, there were only three gays bars in Polk and the Castro maintained its share at 50 percent, annexing upper Market St. (see figure 2.2).

Although Soma maintained or increased its share of bars between 1999 and 2012, it experienced significant qualitative changes reflecting a stylistic homogenization of SF's gay nightlife and a homonormative shift toward respectability.

Polk Gulch's Nonconformist Homosexualities

Polk Street had long been a crossroads between extremes of wealth and indigent transience, bisected by the California Street cable car line to the waterfront and financial district. Long before creative consumption was celebrated, in 1973, the gay enclave had made Polk "the city's new in street" for cosmopolitan heterosexuals in adjacent wealthy neighborhoods, summarized as "asparagus tip sandwiches . . . [for] the hip, the hep, the gay, the mod" (San Francisco Chronicle, quoted in Plaster 2009). By 1999, Polk's reputation had merged with the Tenderloin, "one of the roughest parts of San Francisco, a seedy, crime-ridden mix of drug dealers, homeless drunks and hookers of both sexes" (Wildermuth, 2013).

Polk's 1999 streetscape supported an array of LGBT subcultures little found elsewhere in San Francisco, nor in such concentrated proximity. Its twelve gay bars nestled among straight bars; social service agencies; late-night diners; and mom-and-pop stores selling donuts, pornography, and

District	1999 N	%	2004 N	%	2012 N	%
Polk	13	*25*	6	*13*	3	*7*
SoMa	8	*15*	7	*15*	10	*24*
Castro	19	*36*	24	*52*	21	*50*
SF (rest)	13	*25*	9	*20*	8	*19*
TOTAL	53		46		42	

Figure 2.2   San Francisco Gay Bar Distributions.

stationery. Nighttime sidewalks were always populated by bedraggled figures pushing shopping carts or huddled in dark doorways; men walking alone; strolling groups; transgendered women and male hustlers selling sex; and bouncers and smoking patrons outside nightclubs. This streetscape provoked diverse homosexual desires: "Polk Street is one of the last remaining places where there has been cross-class, cross-gender and cross-sexuality, an inter-action between street cultures" (Fulbright, 2005). For locals, a bar might provide an oasis of sociability, but for male passersby, the scene provoked diverse sexual possibilities—sugar daddy, John/punter, campy queen, hustler, cross-generational, transgender women, or Asians.

Older men met much younger men at Reflections (est. 1987), often for commercial sex. When I first slid onto one of the barstools as a scruffy gradu-ate student, the bartender placed a napkin in front of me: "the gentleman at the end there would like to buy you a drink." Meeting the gaze of a paunchy bald man in a Members-Only jacket, I demurred, sliding the napkin back and hoping not to give offence. "Well in that case," said the bartender as he slid the napkin back to me, "the gentleman at the *other* end of the bar would like to buy your drink." As I retreated, red-faced, a third told me that he'd buy me anything I liked. Polk's scene meant that eye contact between older and younger men on Polk was intense, prompting men to consider cross-generational desire or for pay.

The White Swallow's (est. 1987) eponymous double entendre belied a camp sensibility in stark contrast to gay styles of hypermasculinity or restrained cos-mopolitanism. To my right sat an elderly dandy, resting one white-gloved hand on the fidgety knee of youth who I took for a hustler. The other ten to twelve patrons, mainly in their fifties to seventies, wore colorful sweaters and slacks. A florid, pudgy pianist with frosted hair embellished classic songs with bawdy lyrics, while patrons joined in with off-key bellowing and raucous laughter.

Diva's (est. 1988 as Motherlode) advertised itself as the premier trans-gender club in America. Asian women in sequined ball gowns performed duets for older men of indeterminate sexual orientation and two white trans-gendered women sitting alone. Upstairs, couples swayed in the strobe-lit darkness, white men in their fifties and sixties wearing business attire danced with young brown-skinned women in low-cut dresses and high heels. A young woman beside me gestured to her swooping neckline: "They're real, here, feel them," she insisted, taking my hand, "but it all works downstairs, believe me," she said, echoing newspaper sex ads by transgender women with penises. Women of color smoked on the sidewalk outside or lingered on a busy corner well-known as a prostitution stroll. As I passed one with breasts practically exposed, she purred "Hey baby, wanna party?" The Polk streetscape thus prompted male passersby to consider whether they were sexually interested in transgender women or paying for sex.

N'Touch (est. 1992) was the only gay bar for Asian men in North America. Patrons, mainly East or Southeast Asian, ranged from stiff young Asian Americans in the baseball caps of any fraternity brother to flamboyant Asian immigrants with bleached hair in trendy nightclub fashions. Caucasian patrons, older on average, were as often objects of desire as dismissed as fetishistic "rice queens." The presence of N'Touch on Polk created a field of desire between and among white and Asian men. An Asian man's interest in other men was not apparent until he neared N'Touch, nor a white man's desires for Asian men, as when an Asian man encouraged me to change my plans: "Oh that's too bad—you should!" before leaving with a wink.

The gay streetscape, much diminished in 2004 from the loss of half Polk's bars, was gone by 2012. A neighborhood famed for its activism to resist gentrification did not rally to defend its gay bars (Robinson, 1995), while N'Touch's 2008 closure left 32 percent of Asian city without an Asian gay bar. By 2010, Polk had the largest concentration of dance bars for young heterosexuals, and neighborhood groups successfully reined in its rowdy street scene with restrictive zoning in 2013 (Wildermuth, 2013).

Soma's Nonconformist Hypermasculinity

Soma (South of Market) has long faced development pressures eroding its light industry and single resident occupancy hotels (Hartman, 2002; Rubin, 1998). Compared to Polk Gulch, Soma was stylistically homogenous, facilitating a singular meaning of homosexuality. Like Polk Gulch but unlike the Castro, Soma's hypermasculine "leather" sexuality was a counterculture of fraternal libertinism, working-class romanticization and fetish sex that bridged social divides and created solidarity between strangers (Rubin, 1998). A shadow of its 1980s-self, Soma still hosted sex clubs, alleys notorious for public sex, and accounted for 15 percent of the City's gay bars, six of which reflected its historic styles. Folsom's sidewalks were mixed, groups of heterosexual partygoers in their twenties and men in their thirties to fifties in leather chaps and caps with smirking direct eye contact. Two men incredulously discussed a resident who threw water from their new condo onto men having sex below: "Don't move here, fucking yuppies!" Left unspoken was the likelihood that the yuppies were also gay.

Soma staff and patrons showed their commitment to the district's countercultural aesthetic in ways that could not be removed like clothing. Punk haircuts, facial piercings and tattoos, and long, unkempt motorcycle-gang beards precluded conventional employment for some. Folk accounts of Soma implicitly invoke working class marginality as an explanation for its decline, yet our conversations with patrons revealed lifestyle commuters adopting a style to signal affiliation with radical sexuality: the PhD in coveralls and work boots, the Stanford graduate with a literary tattoo, the shirtless investment banker with pungent body odor. Only in Soma or Polk would such men rub elbows—or more—with actual homeless men.

At the Eagle Tavern, for instance, crowded evenings frequently afforded scenes of mutual masturbation and oral sex. It sported old advertisements for motorcycles, leather bars around the world, rock music, and working-class beer brands. Its Sunday afternoons were packed with leather jackets, bulging crotches, tight Levis, high boots, bared hairy chests, and cigars. We noted, however, that much of the full-mouth kissing or prolonged hugging appeared to be affectionate greetings rather than sexual activities per se, reflecting the higher degree of public physical intimacy men had with each other in Soma compared to the Castro or Polk (also observed by Hennen, 2008).

Not all of the Soma bars fostered a visible leather aesthetic—patrons or staff at My Place rarely wore leather. Yet, the participants created a scene that hewed to Soma's aesthetic of casual sexual contact. Men stared at each other openly, a casual curiosity that seamlessly gave way to disinterest or lust—locking eyes with another man for more than two seconds signaled interest that provoked them to approach. Men had noticeably more conversation with strangers than in other neighborhoods. The narrow backroom lit by a single red bulb was crowded even at 8:15 p.m.; as a man began performing fellatio on another, attracting a huddle around the duo, the impassivity of their faces belied by their shifts of position.

Year 2004 marked the nadir of Soma's leather scene. Two of the district's leather bars closed, while one of the oldest became a venue for mostly heterosexual events. Public sex was curtailed in all Soma bars in 2003 by a joint crackdown by the San Francisco Department of Public Heath, San Francisco Police Department, and state Alcoholic Beverage Control (ABC). This marked the extinction of one of the ethics of Soma sociality. With public sex confined to private clubs and sporadic parties after 2004, the gay passersby increasingly reflected a cosmopolitan aesthetic and men in leather chaps walked directly into one bar rather than strolling among them.

My Place was shuttered in 2003 by the ABC, replaced by the homonorma-tive Cip Lounge, whose website described it as a "dreamworld of inventive cocktails, eclectic wines . . . decadent champagnes and inspiring sights and sounds." The backroom became a wheelchair-accessible restroom, and a sign out front underscored the bar's past and its new present: "Please respect our neighbors! No public urination. No sexual shenanigans. No noise. Remember: People live here." Homonormative people do not do these things, and those who do them are not neighbors or, implicitly, people. These rules were formally enforced by bouncers with flashlights and informally by the disruptive presence of bachelorette parties I observed in 2006.

By 2012, the neighborhood had rebounded as a diverse gay and straight nightlife district, including a bar for South Asian gay men and admirers, and a "white trash" themed gay bar famed for its comfort food. Three attempts to open leather bars at My Place's address failed in six years—during my visits in 2008 and 2010, I was the only patron in leather. It became Driftwood in 2012, a craft cocktail bar of reclaimed wood and fireside library that encourages patrons to play their own vinyl records. As San Francisco's gay newspaper summarized its cosmopolitan respectability, "While it's easy to snub one's nose at gay bar venues 'going straight,' Driftwood pretty much embodies the future of nightlife; a hybrid of gay and straight, just like the bar's new owners" (*Bar Tab*, 2013).

The Castro's Metrosexual Homonormativity

As the most vibrant institutional enclave of the gay rights movement, the Castro redefined what it meant to be gay by politicizing identity as urban voters (Armstrong, 2002). It remains the iconic 24/7 gay village celebrated by creative cities promoters, packed with juice bars, coffee shops, bars, boutiques, and clothing stores. In 1999, its nineteen bars represented a third of the city's total and its largest concentration. From 2004 onward, it dominated, with more than half the city's gay bars.

First-wave Castro settlers built a protective ghetto to escape physical violence and discrimination (Levine, 1979), with a style and a masculine politics not dissimilar to Soma's (Levine, 1998). In 1999 as in 2012, its sidewalks and thronged with tourists and "bridge and tunnel" visitors to its restaurants and bars, while clutches of under-twenty-one youths sat on stoops or made conversation on the street. Many bars reflected a self-conscious iconic minimalism in their names and décor: The Café, Blue, and Home all featured clean lines and strategic lighting. The ambiguous "I'm going to *The Bar*" distinguished insiders from outsiders. Moby Dick had an exuberantly intoxicated crowd in designer denim and sporty retro T-shirts, while in the cavernous Midnight Sun, the first video bar, clean-cut men wearing khakis and polo shirts sipped cocktails in front of TV screens.

Castro patrons exemplified the "metrosexual" look also trendy among stylish, fastidious heterosexual men. Clothes were stylishly new, well-groomed hair and eyebrows, colognes frequently worn. Compared to Polk and Soma, there were more glances than talking among strangers, and more talking than touching. Castro nightlife-goers disdain public sex as undisciplined or reckless, but in 1999 there was still cruising for sex in the nearby Collingwood Park after 2 a.m.—sex that took place in nearby apartments or, perhaps, in cars.

The Café was the largest dance bar in the district. Once a lesbian bar, it had transitioned to young gay men, reflecting men's dominance in the Castro. It was often called a "tourist bar," a destination for gay visitors from local suburbs and foreign countries alike. Although the young men we interviewed often wore expensive designer labels, most had multiple low-wage service jobs. Groups of men huddled together, duos talking mouth to ear over the din of the music in the crowded bar. The dance floor was packed even at the early hour of 10:30 p.m.—and there were lines to get near a bartender. When I approached a young man who had been looking at me he fled, as if my approach signaled something more than an introduction between strangers. In the Castro, men look but avoid being touched by unwanted contact with strangers.

Although the homonormative style dominated the Castro in 1999, it was not stylistically homogenous. The Pendulum was the only bar in the city for gay African Americans, where stylistic practices included baggy jeans, R&B music, and logos of urban streetwear. The spacious Detour had industrial design, loud repetitive music, and a reputation for heavy drug use—and was the only place we witnessed penetrative sex in any bar, gay or straight. Daddy's was the remaining leather bar in the neighborhood, favored by men in their fifties with close-cropped gray hair, tight blue jeans, and black leather vests. The Edge's patrons were edgy only compared to its neighbors: patrons' leather jackets, dress shoes, and gelled hair were a far cry from the motorcycle jackets and shaved heads of Soma. Yet the bar played rock music and featured an enormous papier-mâché penis above the bar, rippling lights radiating from its tip.

By 2004, the Castro expanded down Market Street and all of the nonconformist bars had either been replaced by homonormative ones or had diluted their style. These new bars attracted increased pedestrian traffic with their contemporary furniture and gastronomy, attracting a well-dressed mixed gay and straight audience for drinks and meals. Cementing these Upper Market bars to the Castro in 2002 were two new supper clubs and the new Gay and Lesbian Community Center. Even the organization founded by Harvey Milk that first named the neighborhood "the Castro," changed its name to "Merchants of Upper Market and the Castro." The collapse of the Castro's leatherman heritage was complete with the closures of Daddy's and Leather Image, a combination barbershop and fetish gear store, and the shuttering of sex bar Detour. The Edge transitioned toward the Castro's aesthetic homogeneity, replacing its rock music and giant ejaculating penis with clean black walls and electronic dance music. Though the patrons were more bearish (larger and hairier) than those in other bars, they were otherwise indistinguishable from other Castro patrons in their comportment and clothing. The early-morning public cruising for sex at nearby Collingwood Park waned as adjacent buildings became condos. Subway advertisements in 2008 promoted a new same-sex wedding chapel, while ads for an internet dating service promoted "getting real" about "long term relationships."

Between 1999 and 2012, the Castro underwent a geographic expansion and stylistic homogenization, dominating San Francisco gay life. While Soma survived as a mixed nightlife district, Polk transitioned from heterogeneous gays to homogenous heterosexuals. The homonormative style became hegemonic, reflected in bars and patron practices in all gay neighborhoods.

RESISTING HOMONORMATIVITY

San Francisco is considered by erotic tourists to be one of the most prudish cities in the world. Unlike other civic dens of iniquity, San Francisco has no gay bathhouses, no sleazy back rooms in bars…and a dwindling amount of mischief in the bushes. (*San Francisco Guardian*, 2006)[3]

Changes in the vitality and character of San Francisco's bar districts did not go unnoticed. An important indicator of homonormativity, defined by its "demobilized gay constituency," is resistance to displacement. These included unsuccessful protests over the closure of the backroom bars in Soma (2003), protests over the closure of the Pendulum and a boycott of the owner's other Castro bar (2005), divisive debates about the gentrification of gay neighborhoods that ignored gay working class and men of color (2008–2009), and the successful defense of two Soma leather bars through the zoning and permitting process (2011–2013). The class-inflected erotics of gay style explain how these debates played out in urban placemaking.

Charges of racism erupted when the owner of Badlands, a Castro dance bar, purchased and closed the neighboring Pendulum in 2003, leaving Northern California without a bar for African American men and their admirers. An investigation by the San Francisco Human Rights Commission found the owner had referred to African Americans as "non-Badlands customers," directed doormen to request multiple forms of identification from, engaged in hiring discrimination against and the selective enforcement of dress codes against African Americans.

Social-class presentation was never invoked in public discussions, but helps explain why some African Americans and not others experienced problems. Black men with dreadlocks, in groups, and wearing Afrocentric or urban streetwear experienced trouble, while men of color who defended the owner appeared in normative Castro style. The "no bag" rule was more enforced against backpacks than laptop cases, as I myself experienced in 2002 and 2008, excluding youths. Thus, protest about race implicitly condoned class-based discrimination, as the defeat of a plan to locate a homeless shelter for queer youth in the Castro (see Reck, 2009).

By the time Polk Street's "death" was announced (Plaster, 2007), all but three of the bars were dark and the streetscape gone. Only the protest group Gay Shame explicitly connected mainstream gay identity, race and class discrimination, and gentrification in all three districts (see Sycamore, 2004). Leader Mattilda Bernstein Sycamore described its inspiration from the radical politics of ACT UP (AIDS Coalition To Unleash Power): "misogyny, racism, classism and homophobia: it was all tied together" (Sycamore, 2011), its actions inspiring academics as well (e.g., Halperin and Traub, 2010).

In 2003, Gay Shame protested the closure of My Place by pasting wordy editorials around Soma entitled "Gay Shame Supports Sex in All Bars." They framed the closures in martial terms: "In a city renowned for a teaming [*sic*] gay sexual underworld, public sex and queer visibility are under attack. Gentrification has virtually ended cruising in South of Market alleys, and Polk Street gay bars are being replaced by hip, upscale straight bars" (Gay Shame, 2003). Its flyers in Polk mapped its shift "from trannies, hustlers and queers . . . to hipsters, yuppies and trend seekers" (ibid.), and it crashed a Castro street festival with a protest action titled, "KKKutest in the Kastro." Gay Shame's radical rhetoric against the "violence of assimilation" went unheeded (Sycamore, 2004: 4), and they were the only group to draw attention to the plight of Soma and Polk. Polk's subcultures did not raise a fuss and, as of 2012, no new bars served them. The slow erosion of the city's bars to forty-one in 2012 and thirty-nine in 2014 may represent a shift away from bar socializing, justifying one blogger's "gay bar deathwatch" (Pape, 2013).

The struggles of two of the last old-school Soma bars reveal the perils and possibilities of SF's nightlife regulations. While one person can slow a bar opening, the city's inclusive permitting process also can save institutions through community mobilization. The Eagle closed in 2011 due to a 20 percent rent increase, but gay community mobilization prevented the owner from opening a non-gay bar, transferring its liquor license off-site, or selling the property to condo developers, petitions that were successful in part because of its role as a major site of charity fundraisers for gay and AIDS organizations (Brogan, 2012). Earlier, Hole in the Wall lost its lease and nearly went under because one resident filed multiple petitions to block its one-block move because "this neighborhood has been moving away from its sexual outlaw [demilitarized zone] rep[utation]" (Bajko, 2008). Though the neighbor held up the move for almost a year, sympathetic agents in the Entertainment Commission and the Board of Supervisors helped smooth its reopening. Thus, two of Soma's three remaining leather bars survived with help from a mobilized constituency, albeit one that hadn't mobilized over the removal of public sex in 2003–2004. New bars remade Soma along the lines of the old Polk, a heterogeneous streetscape of same-sex desires, albeit one in which the leather style played only one small part among many.

Debates about gentrification raged in the Castro over chain retail stores and perceptions of an influx of heterosexuals. As the moderator of a symposium on the future of gay neighborhoods summarized, "With gay gentrification, of course one of the great ironies is that now we are seeing this desirable location of the Castro becoming a place that is desirable for a much broader group of people as well, potentially imperiling what we are doing" (GLBT Historical Society of Northern California, 2006: Nov. 28). The open meetings hardly addressed the other gay enclaves—Polk was mentioned four times and Soma once, compared to the Castro's 302 mentions. One panelist contrasted "the Castro's fading historical role in terms of social oppression and stigmas" with current concerns: "Affluent gay professionals now talk about property rights, safety and stability." Thus gentrification, for Castro residents, meant "social preservation" legitimized by property ownership (Brown-Saracino, 2010).

CONCLUSION

"Homo now stands more for homogenous than any type of sexuality." (Sycamore, 2004: 4)

Reductionist understandings of gay neighborhoods have obscured their diverse stylistic practices and relationships to urban revitalization. Gay bars, streetscapes or neighborhoods do not succeed for the same reasons or fall victim to the same processes—or at least, they didn't used to. The nightlife of "respectable gays" thrived even to its dilution by cosmopolitan heterosexuals, as in the Castro, with a stylistic appeal that served as an engine of gentrification from within. Only nonconformist venues with broad appeal to gay "lifestyle commuters" prompted mobilizations to preserve them, as in Soma—but only after some of their nonconformism had been lost. Polk fell victim to gentrification from without, with only one radical group defending its dissident patrons and their practices.

I invoked queer theorists' critique of homonormativity to describe the convergence upon a particular style of gay placemaking that has displaced alternatives. By observing the erotics of gay styles and their geographic deployment, I linked the homonormative performance of individuals to the streetscapes and bars where its institutionalization is visible. The contrast between Polk's failure and Castro's success was about social class, not creativity or enterprise—a neighborhood anchored by wealthy homeowners and celebrated as a site of gay pilgrimage weathered the post-industrialization of the urban economy, while blue-collar and racial minority scenes withered, even when eroticized by lifestyle commuters (see also Collins, 2004;

Talbot, 2004). Gay Shame did protest homonormativity and promote non-conformist "rights to the city" (Prior et al., 2012), but its failures led its most vocal leader to leave SF (Sycamore, 2011). By adding to the cautions that nightlife economies can come at the cost of racial segregation (Talbot, 2004) and homogenization (Chatterton and Hollands, 2002; Prior et al., 2012; Zukin, 1998), this study also suggests that queer theorists have much to learn from these urban trends that affect more than gay citizens.

The homonormative cultural shift says as much about mainstream culture as it does about gays. The convergence between mainstream acceptance of gays and gay cosmopolitanism has opened "post-gay" possibilities for the privileged (Ghaziani, 2010; Nash, 2013), at the cost of further isolating sexual dissidents, the poor, and racial minorities (Collins, 2004; Hennen, 2008; Hubbard et al., 2008; Prior et al., 2012). The gay lifestyle commuter's spatial capital gives him access to ever more nightlife scenes, perhaps at the expense of any particular attachment to one. His "liberation" (Kelly et al., 2014) may cause the collapse of the scenes that also served others, paralleling the collapse of community institutions in African American neighborhoods after the suburbanization of the black upper-middle class (e.g., Pattillo-McCoy, 2000). If institutionalized streetscapes that foster serendipitous erotic possibilities are important, as Gay Shame argued, then websites and monthly parties in shared spaces cannot replace 24/7 establishments, especially for those gays without the spatial or racial capital to travel comfortably in cosmopolitan circles.

The generational shift away from gay placemaking and toward the temporary performance of privatized gay identities means that the streetscapes of gay enclaves may no longer be important sites of subcultural socialization. Further research must not assume that this privatization was inevitable, but assess the value that internet publics and ephemeral spaces have, both for nonnormative gays, racial minorities, and privileged consumers. Though folk accounts blamed the Internet for the collapse of cruising for sex in public or gay bars, it could just as easily have educated newcomers, just as it currently publicizes homonormative critiques. What has been gained, perhaps, is a stronger unity of purpose among the cosmopolitan mainstream, gay and straight, reflected in their consolidated command of city nightlife and shared support for gay marriage. But in the gay capital of San Francisco, the "new homonormativity" has become, spatially speaking, the only game in town.

EPILOGUE 2020

The trends identified in this chapter have continued apace. However, San Francisco's voters and elected officials have approved significant measures to preserve LGBT cultural heritage, including bars and gay neighborhoods. In 2014, the City began recognizing cultural districts, a process that was formalized in 2018; each of the City's historic gay neighborhoods was so organized in 2017–2019 (Elison, 2019). City voters also established the Legacy Business Registry and Preservation Fund in 2015 to support businesses that are more than thirty years old and can prove they are "have made a significant impact on the history or culture of their neighborhood." The fund provides grants directly to businesses and financial incentives to landlords for providing lease renewals of longer than ten years; gay bars have been among the first businesses so recognized (Office of Small Business, 2016).

By the end of 2019, Polk Gulch's only gay bar remaining was The Cinch, which advertised itself on Facebook as "the only surviving gay bar from a bygone era where almost every bar on Polk Street was Gay." Diva's, the Bay Area's only bar dedicated to transgender women and their admirers, closed earlier that year, one year after the establishment of the Compton's Transgender Cultural District in the southeastern part of the Tenderloin (Kost, 2019; Elison, 2019). In the adjacent part of the Tenderloin, San Francisco's oldest gay bar, The Gangway, closed in 2018, described as a haven for "working-class patrons from diverse backgrounds" and "the best damn seedy dive" by one admirer (Phillips, 2018; Avery, 2018). The passage of places in Polk and the Tenderloin did not go unremarked; a 2018 "March to Remember and Reclaim Queer Space" took nearly 200 attendees past many of the bars detailed in this chapter, including N'Touch, White Swallow, Kimo's, Rendezvous, Giraffe, and Polk Gulch Saloon (*Bay Area Reporter*, 2018).

In Soma, the Board of Supervisors established the "Leather and LGBTQ Cultural District" in 2018. It includes the historical and artistic exhibits in Ringold Alley, designated the "San Francisco South of Market Leather History Alley" (Madison, 2017). Gentrification has continued apace, however, with these installations and proposed ones outside the Eagle being funded by developers as part of the public amenities they must provide in order to build new condos. Of these public-private partnerships, leather culture anthropologist Gayle Rubin described them as "reshaping central city landscapes in ways that generally favor the affluent, the white, and the conventional" (Meronek and Clark, 2018). Soma's Lone Star Saloon was part of the inaugural class of nine legacy businesses (Brinklow, 2016), while the Eagle was added one year later. The Stud, faced with a tripling of rents, transitioned in ownership to a cooperative that has worked to find a new spot for the club that was registered as a Legacy Business in the first year of the registry's existence (Hemmelgarn, 2016). While none of the old leather bars have so far closed, a new bar opened two and a half blocks from the Leather Cultural District's edge. In 2019, this queer bar, co-owned by lesbians and a transgender man, opened, cultivating a diverse slate of entertainers and patrons, especially African American, lesbian, and transgender (Silvers, 2019).

In the Castro, the nonprofit Leather Alliance that organized the successful campaign for the Leather and LGBTQ Cultural District acted as the umbrella organization for the establishment of the Castro LGBTQ Cultural District in 2019. The district's official boundaries reflected the spread of the Castro during the 2000s, including businesses in adjacent Dolores Heights and trailing northwest up Market Street as far as the gay bars in Upper Market. Although it was the last of three LGBTQ-themed cultural districts in the City and the youngest of San Francisco's three gay neighborhoods, it continued to eclipse its older and less commercially viable, sisters. As committee chair Jesse Oliver Sanford told journalists, a cultural district was necessary because "it is the densest and longest-standing LGBT neighborhood in a major city"— a statement that is not quite accurate (Sabatini, 2019). Supporters hoped that the funds could help address the neighborhood's retail vacancy problem, homelessness, and the declining gay character of new businesses and residents (Barmann, 2019). Organizers also appointed outreach and inclusion co-chairs to address the Castro's "difficulties with diversity." In the words of co-chair Shaun Haines, "There's work to be done in cultural competency around a number of vectors. We've heard this from communities of color, from women, from trans communities, from the senior community."

LGBTQ businesses in or near all three neighborhoods' cultural districts have taken advantage of listings on the Legacy Business Registry; thus far none so listed have gone out of business, although The Stud will almost certainly have to relocate soon. Time will tell whether these strategies and future ones will be enough to preserve the remaining LGBT character in San Francisco's historic gay nightlife districts as the region continues to experience intense gentrification, or whether these significant measures will have proven too little, too late for the most vulnerable.

NOTES

1. Reprinted from 2015. *Urban Studies* 52(16):3144–33159; epilogue added 2020.
2. (Sledge, 2000).
3. (Marke B., Sept. 20–26).

REFERENCES

Andersson, Johan. 2011. "Vauxhall's Post-industrial Pleasure Gardens: 'Death Wish' and Hedonism in 21st-Century London." *Urban Studies*, 48(1):85–100.

Armstrong, Elizabeth A. 2002. *Forging Gay Identities: Organizing Sexuality in San Francisco*. University of Chicago Press

Avery, Dan. 2018. "San Francisco's Oldest Gay Bar Closes After 108 Years." *New Now Next*, Jan 30.

Bajko Matthew S. 2008. "Appeals delay SOMA bar's relocation." *Bay Area Reporter*, San Francisco, Mar 27. Available from: http://ebar.com/ (accessed 29 June 2014).

Bar Tab. 2013. "Driftwood." *Bay Area Reporter Gay Nightlife Guide*. Available from: http://www.bartabsf.com (accessed 29 June 2014).

Barmann, Jay. 2019. "Five Reasons Why the Castro and North Beach Have So Many Vacant Storefronts." *SFist*, Mar 30.

Bay Area Reporter. 2018. "March to Reclaim Queer Spaces." Mar 14.

Beauregard, Robert A. 1986. "The chaos and complexity of gentrification." In *Gentrification of the City*, edited by N. Smith and P. Williams. Boston: Allen & Unwin, pp. 35–55.

Berlant, Lauren and Michael Warner. 1998. "Sex in Public." *Critical Inquiry*, 24(2):547–566.

Borden, Mark. 2000. "The Best Cities for Business". *Fortune*, 142(13):218–232.

Bourdieu, Pierre. 1984. *Distinction: A Social Critique of the Judgment of Taste*. Harvard University Press.

Boyd, Nan A. 2005. *Wide-Open Town: A History of Queer San Francisco to 1965*. University of California Press.

Brekhus, Wayne. 2003. *Peacocks, Chameleons, Centaurs: Gay Suburbia and the Grammar of Social Identity*. University of Chicago Press.

Brinklow, Adam. 2016. "Here are San Francisco's Very First Legacy Business Recipients." *SF Curbed*, Aug 11.

Brogan, Scott. 2012. "SF Eagle will re-open." *Bay Area Reporter*, Sep 6. Available from: http://ebar.com/ (accessed 29 June 2014).

Brown, Gavin. 2009. "Thinking Beyond Homonormativity: performative explorations of diverse Gay Economies." *Environment and Planning A*, 41(6):1496–1510.

Brown, Michael. 2014. "Gender and sexuality II There goes the gayborhood?" *Progress in Human Geography*, 38(3):457–465.

Brown-Saracino, Japonica. 2010. *A Neighborhood That Never Changes: Gentrification, Social Preservation, and the Search for Authenticity*. University of Chicago.

Cavan, Sherri. 1966. *Liquor License: An Ethnography of Bar Behavior*. Chicago: Aldine.

Centner, Ryan. 2008. "Places of Privileged Consumption Practices: Spatial Capital, the Dot-Com Habitus, and San Francisco's Internet Boom." *City & Community*, 7(3):193–223.

Chatterton, Paul and Robert Hollands. 2002. "Theorising Urban Playscapes: Producing, Regulating and Consuming Youthful Nightlife City Spaces." *Urban Studies*, 39(1):95–116.

Clark, Terry Nichols. 2003. *The City as an Entertainment Machine*. Greenwich: JAI Press.

Clendinen, Dudley and Adam Nagourney. 1999. *Out for Good: The Struggle to Build a Gay Rights Movement in America*. New York: Simon & Schuster.

Collins, Allan. 2004. "Sexual dissidence, enterprise and assimilation: bedfellows in Urban Regeneration." *Urban Studies*, 41(9):1789–1806.

Doan, Petra L. and Harrison Higgins. 2011. "The Demise of Queer Space? Resurgent Gentrification and the Assimilation of LGBT Neighborhoods." *Journal of Planning Education and Research*, 31(1):6–25.

Duggan, Lisa. 2002. "The New Homonormativity: The Sexual Politics of Neoliberalism." In *Materializing Democracy*, edited by R. Castronovo and D. Nelson. Durham: Duke University Press, pp. 175–194.

Elison, Meg. 2019. "San Queer Cultural Districts Take Shape." *Bay Area Reporter*, Aug 14.

Flanigan, Kathy. 2012. "Tolerant Times Bring Change to Gay Bars." *Journal Sentinel*, Milwaukee, WI, Jun 9. Available from: http://www.jsonline.com (accessed 21 March 2014).

Florida, Richard L. 2003. *The rise of the Creative Class: and how it's Transforming Work, Leisure, community and Everyday Life*. New York: Basic Books.

Fulbright, Leslie. 2005. "Polk Gulch Cleanup Angers Some: Gentrification Pushing Out 'Hookers, hustlers.'" *San Francisco Chronicle*, Oct 12.

Gay Shame. 2003. "Gay Shame Supports Sex in All Bars." Available from: http://www.gayshamesf.org/sexinbars.html (accessed 16 June 2009).

Ghaziani, Amin. 2010. "There Goes the Gayborhood?" *Contexts*, 9(4):64–66.

Ghaziani, Amin. 2014. "Measuring Urban Sexual Cultures." *Theory and Society*, 43:371–393.

GLBT Historical Society of Northern California. 2006. "Queer in the City - GLBT Neighborhoods." Available from: https://www.youtube.com/user/glbt1history (accessed 24 June 2010).

Goffman, Erving. 1951. "Symbols of Class Status." *The British Journal of Sociology*, 2(4):294–304.

Gotham, Kevin Fox. 2005. "Tourism Gentrification: The Case of New Orleans' Vieux Carre (French Quarter)." *Urban Studies*, 42(7):1099–1121.

Grazian, David. 2007. *On the Make: The Hustle of Urban Nightlife*. University of Chicago Press.

Hae, Laam. 2011. "Dilemmas of the Nightlife Fix Post-industrialisation and the Gentrification of Nightlife in New York City." *Urban Studies*, 48(16):3449–3465.

Halperin, David M. and Valerie Traub. 2010. *Gay Shame*. Chicago: University of Chicago Press.

Hartman, Chester. 2002. *City for Sale: The Transformation of San Francisco, Rev. Ed.* U. California.

Hebdige, Dick. 1981. *Subculture: The Meaning of Style*. New York: Routledge.

Hemmelgarn, Seth. 2016. "Stud, Castro Country Club Get Legacy Status." *Bay Area Reporter*, Nov 30.

Hennen, Peter. 2008. *Faeries, Bears, and Leathermen*. University of Chicago Press.

Howe, Alyssa C. 2001. "Queer Pilgrimage: The San Francisco Homeland and Identity Tourism." *Cultural Anthropology*, 16(1):35–61.

Hubbard, Phil, Roger Matthews, Jane Scoular, and Laura Agustin. 2008. "Away from Prying Eyes? The Urban Geographies of Adult Entertainment'." *Progress in Human Geography*, 32(3):363–381.

Hunter, Marcus A. 2010. "The Nightly Round: Space, Social Capital, and Urban Black Nightlife." *City & Community*, 9(2):165–186.

Kane, Peter L. 2013. "Best Gay Bars Not in the Castro." *The Bold Italic*. Available from: http://www.thebolditalic.com (accessed 28 June 2014).

Kelly, Brian C., Richard M. Carpiano, Adam Easterbrook, and Jeffrey T. Parsons. 2014. "Exploring the Gay Community Question: Neighborhood and Network Influences on the Experience of Community among Urban Gay Men." *The Sociological Quarterly*, 55(1):23–48.

Kost, Ryan. 2019. "Last Dance at Divas." *San Francisco Chronicle*, Apr 3.

Levine, Martin P. 1979. "Gay Ghetto." In *Gay Men*, edited by M.P. Levine. New York: Harper and Row, pp. 182–204.

Levine, Martin P. 1998. *Gay Macho*. Kimmel M (ed.). NYU Press.

Lewis, Nathaniel M. 2013. "Ottawa's Le/The Village: Creating a gaybourhood amidst the 'death of the village.'" *Geoforum*, 49:233–242.

Madison, Alex. 2017. "SOMA Leather Alley Dedicated." *Bay Area Reporter*, Jul 26.

Marke B. 2006. "Oral Histories: Tales of the Early '90s Underground Gay Sex Club Scene." *San Francisco Bay Guardian*, Sep 20.

Meronek, Toshio and Cole Clark. 2018. "How Gentrification is Eroding San Francisco's Historic Leather Scene." *them.*, Oct 1.

Murray, Stephen O. 1996. "The Promiscuity Paradigm, AIDS, and Gay Complicity with the Remedicalization of Homosexuality." In *American Gay*, edited by S.O. Murray. University of Chicago Press, pp. 99–125.

Musto, Michael. 2010. "RIP Gay Bars." *Village Voice*. Available from: http://blogs.villagevoice.com (accessed 21 March 2014).

Nash, Catherine J. 2013. "The age of the 'post-mo'? Toronto's gay Village and a New Generation." *Geoforum*, 49:243–252.

Office of Small Business. 2016. "Legacy Business." *City of San Francisco* (accessed 4 February 2020).

Pape, Allie. 2013. "Gay Bar Deathwatch." *Eater SF*. Available from: http://sf.eater.com/ (accessed 1 July 2014).

Pattillo-McCoy, Mary. 2000. *Black Picket Fences : Privilege and Peril among the Black Middle Class*. University of Chicago Press.

Phillips, Justin. 2018. "SF's Oldest Gay Bar Closes After Five Decades." *San Francisco Chronicle*, Jan 29.

Plaster, C. Joey. 2009. "Economic Power to Political Power." *Polk Street History Project*. Available from: http://outhistory.org/ (accessed 30 June 2014).

Plaster, C. Joey. 2007. "The death of Polk Street." *San Francisco Bay Guardian*, Aug 29.

Podmore, Julie. 2013. "Critical commentary: Sexualities Landscapes Beyond Homonormativity." *Geoforum*, 49:263–267.

Prior, Jason, Spike Boydell, and Philip Hubbard. 2012. "Nocturnal Rights to the City: Property, Propriety and Sex Premises in Inner Sydney." *Urban Studies*, 49(8):1837–1852.

Reck, Jen. 2009. "Homeless Gay and Transgender Youth of Color in San Francisco: 'No One Likes Street Kids'—Even in the Castro." *Journal of LGBT Youth*, 6(2–3):223–242.

Roberts, Marion, Chris Turner, Steve Greenfield, and Guy Osborn. 2006. "A Continental Ambience? Lessons in Managing Alcohol-related Evening Entertainment." *Urban Studies*, 43(7):1105–1125.

Robinson, Tony. 1995. "Gentrification and Grassroots Resistance in San Francisco's Tenderloin." *Urban Affairs Review*, 30(4):483–513.

Rubin, Gayle S. 1998. "The Miracle Mile: South of Market and Gay Male Leather 1962-1997." In *Reclaiming San Francisco*, edited by J. Brook. San Francisco: City Lights, pp. 247–272.

Sabatini, Joshua. 2019. "SF to Form Castro Cultural District to Protect LGBTQ Heritage." *San Francisco Examiner*, Jun 23.

Schulman, Sarah. 2012. *The Gentrification of the Mind*. University of California Press.

Shaw, Robert. 2013. "'Alive After Five': Constructing the Neoliberal Night in Newcastle Upon tyne." *Urban Studies*, 52(3):456–470.

Sides, Josh. 2009. *Erotic City: Sexual Revolutions & the Making of Modern San Fran.* Oxford University Press.

Silvers, Emma. 2019. "Jolen's in S.F. is a New Kind of Queer Bar." *San Francisco Chronicle*, Feb 27.

Sledge, Buck. 2000. "Clubs and Bars." Apr 25. Available from: http://www.sfgate.co m/cgi-bin/article.cgi?f=/g/a/2000/05/02/queer.clubsbars.DTL&hw=castro+neigh borhood+straights&sn=038&sc=354 (accessed 4 March 2009).

Sycamore, Matilda B. 2004. *That's Revolting!: Queer Strategies for Resisting Assimilation*. Brooklyn: Soft Skull Press.

Sycamore, Matilda B. 2011. "We Who Feel Differently." Available from: http://wew hofeeldifferently.info (accessed 26 June 2014).

Talbot, Deborah. 2004. "Regulation and Racial Differentiation in the construction of Night-Time economies: A london Case Study." *Urban Studies*, 41(4):887–901.

Valentine, Gill and Tracey Skelton. 2003. "Finding oneself, Losing Oneself: the lesbian and Gay 'Scene' as a Paradoxical Space." *International Journal of Urban and Regional Research*, 27(4):849–866.

Walker, Richard. 2006. "The boom and the bombshell: the New Economy Bubble and the San Francisco Bay Area." In *The Changing Economic Geography of Globalization*, edited by G. Vertova. London: Routledge, pp. 121–139.

Weiss, Margot. 2011. *Techniques of pleasure: BDSM and the circuits of sexuality*. Duke University Press.

Wildermuth, John. 2013. "Polk Street neighbors seek to Limit Bars." *San Francisco Chronicle*, Feb 25.

Yeo, Su-Jan and Chye Kiang Heng. 2014. "An (extra)ordinary Night Out: Urban informality, Social Sustainability and the Night-Time Economy." *Urban Studies*, 51(4):712–726.

Zukin, Sharon. 1998. "Urban lifestyles: Diversity and standardisation in spaces of consumption." *Urban Studies*, 35(5/6):825.

Chapter 3

Gayborhoods as Criminogenic Space

Vanessa R. Panfil

When criminologists and sociologists discuss criminogenic space, they often intend to discuss how the space or place leads to crime. Criminogenic, at its root words, refers to something that causes crime. Studying criminogenic space has led to advancements in crime prevention and improving resident feelings of safety and self-efficacy. Relatedly, gayborhoods and gay districts serve important roles in LGBTQ+ people's lives, allowing them physical spaces where they can be themselves, meet others like them, and hopefully be insulated from the heterosexism and cissexism of society. Take this description of the many purposes gayborhoods can serve, and the many ways they've been described or conceptualized over time:

> A gayborhood can be a "ghetto" for disadvantaged sexual minorities; the site of real or "imagined communities" of like-minded queer people; a "quasi-ethnic" settlement that promotes identity development; a "safe space" to which queer moral refugees retreat for shelter from heterosexual hostility; a "site of resistance" from which activists can overcome antigay violence; an "urban land market" that promotes economic vitality and revitalization; and an "entertainment district" of consumption and tourism. (Ghaziani 2014:271)

As a queer criminologist, sociologist, and urban ethnographer, I am interested in thinking about gayborhoods and gay districts as so-called criminogenic spaces. I do not, of course, mean to suggest that LGBTQ+ people are prone to offending in gayborhoods, or prone to offending more in general. However, LGBTQ+ people have often been targeted for arrest for their alleged criminality in gay gathering places. There is a well-documented history of police officers raiding places gays and lesbians were suspected to congregate in order to disrupt and prevent public gay life. In post–World War I

New York City, hundreds of gay men were arrested at bathhouses, bars, and theaters and charged with "degenerate disorderly conduct" (Chauncey 1995:146). The famed Stonewall Riots were borne of police harassing LGBTQ+ bar patrons at the Stonewall Inn for their clothing, gender presentation, and sexual identity. Arresting queer and trans people in gay bars for "crimes" committed there would create a criminogenic space by virtue of enforcing law in the gathering places of those targeted by these laws. That is not quite what "criminogenic space" has originally been meant to discuss, but in this case of LGBTQ+ people's overcriminalization, it is still relevant. Additionally, perhaps there are forces at work where perpetrators (sometimes including police officers) target LGBTQ+ people in gayborhoods, and LGBTQ+ people are more willing to physically defend themselves in those areas; the dynamics of violent heterosexism and LGBTQ+ resilience combine to complicate feelings of safety.

To explore the notion of gayborhoods as criminogenic space, I first delve deeper into the criminological concept of criminogenic space to investigate how this concept could be used more productively to explore LGBTQ+ people's experiences with crime and victimization. Next, I explore several relevant themes. Two primary themes include LGBTQ+ people experiencing victimization in gayborhoods—because that is where they are visible and unapologetic; and LGBTQ+ people fighting back when targeted in gay bars and gay districts—some of the few places they thought they could actually be safe, or feel justified in defending their gayness. Another key theme I examine is the relationship of gentrification to crime, victimization, and feelings of safety. Related concerns I discuss include navigating urban risk on the way to/from outreach and advocacy organizations and experiencing state violence while in gay or trans "strolls." I draw from prior interview-based studies I have conducted, as well as existing literature on LGBTQ+ people's experiences in gayborhoods and gay gathering places. Such areas are not just enclaves, but are incubators of culture and interaction, and serve as microcosms that exemplify larger structural processes.

CRIMINOGENIC SPACE: A CONTESTED CONCEPT

As a discipline, criminology has a long history of studying criminogenic spaces. Perhaps the most recognizable example of this would be concentric zone theory, drawn from Park, Burgess, and McKenzie's (1925) study of Chicago. This theory can be found in probably every introductory criminology textbook and reader. It pinpoints the "zone of transition" (what the authors call "the area of deterioration, the so-called 'slum'":148) as the primary location of crime. The zone of transition has buildings such as factories, abandoned warehouses, dilapidated housing, and immigrant tenements, and thus, has high population density and poor and transient residents. It is these features of the environment said to produce crime among occupants.

Other influential works in criminology have taken a similar approach in exploring how the features of neighborhoods might lead to crime commission, and thus, prevention. Ecological approaches to crime include social disorganization theory and broken windows theory. Regarding the latter, broken windows theory suggests that blights such as overgrown lots, litter, boarded-up houses, and broken windows—thought to be visible signs of disorder—send a signal that the neighborhood is not cared for and thus crime will be able to flourish as well (Skogan 1990). The legacy of broken windows theory was evident in sweeping changes to many cities' law enforcement strategies, including zero tolerance policies to arrest people engaging in "public order" crimes such as vagrants, the homeless, street-based sex workers, and even sidewalk booksellers (e.g., Dunier 1999).

Environmental criminology is thus an influential form of criminological inquiry. Other modern applications of the concept of criminogenic space include actuarial assessments of where crime happens most often, in order to intervene and prevent crime. For example, hot spots policing identifies small areas where crime happens often and deploys additional police officers and resources to those areas to target and prevent crime; interestingly, the literature on hot spots policing refers to these areas as "deviant places" (e.g., Braga et al. 2014:633). Ecological interventions such as CPTED—Crime Prevention through Environmental Design—seek to resolve the conditions that are seen as making certain spaces criminogenic and thus dangerous for people to move through. Environmental changes inspired by CPTED might include increased lighting, cameras, and landscaping that produces clear paths. CPTED has also been referred to as "Designing Out Crime" and "defensible space" (ICA 2020).

When I discuss criminogenic space, I mean something a bit different. My thinking and analyses for this chapter have been influenced greatly by Hayward's (2012) discussion of new ways to think about the relationship between space/place and crime/victimization. One of his main critiques is how environmental criminology eschews more humanistic and interactive approaches by focusing on technocratic ones. His argument "prioritizes phenomenological place over abstract space in an attempt to take seriously the cultural and structural relationships that contribute to crime and disorder or, for that matter, community safety and stability" (2012:442). Hayward draws from understandings of space/place used by cultural geographers in advocating for cultural criminologists (and mainstream criminologists) to reconceptualize criminogenic space. Specifically, he says that for cultural geographers, "space is understood almost as if it were a living thing, a multi-layered congress of cultural, political and spatial dynamics" (2012:443). Instead of limiting our exploration to how a place creates opportunities for crime for those living in it, such an approach instead looks at how people living in the space help to shape said space. As Campbell (2012:401) explains:

> A cultural criminological approach emphasises the subjective, affective, embodied, aesthetic, material, performative, textual, symbolic, and visual relations of space, while recognising that the settings of crime are neither fixed nor inevitable but are relational, improvised, contingent, constructed, and contested through an array of creative and dynamic cultural practices, made meaningful within and mediated by wider processes of social transformation.

It is this cultural criminology approach to "criminogenic space" that I employ in this chapter to discuss experiences of LGBTQ+ people. I draw from various sources and studies, but rely heavily on my interview-based and partially ethnographic study of gay and bisexual men who are also gang- and crime-involved.

Criminologists might envision criminogenic spaces for LGBTQ+ people as places where those individuals are more likely to commit crimes, or where they are more likely to be victimized. While I integrate this understanding into my analyses here to help define the scope of my chapter, analytically, I find it to be a static way to think of gayborhoods as criminogenic space. Certainly, if LGBTQ+ people are more likely to spend their leisure time in gayborhoods, they may be more likely to commit crimes there due to increased opportunities. And, certain areas of town may be more conducive to LGBTQ+ people committing crime there because of the purpose of that space. For example, if we were to look at so-called strolls or beats—words sometimes used to refer to particular areas of town where gay or transgender sex workers sell sex, or where gay or transgender people seek anonymous sexual encounters in public settings—the place itself would be considered criminogenic because people intentionally go there to commit crimes. However, this ignores the context, power dynamics, and interactional features of those settings: for example, that gay and transgender sex workers sell sex in siloed strolls because of structural forces that marginalize them in formal labor markets, and strolls can provide them with additional safety when they are surrounded by others like them. (There is also the commodification aspect of this in that clients seeking these transactions and those seeking to provide them know exactly where to go.) This is a very different reading than strolls being sites of crime causation through disorder or through the people who frequent these places. Thus, I hope to contextualize my analyses throughout to not suggest that LGBTQ+ people are somehow more susceptible to offending in gayborhoods by virtue of their existence, but through interactional social processes that occur in these settings.

EXPERIENCING VICTIMIZATION IN GAYBORHOODS: BECOMING A VISIBLE TARGET

For many LGBTQ+ people, gayborhoods or districts known to be gay-friendly—such as those with a high proportion of gay bars, clubs, restaurants, and gay-owned retail stores—have an important role in making them feel welcome, safe, and able to be themselves. LGBTQ+ people often feel they can be "out, loud, and proud" in gayborhoods and gay districts, and will be protected by other LGBTQ+ people either indirectly, through safety in numbers, or directly, in the case of defending "our own" should a conflict happen. There may also be the assumption that homophobic people avoid gayborhoods because they find what happens there to be distasteful, thus reducing the likelihood that gayborhood patrons will be victimized. However, there is a paradoxical element to this: while gayborhoods allow for feelings of safety and greater freedom of expression, they can facilitate LGBTQ+ people becoming visibly queer, and thus potentially becoming a target. In this way, gayborhoods can be conceptualized as criminogenic space in that they concentrate and expose LGBTQ+ people to potential perpetrators—that is, criminogenic for those seeking to do harm to a population that isn't necessarily visible otherwise.

Perhaps an example will better illustrate the issue of "becoming visible." Gay and bisexual male participants in a prior study of mine (Panfil 2017) described strategies to avoid anti-gay harassment, one of which was to avoid neighborhoods or areas they thought were dangerous for gay men. Another was to be very aware of their gender presentation when moving through those districts, such as modifying their gender presentation to remove any stereotypically feminine gestures, which they thought would mark them as gay. In their experience, presenting in a masculine or neutral way meant that they didn't attract any unwanted attention, and were not harassed for being gay. One participant, Silas, explained that he did not feel safe being openly gay or visible in his neighborhood. He said, "I think I can hide it [my sexuality] pretty well, so as long as I walk with my head down, and don't talk, or say anything to anybody, I'm fine." He added, "I wouldn't hang a gay flag on my porch." In contrast, when in the gay parts of town near his neighborhood, he said, "I'd be more comfortable. I'd walk however I wanted to, talk however I wanted to, do whatever kind of hand gestures I like" (171). In his neighborhood where he wanted to ensure his safety, Silas eschewed both covert and overt signals of his sexual identity, ranging from the subtle, like hand gestures, to the more obvious, like hanging a rainbow flag.

On this latter point, rainbow flags mark not just the person, but the dwelling: someone may choose not to mark their home as one inhabited by LGBTQ+ people to avoid both violent victimization and property crime (e.g., vandalism or burglary). Similar thought processes likely occur when deciding on car bumper stickers. I personally do not live in a gayborhood, but I am very heartened and feel safer seeing other rainbow flags in my neighborhood, since I feel as though there are allies or people like me nearby who contribute to a more accepting culture (and at our house, we fly the Progress pride flag).

LGBTQ+ people may also encounter risk on their way to or from community organizations that provide services, outreach, and advocacy. While not strictly a gayborhood as these organizations may be decentralized and in various locales, these organizations represent a physical place that offers affirmation, empowerment, and resources in the ways gayborhoods aim to, and would-be clients must travel to them. In my research with LGBTQ+ youth who had to traverse perilous urban environments to reach the after-school drop-in youth center, that was their main complaint: just getting to the center—the neighborhoods they had to pass through and the people they encountered in them. Their movements were complicated by the same issue raised by Silas in a different study mentioned earlier: that an unfamiliar neighborhood will carry unknown risks relevant to being out (or visibly gay). Although urban risk may not be an issue everywhere, I raise this to remind scholars that in order to access needed and wanted services, individuals may have to travel through dangerous neighborhoods just to get to "safe space."

When discussing perpetrators of physical and sexual violence, it is important to note that these individuals may be members of the general public, but also may be agents of the state. Unfortunately, state harassment of LGBTQ+ people did not stop after the Stonewall Riots in 1969, nor after the U.S. Supreme Court struck down all remaining sodomy laws criminalizing same-sex sexual activity in *Lawrence v. Texas* (2003). While violence at the hands of law enforcement can occur when LGBTQ+ people are going about their business in gayborhoods, LGBTQ+ people are perhaps particularly susceptible to police violence when they are accused of engaging in crime (whether the accusation is valid or invalid), or are engaged in low-level but visible forms of criminalized activity. One such example is related to gay and transgender people selling sex on the street, in a location sometimes referred to as a "stroll." In my study, men knew exactly where "the stroll" (or sometimes "the beat") was in town, providing an exact street intersection. People on strolls and beats can also be targeted by police officers not just for arrest for engaging in so-called public order offenses, but for physical and sexual violence, either on the streets, in a police car, or in jail. Violations can range from verbal harassment to requesting sexual services in exchange for no formal arrest to forcible rape. Injustices such as these occur in the United States and globally, especially in countries where statutes already criminalize same-sex sexual contact (see, for example, Amnesty International 2001). For example, in Sri Lanka, several laws criminalize LGBTQ+ people's conduct and presentation. The street in capital city Colombo where gay and transgender sex workers congregate was referred to as "the road." While they might sell sex there, they may also be in the road to buy goods or visit with friends. On the road, not only would customers and residents rob, beat, or rape them, police would also harm them. Police may call them anti-LGBTQ slurs like "ponnaya," falsely accuse and jail them even if they are not actively selling sex, beat them, coerce sexual favors or force bribes to avoid arrest, steal from them, publicly shame them, sexually assault them, and blame them for their own victimization by questioning why they were in the road (Nichols 2014).

The false and damaging assumption that transgender women are always looking to sell sex has been used as a broad law enforcement strategy: transgender women, particularly transgender women of color, are likely to be stopped for suspected vagrancy, loitering, drug possession, and solicitation or manifestation of prostitution simply for talking to someone or walking on the side of a road. Advocates and activists have referred to this "offense" as "walking while trans" (Kellaway 2015). This strategy, consistent with a broken windows sort of ethos, targets transgender people for alleged "quality of life" offenses when they are merely existing.

Paradoxically, LGBTQ+ groups and establishments in gayborhoods have teamed up with law enforcement to try to effect greater safety, reduced victimization, and increased legitimacy, despite challenging relationships with police historically. Moskowitz (2017) remarks on the irony that "Stonewall Inn, once synonymous with anti-cop riots, now welcomes the cops with semiautomatic weapons that regularly stand outside its doors"; Hanhardt (2013: 3) explores the "neighborhood-based convergence of anticrime and LGBT rights strategies" in depth, including the ways LGBTQ groups have tried to distance themselves from so-called criminal elements, which may include urban queer and trans youth of color, a point I return to later. Regardless of one's political orientation toward law enforcement participation in queer rights demonstrations, it is important to note that in gay meccas and cities with gayborhoods, a gay person may feel more comfortable calling the police to report victimization that has happened to them, or more comfortable seeking medical care. These dynamics are stimulated by the cultures of gay meccas: for example, LGBTQ+ people may have seen a contingent of police officers in the Pride parade, or the city may have LGBTQ+ liaison officers active in the community, or community organizations may encourage victims to seek justice against perpetrators. Combined with their perhaps greater likelihood to be out personally, and thus not fear being outed or suspected as gay by reporting, factors like these support reporting anti-gay victimization.

GAYBORHOODS AS DEFENSIBLE SPACE

Recall that using environmental design to prevent crime and victimization can be referred to as "defensible space"; in general, that term refers to an area whose physical attributes facilitate inhabitants' abilities to keep themselves and their neighborhoods safe (Newman 1996). Here, I am using the term a bit more colloquially and focusing on an assumption that precedes designing out crime: that LGBTQ+ people may see gayborhoods as places worthy of defending because of what it provides for those who use the space. In terms of interpersonal violence in gayborhoods, they may defend themselves directly because they feel they are entitled to be "out, loud, and proud" in those areas.

In my study with gay gang- and crime-involved men, gay bars and gay districts played a role in making these men feel justified in fighting back against anti-gay harassment in those areas. For one participant in my study, a chance encounter with some homophobic young men served effectively as a gang initiation, since he proved his fighting prowess alongside the gang he had begun to spend time with. Imani recalled,

> You know how those college kids get drunk, and they were [in the gay bar district] just being reckless, saying "fag this" and "fag that," and [my posse] just had to tear 'em up. And I was there, so I had to help. . . . They was up on a balcony and they was like, throwin' stuff down, so me, I gets mad, I'm like, "Bitch, don't be throwin' stuff down the thing," I swear to God, I started throwin' rocks up there. . . . So they come down the stairs. They started followin' us, callin' us fags and stuff. . . . We just took it upon ourselves to attack 'em. . . . They thought they was gonna get us! I don't know why they think gay people cain't fight. We was beatin' them up. That was crazy. (2017:184)

While Imani seems to mark the college males' behavior as "reckless" in general, his point is that people engaging in anti-gay verbal and physical harassment in gayborhoods are not treading lightly and are inviting trouble, as gay people in these areas would expect to not be harassed there. This point is made more clearly by the following interaction with Reese:

Reese: I fought with a couple of people, like the [gay] bar would get crowded or whatever, we seem to have a lot of straight people come in there, and they thought they was running the show, because we actually have lesbians and gays in there, kissing or whatever, and that pissed them off. Well if we pissed you off, get the fuck out!. . . . He came in our bar, where we can be comfortable, you can get comfortable or you can leave, and he was like, "Shut the fuck up you little faggot," so that instantly puts me off and we started fighting. . . . He disrespected me!

VP: And he called you a faggot right on your turf?

Reese: Yeah, yeah, I could see if I was on his turf, but he was on mine.

VP: Okay so let's imagine that scenario. If you went to a straight bar—

Reese: (rolls his eyes and starts shaking his head)

VP: I know, but let's say you did. You went to a straight bar and he called you a faggot there, would you have fought him at the straight bar?

Reese: Most likely. . . . If I get that, it will not even really be if they call me a faggot, because if you're just like, "Yeah whatever, fag," I'm fine, but if you're doing it as being disrespectful, then that will piss me off and if I can, I'm gonna fight you, and if I can't, then I'll be pissed off and leave.

VP: So would you ever fight with someone [when] you knew you weren't gonna win?

Reese: Yeah, I have . . . It's more about the respect, like if I give you respect, I demand respect back. (2017:177)

Reese first sets up the most basic issue: that gay bars are places specifically intended for LGBTQ+ patrons, where they should feel comfortable engaging in any activities there that are seen as typically acceptable within such a setting, including showing same-sex affection. Reese's description implies that gay bars are one of the few places in society where straight people are not "running the show," should not expect to do so, are not entitled to do so, and should leave if that fact is not to their liking. LGBTQ+ people should not be harassed for being themselves in spaces literally created for them. He connects his and the community's symbolic ownership by saying "our bar," explicitly noting it's a place where they can "be comfortable." When LGBTQ+ people are faced with victimization in so many contexts, gay bars, clubs, and restaurants become safe spaces to call their own. Reese's narrative also suggests that a heterosexual man in society may have the right to object to same-sex displays of affection on "his turf," and presumably, anywhere that is not a gay establishment could be "his turf." While I don't think Reese thinks straight people should feel entitled to harass LGBTQ+ people on the streets and in public accommodations, he is trying to draw an analogy, effectively saying, we didn't bring this to you, you brought yourself here to us, so get right with your behavior. The disrespect communicated by the man's aggressive threat and anti-gay slur were aimed at Reese directly, but as it occurred in a gay bar, the broader gay community was also implicated. The circumstances of this scenario provided Reese with the motivation and justification to fight back; to defend queer space for his and other patrons' use, free of anti-gay harassment.

These examples illustrate how the presence of gay districts and gay establishments can allow LGBTQ+ people to feel justified and empowered to defend themselves in such spaces. Take this example from Steve, who severely beat his harasser:

> I was walking in the gay district, and this guy was like, "Oh, you faggot." And it kinda pissed me off, so I showed him how big of a faggot I was. . . . I don't really look gay, not most of the time, but if I'm walking with a guy, I'll hold his hand or whatever, and [if] someone says something, I'll pretty much, just cuss them out. And if they wanna come at me, it happens, but not really. I wouldn't say it happens a lot. . . . I walked out of the gay bar, and I used to wear a necklace that was a rainbow, and he called me a faggot, so it kinda upset me, so I just told him, "Faggots can do whatever, it's a free world." . . . He swung on me first. I dodged it, and beat him up. And I didn't stop until I felt I was comfortable with it, until I seen enough blood [coming out of his] nose, eye, ear. And I kicked him a couple of times until I seen blood, and then I finished beating him until I was happy. Made sure he never called one of us a faggot again. [Maybe] he just didn't feel comfortable around gay people. I don't know, maybe he was gay hisself, and he was just upset because he couldn't walk around, go to a gay bar. (2017:182–183)

Steve's narrative first sets up a contrast about visibility: while he mentions that he does not "look gay" normally, being in the gay district, wearing rainbow jewelry, holding another man's hand, and leaving a gay bar all visibly marked him as a gay man, which a homophobic harasser then seized upon. While Steve did not fight back until the other man tried to strike the first blow, his subsequent beating of the man was done to prevent future harassment of other LGBTQ+ people, and to secure their ability to "do whatever" in this world. It is especially interesting that Steve suspects this homophobic man of internalized homophobia, with his anger stemming from his perceived inability to use gay space in the ways that Steve and his companion were enjoying.

While all of these examples involved an element of self-defense, they also all involved more symbolic reasons to fight back against anti-gay harassment in gay districts: defending other gay patrons' rights to enjoy the space, free of victimization. One important caveat is that all of the men in this particular study were already involved with gangs and/or crime; other LGBTQ+ people who are not gang- or crime-involved may not respond to anti-gay harassment with violence. However, other individuals may be willing to respond physically under similar circumstances, such as being threatened, targeted, or harassed in areas where they want to feel safe and be shielded from victimization. One example to buttress my claim comes from the group Street Patrol operating in San Francisco in the early 1990s. They were one such street patrol group in the city, and other cities with gayborhoods (like New York City) had similar groups. Their May 1991 newsletter advertising their group (pictured in Hanhardt 2013:179; emphases in original) stated the following:

> Street Patrol is a group dedicated to stopping the violence against us, commonly known as queer-bashing. To end the harassment, threats, and physical assaults, we patrol the streets of the Castro.
>
> Street Patrol is not out to enforce the law and clean up the streets, nor are we claiming the Castro as "our turf." Rather, Street Patrol intends to make the Castro a place where queer people can hang out without being targeted for violent attack.
>
> Street Patrol *does not:*
>
> • escalate violence
> • act as a vigilante squad
> • carry weapons, drugs, or alcohol
>
> Street Patrol *does:*
>
> • patrol in front of bars and clubs where bashings happen
> • intervene in bashings as they occur
> • make citizens' arrests
> • discourage bashings before they happen
> • train in street combat techniques with the Guardian Angels
> • dish, cruise, and window-shop shamelessly

It is especially interesting that Street Patrol is obviously responding to claims or assumptions of its group's criminality, stating, for example, that it is not a vigilante organization nor do its members carry weapons or drugs. I believe that the statement disavowing the Castro gayborhood as the organization's "turf" (which actually seems a bit disingenuous considering their mission) was likely a strategy to differentiate it from a street gang, especially since gang violence was a major sociopolitical concern in cities in the early 1990s. Their strategy to paint themselves as a community defense organization, one that is primarily reactive (though with the hopes of prevention) and seeks to keep the streets safe, likely helped to increase their legitimacy, as this was a prevailing discourse of the time. This was also part of a larger gay rights movement strategy to ease the assumptions of criminality among LGBTQ people and lay it instead with homophobic harassers. Hanhardt (2013) notes that these street patrol groups sometimes exploited state processes of criminalization when making reports to law enforcement so that even if an anti-gay harasser wouldn't be arrested, he might at least be harassed and searched by police.

In his ethnographic study of Chicago gayborhood Boystown, Greene (2018) observed how LGBT youth of color who access gayborhoods and gay districts may create queer street families, a form of chosen families, to help them navigate streetlife and stay safe during their time in gayborhoods. Members of these families defended each other from harassment and violence committed by local residents and police. One twenty-two-year-old black trans woman explained, "When we are on these streets . . . we got nobody but us. They may get on my nerves at times, but we always look out for our own" (176). A twenty-one-year-old Latino gay man remarked, "when the chips are down, and my boys are in trouble, I got their back, and I know they got mine. We're family, and family will go down for one another" (176). Similarly, the men in my study who belonged to gay gangs identified these groups as their families, asserting that they will not tolerate anti-gay harassment or victimization of LGBTQ+ people, but especially the members of their chosen families (Panfil 2017).

GENTRIFICATION AND GAY GATHERING PLACES

The language addressing gentrification lends itself to discussions of crime, victimization, and safety. Gentrification is not always a seemingly detached process by which someone affluent buys a building and raises rents, pricing out prior tenants. It is often deliberate and systematic, involving not just real estate developers and venture capitalists, but land seizure and forced removal of residents who are deemed undesirable through actions enacted by the state such as a "war on homelessness" (Ferrell 2018). Some conversations about gentrification that include such actions and related ones actually describe gentrification as state violence.

Related language has been used by queer observers studying gayborhoods and gentrification. For example, Moskowitz (2017) suggests that "LGBTQ people have both been victims and perpetrators of gentrification," marking gentrification as a social, cultural, and economic offense committed against the community, even if some queer people may benefit from it (Moskowitz's book on gentrification and inequality is called *How to Kill a City*). In writing about his own experiences frequenting Christopher Street in New York City and how it has changed over time as a result of gentrification, author Darnell Moore (2019) writes:

> To some, such swift changes in the neighborhood signal progress. For others, however, progress can feel a lot more like death—death of culture and spirit, death as a consequence of economic and political calculations that have pushed out the black, brown, working-poor, and middle-class people who once infused the area with energy.

Indeed, gentrification has served to make neighborhoods less diverse while pushing out "undesirables."

While gentrification of gayborhoods has been touted as a chance to improve quality of life for residents, it certainly has not benefited some LGBTQ groups of people, including transgender people of color, queer youth of color, sex workers, and HIV-positive people (Moore 2019). White middle- or upper-class gays and the businesses they own or frequent tend to reap the benefits of gentrification and of partnering with law enforcement in their communities, asking for certain groups of allegedly dangerous or troublemaking individuals to be removed in a classic "not in my backyard" stance on "improving" the neighborhood. Regarding Christopher Street and the West Village areas in Greenwich Village (NYC) specifically, an anticrime rally held in 2002 was named "Take Back Our Streets." The rally organizers, which included residents, business owners, politicians, and local organizations, were advocating for enforcing "quality of life" laws. They claimed that their neighborhoods had been taken over by gang members, drug dealers, those involved in street prostitution (including allegedly "hostile transgender prostitutes," as people purported to be selling sex were presumed to be transgender), and "rowdies," which was later elaborated to be groups of African American and Latinx LGBT youth (Hanhardt 2013:1–2).

In Chicago's Boystown gayborhood, a 2011 clash of demonstrators illustrated similar tensions. About fifty residents, most of whom were white gay men, gathered late at night to engage in a "positive loitering walk" through the neighborhood to bring attention to a recent spate of violent crimes. Another group, this one consisting of queer youth of color protesting police violence, "shouted at the positive loiterers through megaphones, accusing local residents of policing queer youth out of the neighborhood by making their presence the scapegoat for the upsurge in crime" (Greene 2018:169). The initial collision culminated in one white gay man yelling "Get the *fuck* out of my neighborhood" (169). Counter-protestors followed the positive loiterers along their walk, leading the loiterers to feel as though their protest had been "coopted and derailed," while the queer youth wanted "not only to defend their presence in the gayborhood, but also to demand recognition from local residents as legitimate stakeholders within the community" (169). Contemporaneously, a Facebook page to "Take Back Boystown" was flooded with comments attributing the rise in crime to the actions of LGBTQ youth of color. Some made explicit, racist contrasts between the "gay whites with hard earned money" who "built and created" Boystown and the "savage monkeys" allegedly responsible for its decline (Greene 2018:178). Another indicted the local LGBTQ community organizations: "The Center on Halsted and the Howard Brown Youth Center . . . both cater to the people who commit these crimes. Get rid of them and watch the crime go down and the property values go up" (178). Such comments are direct encouragements of gentrification that is so detrimental: remove necessary services for marginalized people, while marking those individuals as criminal and thus even more unwanted, in order to increase the privileged class's financial holdings. Furthermore, the image of the white gay man angrily yelling at a young black or brown queer person to "get out of his neighborhood" is about as crystallized as the issue can get—not to mention white men asserting their right to "loiter," which would get other groups of people arrested.

Gentrification of gayborhoods has also meant that non-LGBTQ people, businesses, and organizations move in and change the gayborhoods' priorities and climates beyond their demographics. Sociologist Amin Ghaziani recalls his own experience as a resident of a gentrifying gayborhood:

> I myself lived in Chicago's Boystown district for nearly a decade, starting in 1999. I remember feeling uneasy in those years as I read one headline after another about the alleged demise of my home and other gayborhoods across the country. The sight of more straight bodies on the streets became a daily topic of conversation among my friends—an obsession, to be honest. We writhed over stroller congestion on the sidewalks (though gays and lesbians also have kids, the stroller was, and still is, a politically charged symbol of heterosexual invasion into queer spaces). . . . We accosted straight couples who locked lips in our bars ("We risk physical violence if we do that in your bars; you should be more respectful in our spaces"). We sighed when a sex shop would close and, say, a nail salon would open in its place (much like the strollers, these salons were also symbols of change). We fumed when straight residents complained that the Center on Halsted, our queer community center, excluded them in their programming ("Are you really accusing us of reverse discrimination?") (2014: 4–5).

Ghaziani's complaints were not just about cultural change of a neighborhood in transition or linked purely to representation, however; they were tied very directly to feelings of safety, sense of belonging, and comfort. He continued:

> As the years went by, my friends and I bemoaned, perhaps most of all, feeling a little less safe holding hands with our partners, dates, or hookups—even as we walked down what were supposed to be our sheltered streets. I had been called a "fag" on more instances than I still care to remember, and I was shocked at the disapproving looks that I would receive when walking hand in hand with another man. I knew I could not escape this menacing straight gaze altogether, but I was so angry that I had to deal with it in Boystown. *This was supposed to be a safe space.* (2014:5, emphasis added)

In gentrified gayborhoods that have had an influx of heterosexual or upper-class residents, LGBTQ+ residents may no longer feel safe, as they no longer live in an enclave. Seattle Neighborhood Greenways—an advocacy organization whose "initiatives support priorities at the intersection of the built environment and public health" (Santos-Livengood n.d.:3)—conducted a fact-finding examination of LGBTQ community street safety, in order to make recommendations to prevent hate crimes. One interviewee from the LGBTQ community put their opinion extremely plainly: "[Hate crimes] are a product of gentrification" (8). With the processes of gentrification explored here, it would not be surprising if that interviewee was correct.

CONCLUSION

In this chapter, I explored gayborhoods, gay districts, and gay gathering places as criminogenic space in the cultural criminology sense. Primary themes I discussed included LGBTQ+ people experiencing victimization in gayborhoods (sometimes at the hands of agents of the state) and the relationship between visibility and victimization; examples of LGBTQ+ people fighting back when harassed in gay bars and gay districts, since they felt justified and empowered to keep themselves and others safe there; and the complicated relationships of gayborhood gentrification to crime, victimization, and feelings of safety. This issue of feeling safe or unsafe is of particular interest to criminologists, but burgeoning literature has taken it beyond the realm of actuarial risk and considers it from multifaceted perspectives. Taken together, I do not argue that gayborhoods are criminogenic space in a simplistic and positivistic sense (e.g., that gay people are more likely to commit crime in gayborhoods), but instead look at the mechanisms and processes of crime commission and victimization that signal larger structural conditions, as well as the interactional dynamics that are influenced by the spaces in which they occur.

Discussions of criminogenic space, gay meccas, and gayborhoods can prioritize a decidedly urban experience of queerness. This is a critique of much criminological work more generally. Gayborhoods have to have density, which is why they occur in urban zones instead of suburban or rural ones (Moskowitz 2017). However, this does not mean that rural areas have no gay gathering places or ways to become visible; LGBTQ youth and allies in rural areas use public spaces such as high schools, public libraries, town hall meetings, churches, and websites to carve out meaningful space for visible expression and celebration of their identities (Gray 2009). Interestingly, greater acceptance of LGBTQ+ people is predicted to be related to the decline of gayborhoods as gay enclaves. Ghaziani (2014:6) asks, "Will gayborhoods die, a victim of their own success"? Despite gradual improvements in acceptance over time, the United States has seen an increase in violent hate crimes over the past several years—including large spikes for anti-transgender hate crimes—at least partly attributable to federal-level anti-LGBTQ discourse and rollbacks of rights (Treisman 2019). Discussions of crime, victimization, and harassment in gayborhoods, gay districts, and gay gathering places will likely be relevant for a long time, unfortunately for LGBTQ+ people. Whether that fact can be deemed fortunate for the fate of the gayborhood, I hesitate to say.

REFERENCES

Amnesty International. 2001. *Crimes of Hate, Conspiracy of Silence: Torture and Ill-Treatment Based on Sexual Identity*. London: Amnesty International Publications.

Braga, Anthony A., Andrew V. Papachristos, and David M. Hureau. 2014. "The Effects of Hot Spots Policing on Crime: An Updated Systematic Review and Meta-Analysis." *Justice Quarterly* 31:633–663.

Campbell, Elaine. 2012. "Landscapes of Performance: Stalking as Choreography." *Environment and Planning D: Society and Space* 30:400–417.

Chauncey, George. 1995. *Gay New York: Gender, Urban Culture, and the Making of the Gay Male World, 1890-1940*. New York: Basic Books.

Dunier, Mitchell. 1999. *Sidewalk*. New York: Farrar, Straus and Giroux.

Ferrell, Jeff. 2018. *Drift: Illicit Mobility and Uncertain Knowledge*. Oakland: University of California Press.

Ghaziani, Amin. 2014. *There Goes The Gayborhood?* Princeton: Princeton University Press.

Gray, Mary. 2009. *Out in the Country: Youth, Media, and Queer Visibility in Rural America*. New York: NYU Press.

Greene, Theodore. 2018. "Queer Street Families: Place-making and Community among LGBT Youth of Color in Iconic Gay Neighborhoods." In *Queer Families and Relationships After Marriage Equality*, edited by Angela Jones, and Joseph Nicholas DeFilippis (pp. 168–181). New York: Routledge.

Hanhardt, Christina B. 2013. *Safe Space: Gay Neighborhood History and the Politics of Violence*. Durham: Duke University Press.

Hayward, Keith J. 2012. "Five Spaces of Cultural Criminology." *British Journal of Criminology* 52:441–462.

International CPTED Association (ICA). 2020. "Welcome to the ICA." Retrieved May 8, 2020 (https://www.cpted.net/).

Kellaway Mitch. 2015, January 27. "Arizona Appeals Court Overturns Monica Jones's Conviction for 'Walking While Trans.'" *The Advocate*. Retrieved May 13, 2020 (http://www.advocate.com/politics/transgender/2015/01/27/arizona-appeals -court-overturns-monica-joness-conviction-walking-whi).

Moore, Darnell L. 2019, June 15. "The Gentrification of Queerness." *The Nation.* Retrieved May 14, 2020 (https://www.thenation.com/article/archive/stonewall-chr istopher-street-gentrification/).

Moskowitz, Peter. 2017, March 16. "When It Comes to Gentrification, LGBTQ People are Both Victim and Perpetrator." *Vice.* Retrieved May 14, 2020 (https:// www.vice.com/en_us/article/nz5qwb/when-it-comes-to-gentrification-lgbtq-peopl e-are-both-victim-and-perpetrator).

Newman, Oscar. 1996. *Creating Defensible Space.* Retrieved May 12, 2020 (https:// www.humanics-es.com/defensible-space.pdf).

Nichols, Andrea J. 2014. "Intersections of Gender and Sexuality in Police Abuses Against Transgender Sex Workers in Sri Lanka." In *Handbook of LGBT Communities, Crime, and Justice,* edited by Dana Peterson and Vanessa R. Panfil (pp. 165–182). New York: Springer.

Panfil, Vanessa R. 2017. *The Gang's All Queer: The Lives of Gay Gang Members.* New York: NYU Press.

Park, Robert E., Ernest W. Burgess, and Roderick D. McKenzie. 1925/1967. *The City.* Chicago: University of Chicago Press.

Santos-Livengood, Christie. n.d. *LGBTQ Street Safety in Seattle: A Practicum Report.* Seattle: Seattle Neighborhood Greenways.

Skogan, Wesley G. 1990. *Disorder and Decline: Crime and the Spiral of Decay in American Neighborhoods.* Berkeley: University of California Press.

Treisman, Rachel. 2019, November 12. "FBI Reports Dip In Hate Crimes, But Rise In Violence." *NPR.* Retrieved May 15, 2020 (https://www.npr.org/2019/11/12/7785 42614/fbi-reports-dip-in-hate-crimes-but-rise-in-violence).

Chapter 4

Gay Collective Sex in New York City from the Late 1800s to Today

The Triumph of Collective Intimacy

Étienne Meunier and Jeffrey Escoffier

Collective sex practices have played a key role in the development of gay culture and urban gay spaces for at least a hundred years. Because normative sexual and courtship scripts have for long precluded same-sex relations, homosexual activity could only be found outside of the domestic sphere (Foucault 1982; Gagnon and Simon 2011). Thus, for earlier generations of gay men, knowledge of how to identify or communicate with others like themselves emerged in male-segregated settings such as men's restrooms, gyms, locker rooms, bathhouses, bars, parks, or in men's congregate living spaces. Despite these spaces playing a key role in the development of gayborhoods, internal debates over the importance of collective sex venues—brought on by the HIV/AIDS pandemic or civil rights gains such as marriage equality—have caused some to question their legitimacy in an era of heightened visibility.

In this chapter, we describe the trajectory of collective sex venues in New York City (NYC) through four waves: pre-Stonewall, post-Stonewall, the AIDS crisis, and today's context. These waves are distinguished by changes in several factors affecting collective sex venues: legal (laws regarding homosexuality or sexual establishments), material and economic (urbanization and gentrification), political (the evolution of gay social movements), sociocultural (attitudinal changes toward sexuality and homosexuality), and biomedical (HIV/AIDS and its treatment). Table 4.1 provides an overview of the four waves of collective sex and relevant factors, which we further describe through this chapter. Through these waves, gay collective sex practices have been met with adversity in many forms, being perceived as immoral during the late-Victorian era or as a threat to the public health during the AIDS epidemic. Since the 1990s, they have

Table 4.1   Trajectory of Gay Collective Sex in New York City from the Late 1800s to Today

Wave	Late 1800s to Late 1960s	Stonewall to Early 1980s	Onset of AIDS to Late 1990s	Development of HAART to Today
Legal	*Anti-sodomy laws	*Gradual legalization of homosexuality	*Outlawing of commercial sex venues (public health laws)	*Same-sex civil rights (marriage, parenting rights)
Material & Economic	*Urbanization *Development of public space & establishments	*Gay urban migration *Visible gay neighborhoods *Nightlife industry	*Urban renewal and gentrification *Zoning regulations	*Postindustrial, global economy *Gay consumerism
Political	*Emergence of gay movement	*Gay liberation movement *Radical sexuality and politics	*AIDS activism	*Homonormative movements *Queer defense of public sex
Sociocultural	*Victorian sexual values *Emergence of gay underground	*Sexual revolution *Gay urban culture	*Renewed sexual conservatism in light of HIV/AIDS	*Global sexual recreation & travel market
Biomedical	*Homosexuality considered a mental illness	*Removal of homosexuality from DSM	*HIV/AIDS	*HAART *Treatment as prevention (U=U) *PrEP and PEP
Sex Venues	*Parks *Public toilets *YMCA *Public baths	*Public environments *Gay bathhouses *Sex clubs	*Underground sex clubs *Roaming parties	*Private sex parties *Resorts, retreats *Large bathhouse & clubs

been perceived as an obstacle to urban renewal and gentrification and considered an undesirable from which normative gay politics have tried to dissociate. Nevertheless, as we will show by describing today's private sex clubs in NYC, collective sex has remained alive among gay men and other LGBTQ groups, showing the continued relevance of these practices and spaces for sexual minority individuals. We argue that these spaces have survived because they foster collective intimacy—they create a sense of sharing, knowing, and caring among sexually marginalized groups. The capacity for collective intimacy is what may keep distinguishing queer from heteronormative cultures, and what will sustain the continued need for LGBTQ spaces.

This chapter navigates between the works of LGBTQ studies scholars and historians and data collected through Meunier ethnographic research. Between 2010 and 2015, Meunier conducted participant observation at collective sex venues in NYC by working as voluntary staff member. Observation and unstructured conversations with organizers and attendees of these venues aimed to describe their organization and patterns of interaction. He also conducted in-depth qualitative interviews in private with four event organizers and twenty regular attendees to learn about their perspective on collective norms at sex parties, as well as their motivations for attending. Some results from this study have been reported in other publications (Meunier 2014a,b, 2016, 2018). All procedures were approved by the Institutional Review Board (IRB) at Rutgers, the State University of New Jersey.

BEFORE STONEWALL: SEXUAL INTIMACY IN PUBLIC

Pre-Stonewall collective sex practices emerged primarily out of legal necessity. Until the late twentieth century, sodomy laws were enforced by most European and North American police jurisdictions, and homosexuality was considered a mental illness. Homosexual sexual relations—whether in private or public—were considered felonies, punishable by imprisonment. Even sharing a bed in your home with a partner of the same sex was extremely risky because neighbors or family could—and often did—report people they knew or suspected to be homosexual to authorities (Bérubé 2003; Chauncey 1994). The home was not a safe space for sexualities that deviated from the socially dominant values of marriage and procreation during the late nineteenth century. Further, few people had access to a truly private space since women and young men typically lived with their families, and single men often lived in cramped quarters. Sexual minorities thus had to turn to public environments in rapidly growing cities to find one another.

"Cruising," that is, looking for sex partners among strangers, has been an activity of male homosexual life for centuries or possibly longer (Escoffier 1998a). In a world where homosexual desire and conduct are stigmatized and criminalized, cruising is one of the most common ways for men with homosexual desires to find sexual partners and thus a precondition for congregation and community formation. While we do not know exactly when cruising emerged, historical documents note that such activities took place in most public sites of cities—in the gymnasiums of Athens in the era of Socrates, Alcibiades, and Plato (Reeve 2006), in the Rome of the Caesars, or in the alleys of Florence during the Renaissance (Rocke 1998). In large cities during the nineteenth century, homosexual cruising grounds overlapped with city districts that had large concentrations of sex workers.

Early urban ethnographers have documented how urban life and the routine activities of people allowed for zones to emerge where marginal cultures took shape (Heap 2003; Rubin 2002). Red light districts, vice districts, sex districts, or "interzones" (as Kevin Mumford called those areas characterized by racial intermixing) emerged in cities—even small cities that can provide some minimum degree of anonymity (Mumford 1997:xi–xix). They arise where strangers, travelers, or people unattached to families either mix or transition from one status to another: train stations, bus terminals, tourist spots, entertainment centers, and so on (Chauncey 1994; Turner 2003). It is in these places that brothels, theaters, bars, nightclubs, and hosts of businesses emerge to service these "strangers" and unattached people. The gendered aspect of these sexual zones reflects a social norm which reserved the public sphere for men and relegated women to the private sphere, except for those considered morally corrupt or sex workers (Gilfoyle 1994; Mumford 1997). With greater access to the city, men were better able to use urban areas in creative ways to find one another for sex.

In NYC, historians have found accounts of cruising as early as the 1840s—City Hall Park, at that time, was known as a homosexual cruising ground (Gilfoyle 1994:135–38). By the 1920s, the largest parks of Manhattan and Brooklyn had popular gay cruising spots (Chauncey 1994). Providing places to sit down or wander around, alone or in groups, parks were good places for gay men to congregate or inconspicuously look for sex partners. Parks were often a point of entry into the clandestine gay world; a newcomer to the city may not have easily found gay establishments but going to the parks was an easy way to find gay men to connect with. With the development of public and commercial areas and transportation hubs, public bathrooms became commonplace in malls, parks, and train, bus, or subway stations. Public bathrooms, known as "tearooms" by gay men, provided an inconspicuous place for furtive homosexual activity—as Humphreys later documented (1975). Records of a large wave of police arrests in NYC's public bathrooms in 1896 show that they were a popular place for homosexual sex early on (Chauncey 1994).

Urbanization also brought new types of establishments that would become meeting grounds for gay men, like men's housing, gymnasiums, and bathhouses (Chauncey 1994). The Young Men's Christian Association (YMCA) began building, in the late nineteenth century, dormitories, and gymnasiums in large cities for single men traveling for work or immigrating. By World War I, YMCAs were widely known by gay men to be a center of sex and social life, providing common areas to socialize, and swimming pools and communal showers where full nudity was the norm. In cities like NYC, different waves of immigration brought the public bathhouse (since many buildings had no running water) along with the more male-centric traditional institutions of the Turkish or Roman baths.

Eventually, entrepreneurs opened exclusively gay baths, which screened patrons to ensure that only those looking for homosexual activity came in. This type of gay bathhouse has existed since at least the early 1900s, as evidenced by the records of police raids in NYC in 1903 (Chauncey 1994).

Before bars, gay bathhouses were the first commercial venues to cater exclusively to gay men (Bérubé 2003). Despite the occasional raids, they were probably the safest place for men to have sex with one another. Within their walls, they created a world where homosexuality was the norm, and where patrons could let their guard down and express their desires freely.

In the decades preceding Stonewall, gay culture's footprint on urban landscape became increasingly clear. Yet, despite some fictional accounts like that by Rechy (1963), many Americans were unaware of the existence of the underground subculture populated by drag queens, straight male hustlers, and homosexual men in large U.S. cities. Sociologists Weinberg and Williams identified the two main cruising areas in Manhattan during the 1960s and early seventies: the Times Square/42nd Street area and Greenwich Village. According to them, the Times Square/42nd Street area was where "mainly the poor and footloose young. Black drag queens . . . as well as young hustlers" cruised in movie houses, the street, and the Port Authority Bus Terminal (1974:43). The main cruising areas in the Village ran from Washington Square Park to the western end of Christopher Street to "the piers" and "the trucks" on the waterfront—two of the most notorious sites where sexual encounters regularly took place (Weinberg 2019). "The trucks" were "left unattended at night" and would often "become the scene of orgies that continue for hours with a stream of new participants" (Weinberg and Williams 1974:45). Many other sites existed throughout NYC, including locations on the subway system, street corners, bars, and after hours clubs (Delph 1978).

In their uses of public space and commercial establishments, gay men were conducting intimate—what would ordinarily be private—sexual activities in public. Like anyone deviating from the dominant sexual standards, they could not live their sexual lives in the truly private space of the home. They had to seek out intimacy in secluded areas within the space of the city—in alleys, behind bushes, in restrooms, and clandestine establishments. Their activities created bounded spaces in public grounds within which it was relatively safe to have homosexual activity. Because gay men needed each other to create these designated spaces for cruising, they could only enjoy sexual intimacy in the co-presence of others. Therefore, in the early years of gay culture, sexual "privacy" for homosexual men, who protected themselves through anonymity, did not mean secluding yourself with a loved one in a closed space like a bedroom; privacy meant creating a space where homosexuality was momentarily the norm, away from the eyes of the general, non-gay public, and from the intrusion of the police and public authorities.

These collective sex sites have also contributed to the formation of the gay social world (Escoffier 1998a, 2017). In many cities, the neighborhoods where gay men cruised at the turn of the twentieth century evolved into the gay neighborhoods we know today. There, some men sought quick, anonymous sex, while others developed more lasting relations. By seeking out sex partners in public and commercial places, men were in contact with a large network of men attracted to men, and many "ended up being socialized into the gay male world" (Chauncey 1994:179). Social interaction in these places has led to the formation of gay social movements and the collective sexual practices served as means of political affirmation during the 1970s (Escoffier 1998a).

STONEWALL TO EARLY 1980s:
COLLECTIVE SEX AND GAY LIBERATION

The second wave of gay collective sex came along with broad societal changes that affected the sexual mores both for the mainstream and for sexual minorities. After World War II, the invention of the birth control pill, large-scale entry of married women into the labor force, decline of the family wage, increased divorced rates, and the emergence of a new consumerism instigated changes in sexual attitudes. Three major political-cultural shifts also spurred many of the changes in American sexual attitudes: the explosion of youth culture that reinforced the thirst of young men and women for sexual experience before marriage; the emergence of feminism and the women's movement; and the gay liberation movement arising from the dramatic Stonewall rebellion in 1969 (Escoffier 2003). Each one of these developments spurred new forms of non-reproductive sexual relations.

During the late 1960s and 1970s, many jurisdictions throughout the United States and the rest of the world began to repeal their anti-sodomy laws, thus ending the criminal prosecution of homosexual sex. Further, in 1974, the American Psychiatric Association removed homosexuality from the *Diagnostic and Statistical Manual of Mental Disorders* (DSM), ending the notion of homosexuality as an illness. While some sections of the gay and lesbian social movement of the 1960s and 70s took an "integrationist" stance emphasizing the similarity between homosexual and heterosexual people, sex radicals rejected traditional sexual values and promoted sexual exploration as a political tool. Heterosexual institutions like marriage and the family had been the basis of the oppression of homosexuals and had to be challenged along with values like monogamy, modesty, and sexual privacy (Moore 2004). For such groups, breaking with repressive traditional sexual values was the way to achieve "sexual liberation." Promiscuity was political: if sex—especially gay sex—was something positive and pleasurable, then the more the better (Crossley 2004; Gove 2000). Group sex was a way to explore new configurations of sexuality and intimacy. Sexual experimentation was central to many emerging subcultures that explored bondage-discipline-sadomasochism (BDSM), leather, fisting, and other fetishes.

In this context, sex venues were sites of this sexual experimentation that challenged normative values. In some places, like San Francisco in the 1960s (D'Emilio 1998), sex clubs were places where gay social movements and sexual subcultures converged. Because of the specific history of sexual policing in the city, sexual subcultures like the leather subculture were particularly involved in activism and community organizing (Rubin 1998). Semi-private sex clubs like the Catacombs were established by members of the subculture to provide a space that would foster community formation and sexual exploration (Rubin 1991). In NYC, sex clubs like the Mineshaft were communal spaces for people into these liminal forms of sexuality (Brodsky 1993). Before the 1960s, sex venues like bathhouses allowed men to explore their homosexual desires and to connect with an emergent gay world; the radical sex clubs of the 1960s and 1970s allowed more organized sexual subcultures to push the boundaries of sexuality.

The increasing legitimacy and visibility of gay sexualities and communities would change the urban landscape. Urban enclaves where gay people had been meeting for a long time became more delineated and visible. In gay neighborhoods, restaurants, bars, and shops openly catered to a gay clientele. In these areas, LGBTQ individuals could feel safer to express their sexual and gender identities in public. Secluded beach towns like Cherry Grove and the Pines on Fire Island, New York, were becoming small gay worlds visited by large numbers of gays and lesbians in the warm months (Newton 1995). In large cities, certain areas became almost exclusively used for gay public cruising, like the West Side Piers in NYC, which brought together crowds of gay men sunbathing naked and having sex in large open spaces on the waterfront. Sexual establishments, previously operating underground, could also bloom into larger, more visible legitimate businesses. These included pornographic movie theaters, many of them being places where men had sex (Delany 1999; Escoffier 2017).

Through the 1970s, commercialized sexual recreation became a profitable business. With the steady migration of gay men to urban gay enclaves, a wide range of gay establishments were becoming economically viable, and commercial sex venues could grow into large entertainment complexes. Bathhouses sought to cater to as many needs as possible: besides providing a space for sex, some of them had gyms, restaurants or snack bars, dance floors, or stages for shows with popular singers. The Continental Baths in NYC was famous for showcasing upcoming stars like Bette Midler (Bérubé 2003). Some gay entrepreneurs rose to prominence by developing large-scale venues and events bridging dance clubs and sex clubs. An example is Bruce Mailman who opened the New St. Marks Baths in NYC in 1979—claiming to be the largest gay bathhouse in the world—and the Saint in 1980, a multimillion-dollar nightclub with darker sections were men had sex (Moore 2004). Group sex was no more a clandestine affair, it was now a profitable business that nightlife entrepreneurs advertised and promoted, and which was tied to urban club culture (Mitchell Forthcoming).

From the early gay bathhouses of the first half of the twentieth century to the radical sex clubs of the 1970s and finally to the large-scale sex clubs of the early 1980s, gay group sex shifted between affirmation, experimentation, and commodification. For some sections of urban gay communities, group sex had become normalized and less political or exploratory. For the gay "clone" in NYC, described in Martin Levine's ethnography (1998), group sex venues were just one part of the gay "circuit." Gay men visited bathhouses, backrooms, adult theaters, or sex clubs just as routinely as they did bars, restaurants, gyms, and discos. Cruising and group sex were part of the sexual script of the subculture, no longer an experimentation. The commercialized gay sexual entertainment industry that was taking shape and growing in importance at the turn of the 1980s had, however, to go on hiatus because of the onset of the AIDS epidemic.

ONSET OF AIDS TO LATE 1990s:
THE CRACKDOWN ON COLLECTIVE SEX

The AIDS epidemic provoked a devastating crisis—one that was political, cultural, and sexual. For LGBTQ people, AIDS was a historical trauma that shattered the experience of sexual freedom and disrupted patterns of identity and community that had been prominent in the 1970s. In addition to striking down hundreds of their friends and fellow community members, AIDS led to a decline in sexual minority men's participation in community institutions and negatively associated sexuality with fears of disease and death (Groff and Hardy 1999; Rofes 1996).

The impending epidemic provoked debate and conflict over what aspects of the "gay lifestyle"—either sexual practices or recreational drug use— might have contributed to the pattern of immune deficiency among gay men (Epstein 1996; Seidman 1988). The "lifestyle" argument had dramatic public health implications as it suggested that prevention could only be achieved by modifying the whole lifestyle itself: stop partaking in nightlife, reduce the number of sex partners, stop using drugs, and so forth. Many observers attributed the outbreak to sexual promiscuity, the frequent patronage of bathhouses and other public sex venues, along with the general availability of sexual activity in the urban centers of San Francisco and NYC. Sexual practices popular among gay men were especially scrutinized: fellatio, fisting, anal sex, and casual sex with strangers and with multiple partners.

Public health authorities believed that sex venues were potentially sites of transmission for the virus and many jurisdictions in the United States and globally began to take measures to close them down. In 1984, New York State added a clause under its sanitary code that forbids any commercial establishment from allowing "sexual activities where anal intercourse, vaginal intercourse or fellatio take place" on the ground that they "constitute a threat to the public health." The law stipulates that local health officers "may close any such facilities or establishments as constituting a public nuisance" (New York State 2000). Large commercial venues in NYC like the New St. Marks baths, the Saint, and Plato's Retreat (the latter which catered mainly to heterosexual men and women) were promptly ordered to close by 1985 (Moore 2004). Between then and the late 1990s, the NYC Department of Health and Mental Hygiene (DoHMH) was instrumental in closing most bathhouses, adult theaters, sex clubs, and gay bars where sexual activity happened, and in making sure that those that remained enforce a "no-sexual-activity-allowed" policy (Elovitz and Edwards 1996). Between 1985 and 1995, there was a great decrease in the number of gay bathhouses in NYC, Los Angeles, and San Francisco (Woods, Tracy, and Binson 2003). The gay cruising culture, which had benefited from a climate of permissiveness for a time, had to deal once again with illegality and move back to clandestinity.

Not everyone in public health circles endorsed this prohibitive stance on collective sex venues, and many actually emphasized their importance in HIV prevention. By the mid-1980s, it became clear that the virus was transmitted through blood or certain high-risk sexual acts, not through lifestyle. The amount of sexual activity or number of partners one had would not lead to HIV transmission as long as risk was prevented, mainly by using condoms for anal or vaginal intercourse. With this knowledge, in 1983, gay grassroots organizations developed safer-sex guidelines and started promoting them in the gay community (Escoffier 1998b; Epstein 1996). Sex clubs and bathhouses were a good place to reach out to men at risk for HIV and to educate them about safer practices, and managers of these establishments contributed by posting information and distributing pamphlets about safer sex, handing out condoms, and encouraging their patrons to use them. Within a few years, these efforts resulted in "shifts in sexual practice unprecedented in their scope, speed, and efficacy" (Rubin 1997:116). Nevertheless, the notion that promiscuity leads to AIDS prevailed in the United States, and the sex venues' efforts at creating a safer-sex culture were cut short, as they were forced to close.

As authorities shut down sex venues in NYC, HIV and LGBTQ activists feared that these measures would move cruising back underground. Other concerns by those doing HIV prevention outreach were raised as "the focus shifts away from what is safe or unsafe, to what one can get away with" (Gendin 1996:113). Indeed, in order to survive, the gay cruising culture had to be adaptable and flexible (Colter et al. 1996), and collective sex in NYC widely moved to underground venues. Owners and managers of bathhouses and sex clubs started looking for noncommercial places to direct their clientele, like private lofts or apartments. For at least two decades into the AIDS epidemic, underground clubs routinely opened for short periods of time until authorities found out about them and shut them down. Today, underground clubs have shifted into sex parties, events that promoters can take to different spaces every time they hosted them, sometimes revealing the exact location to patrons only the day of events. Although there is less policing of sex venues, public health surveillance of these establishments between approximately 1985 and 2005 greatly shaped today's NYC cruising culture.

Collective sex venues thus stopped being visible establishments of gay neighborhoods and began operating in the margins of society. The relocation of collective sex, from public sites to more private locales, was primarily the result of public health policy, but it also served economic purposes. For city reformers and many neighborhood organizations, adult establishments (including sex-on-premise venues but also sex shops, porn stores, or strip clubs) are undesirable places when trying to attract middle- and upper-class residents, families, and tourists. The 1990s "quality of life" campaign of NYC Mayor Rudy Giuliani adopted zoning resolutions for adult establishments, forbidding them to be closer than 500 feet from one another, and from schools, churches, day care centers, and residential districts (City of New York 2012). In combination with the public health law from 1984, these zoning resolutions were the last blow to the sex venues that were still holding on. In these years, the city also renovated the public grounds where gay men used to cruise, most notably the West Side Piers in the West Village, making them more open-spaced, removing places where people could seclude themselves, and closing them at night. Though, in 2019, a federal court judge ruled that enforcement of the zoning resolutions is unconstitutional (Brown 2019), the damage had already been done for most adult business. NYC's situation is thus similar to what Orne observed in Chicago; collective sex used to be central in Boystown's establishments, but now "exist[s] on the periphery in the shadiest spaces, the darkest bars in the deepest night" (Orne 2017:11)

COLLECTIVE SEX IN NYC TODAY:
FOSTERING COLLECTIVE INTIMACY

Public health and zoning regulations in NYC did not completely eradicate commercial establishments where sexual activity occurs but changed what these venues could offer to their clientele. Some took measures to restrict sexual activity or at least obscure it. For example, some cruisy gay bars posted signs saying sex is not allowed while gay bathhouses offered poor and unused gym equipment to qualify as "health clubs." At times, the fear of inspections from authorities has led venues to more actively prevent sex, for instance, following a June 2011 raid at the NYC Eagle when twenty police officers and inspectors arrived unannounced (Baker and Meenan 2011). While the inspection only resulted in fines unrelated to sexual activity, the owners took measures to prevent patrons from having sex in the months that followed. Employees of the bars started walking around with flashlights and fake police badges (participants in Meunier's ethnographic work referred to them as the "sex police"), breaking up groups of men who were engaging in any form of sexual activity:

> They flash their lights, break it up, and they'll come back a few minutes later if they think people are still doing that. I think the time I got kicked out for having sex was because I didn't stop when they asked me to.

Though people keep having sex in certain gay establishments in the city, the policing of activities can make some uncomfortable. As a regular sex-party attendee put it: "I don't like fooling around in places that aren't devoted to sex because I'm very uncomfortable that I might get in trouble with the establishment or with the authorities." Such limitations make private sex parties in NYC more appealing than cruisy bars or bathhouses. Sex parties include a wide range of collective sex events held occasionally in various private or unlicensed spaces, thus remaining out of the target of authorities. They range from small parties in private homes or hotel rooms, to events like the Black Party that easily host over a thousand people for dancing and sex. What seems the most reliable and steady venue for gay collective sex in NYC today is what we call "private sex clubs": spaces that host events with about 100 to 200 patrons and largely emulate commercial sex clubs.

As collective sex practices move into different venues, the norms surrounding them must necessarily adapt to the environment in which they take place. Indeed, different symbolic interactionist studies of collective sex environments in the 1960s and 1970s showed how the spatial organization of public bathrooms (Delph 1978; Humphreys 1975), parks and rest areas (Corzine and Kirby 1977; Ponte 1974; Troiden 1974), or bathhouses (Weinberg and Williams 1975) each led to distinct norms of sexual and social interaction. Private sex clubs are similar to bathhouses in that they create a space of unrestricted sexual freedom; however, where bathhouses are structured to keep sexual interaction impersonal (Tewksbury 2002; Weinberg and Williams 1975), private sex clubs foster a sense of sociability and community (Meunier 2014a). As we will show, in the description of private sex clubs' organization below, sex-party promoters, in their attempt to create a place of sexual freedom that is protected from unwanted intrusions and authorities, have created environments that foster a sense of collective intimacy among their clientele.

Organizers of collective sex venues in NYC today have found ways to attract a clientele while operating clandestinely. Private sex clubs are held in private, non-commercial establishments that remain invisible from passersby. Most venues have no signage, and venue managers ensure that patrons do not attract unwanted attention. To know where sex parties are, interested people must be in connection with sex-party promoters. Promoters design events and publicize them in the community, often through social media, hookup apps, email lists, or online party listings. These events can often be highly special-ized, for instance, some cater to specific age groups, to men of certain body types (e.g., muscular "jock" parties or "bear" parties), to specific racial/eth-nic groups (e.g., black and Latin men events), to safer-sex preferences (e.g., condoms or bareback only), or to specific sexual fetishes. As schedule and exact location of sex parties are not made public, one cannot simply show up to a private sex club on any given night expecting to find what they desire. Instead, they have to be "in the know" about when and where events will take place, creating a form of subcultural capital similar to that observed in other areas of nightlife (Thornton 1996). This system of party promotion developed partly because collective sex venues had to operate in clandestinity, a side effect being that those who attend might feel like they must be part of a sexual community in order to know about events.

In addition to restricting access to schedule and location of parties, private sex clubs have other layers of protection against unwanted intrusions. Inside the building, clubs have a lobby area where those who enter are verified against the promoter's email list. Door staff act as "gatekeepers" and ensure individuals are there for the right event, turn away anyone those who do not fit the criteria for admission, and charge the entry fee (often between $25 and $30). Once screened, individuals go to a changing area where they will have to check their clothes. Most events require individuals to be completely nude, or to strip down to their underwear.

After the clothes check, guests enter the social area of the club where people socialize and have drinks or snacks. While alcohol and food are avail-able for free at private sex clubs, these items are never sold—to do so would require a license and risk attracting unwanted attention and possible fines. Many events have a DJ playing music through the night and may have some artists performing at some point. The social area always has people chatting with one another and, in this sense, private sex clubs are only different from gay nightclubs in that people do so in the nude. The lobby area, changing area, and social area create layers of protection between the outside of the club and the sexual play area, ensuring that the place of sexual activity is not easily accessed by unwanted intruders.

In private sex clubs, the play area is usually a large, open space shared by everyone. Because these venues are clandestine and may not have much longevity, owners typically invest little in renovating the premises and the design is less elaborate than licensed commercial establishments. In a gay bathhouse, patrons typically have access to small private bedrooms. Comparatively, guests of private sex clubs cannot seclude themselves in privacy for sexual activity and may often share the few pieces of furniture with other groups of people. In the play area, sex is ubiquitous, and every sight, sound, and smell is shared among everyone present. During the peak hours of a party, the crowd in the play area can get very dense. Body contact is often unavoidable even between those who are not having sex together. The openness and density facilitate movement in the crowd, and many guests can spend much of the time of their visit moving from one partner to another, if only for very short sexual activity.

By creating a small, open space where nudity is required and guests have sex in close proximity with one another, private sex clubs foster physical intimacy among attendees. This physical intimacy often extends to social interactions and leads to interpersonal intimacy. Over the course of a night, people alternate between social and sexual interaction: they may enjoy conversation early on before feeling ready for sex; they might talk while resting in-between rounds of sex; or they enjoy other's company before heading home. Conversation can cover many topics, many of them related to gay life: bars, porn, gyms, nightclubs, sex parties, travel, dating, sex, relationships, coming out, HIV, and so forth. Sexual teasing is common as people might comment on what they had seen one another doing in the play area. Physical gestures of affection are common during casual conversation among regular attendees. Social and business connections, friendships, and romantic relations often begin at parties. Even if they do not have sex together, there is a sense of shared sexual intimacy among many guests.

Sociologists define intimacy as a form of close association characterized by shared knowledge of the other (Jamieson 1998). In heteronormative culture, close intimacy is possible only with a few loved ones, and sex—the most deeply intimate act—should be reserved for the most intimate person in one's life. Yet intimacy is also present at the level of communities, groups, or subculture, as people may feel a close association with others with whom they share a space, personal characteristics, or common interests. In collective sex venues, the intimate act of sex is shared among the like-minded community, creating a sense of collective intimacy. Within the boundaries of the sex club, individual boundaries around the sexual body become more porous to allow for the shared sensual and intimate collective experience. To be clear, people can maintain personal sexual limits and do not have to engage in sexual activity with anyone in the space, but everyone participates in the creation of a shared sexual experience. The result is *collective intimacy*, a sense of close association and shared knowledge and experience among a group of people who might otherwise not know one another.

Private sex clubs set the stage for the development of collective intimacy by favoring large, open spaces to small, private ones; hosting time-restrained events to bring a crowd together at planned intervals; using the privacy or clandestinity of the venue to make people feel like they are part of an "in-the-know" group; using the services of volunteers or hired staff who are part of the sexual subculture of the parties; providing socialization areas; and planning parties around specific concepts so guests share common sexual preferences. Similar to what Jason Orne observed in Chicago's cruisy bars, these organizational features craft what he calls "naked intimacy," which, in turn, fosters "sexy community" (2017). The way guests are brought together at private sex clubs favors repeat encounters, group physical intimacy, and sociability, thus creating a sense of shared detailed knowledge about the other. The features of today's private sex clubs in NYC have taken shape as collective sex adapted to the legal and economical context since the AIDS epidemic. Measures taken against collective sex venues thus may have actually heightened a sense of collective intimacy among people who frequent these establishments.

CONCLUSION: THE CONTINUED RELEVANCE OF COLLECTIVE INTIMACY

As we have shown, collective sex has existed within many layers of the urban fabric of NYC's gay life for well over a century. While cruising was an important driver of the development of gay neighborhoods like New York's Greenwich Village, it has since then moved away from public spaces. The gay bars and restaurants that remain in the Village, Chelsea, and Hell's Kitchen are merely the surface of LGBTQ life in the city. Deeper within, gay men and other LGBTQ individuals find collective intimacy in private sex clubs. In spite of the public health policies from the 1980s and 1990s that successfully removed many outlets for collective sex from the public façade of gay life in the city, the drive for collective intimacy has been resilient. With recent biomedical advances and current political-economic trends, collective sex might find itself stronger than ever. One thing that remains to be seen is how traditions of collective intimacy largely developed in all-male spaces will respond to the growing demand for making collective sex more democratic and diverse.

Collective intimacy has been and still is crucial for LGBTQ cultures and politics as a way to resist the hegemony of the heteronormative way of life.

As Lauren Berlant and Michael Warner put it, sex venues are places where queer people have developed "kinds of intimacy that bear no necessary relation to domestic space, to kinship, to the couple form, to property, or to the nation" (1998:558), and the defense of public sex has been an important aspect of queer theory (Bersani 2002; Califia 2000; Delany 1999; Warner 1999). The collective intimacy that took shape in gay sex venues contributed to the development of the gay liberation movement and the social solidarity that was crucial in AIDS activism. As Warner puts it: "the history of queer public activity is now repudiated on the theory that its purpose has been served" (1999:164) but, without collective intimacy, LGBTQ communities would lose a powerful tool in the defense of sexualities that resist conformity and heteronormative privilege.

The resilience of collective sexuality despite measures aimed at eradicating it demonstrates its importance; however, the relevance of these spaces and practices remains a subject of debate, even among LGBTQ circles. To be sure, there have always been members of LGBTQ communities who were uncomfortable with collective sex. The AIDS epidemic fueled a heightened sense of sexual conservatism within LGBTQ communities. At the height of the epidemic, many LGBTQ writers and activists purported that the gay cruising culture was irresponsible and unhealthy, encouraging their peers to "mature" into more socially responsible lifestyles (for accounts of these arguments, see Epstein 1996 and Seidman 1988).

In the decades to follow, LGBTQ social movements became increasingly connected to neoliberal political values. This "homonormative" movement focused on assimilating gay and lesbian individuals through same-sex marriage and adoption rights (Duggan 2004), and prefers to dissociate itself from collective sex practices as it carries a social stigma. The past few decades have seen increased visibility and tolerance of sexual minorities but only in their "domestinormative" form (Franke 2004). That is, homosexuality has become protected only when it conforms to the dominant views of sex as intimacy; other "deviant" forms of sexuality are still not legitimized. With the rise of homonormativity, the protection of collective sex has gone out of the sight of activism—laws that dismantle gay collective sex remain in operation, unquestioned and unchallenged.

The same neoliberal ideology that supports the homonormative movement has, ironically, also fueled commercialized collective sex. For instance, there is a growing sexual recreation and travel market in which LGBTQ individuals, especially gay men, are important consumers. This post-industrial leisure economy is aided by increased business travel, labor migration, and temporary work, which all require individuals to be mobile and flexible. As such, fleeting forms of pleasure and intimacy can be more practical than relationships grounded by local community or family ties. Under these new economic conditions, sexual recreation services like prostitution, escorting, or sex venues have actually thrived (Bernstein 2007).

While some critics may disagree, the establishment of sexual recreation travel services has been an important part of the economic viability of distinct gay neighborhoods with establishments like restaurants, bars, nightclubs, strip clubs, sex shops, adult video stores, peep shows, sex clubs, and bathhouses. No one goes to iconic gay neighborhoods such as Boystown *because* they are sanitized; even under neoliberal policies, a hint of sexual revelry must remain for these spaces to be successful. Offering sexual recreation increases tourism to LGBTQ neighborhoods and stimulates local economy. Catering to the gay consumer is not only an economic move but also a political one, as it can be a means for a nation to flaunt its acceptance of homosexuality as a symbol of progress (Puar 2007). Thus, neoliberalism and "homonationalism" come together to give new strength to the industry of commercialized gay sexual recreation that appeared in the 1970s but was halted by the AIDS epidemic.

Collective sex has also found new life as advances in HIV treatment have diminished the consequences and spread of HIV. Highly active antiretroviral treatments (HAART), which became available in 1996, now allow HIV-positive people to live longer lives and to prevent forward transmission of the virus. Public health campaigns such as *Undetectable = Untransmittable* now promote the knowledge that people living with HIV who adhere to treatment and reach viral suppression cannot transmit the virus to their sex partners (Prevention Access Campaign, 2016). HIV-negative people can also take HIV treatment as preexposure prophylaxis (PrEP) to prevent infection. Where HIV prevention used to be centered on sexual behavior—number of partners, types of acts, or condom use—today, it is increasingly focused on biomedical strategies. Sexual promiscuity and collective sex might become increasingly acceptable, but mostly among those who have access to biomedical prevention (HIV-positive men who are virally suppressed and HIV-negative men on PrEP).

Though much collective sex in NYC happens in underground clubs, there is a global development of a commercial sexual recreation industry that caters to the post-AIDS gay consumer. Middle- and upper-class gay men may not roam public places in search of sex anymore. These consumers demand sexual recreation that is safe, reliable, efficient, satisfying, and worth their money. Large-scale gay bathhouse and commercial sex clubs can be found in many European or North America cities. Gay male travelers who can afford the cost can also find collective sex at "all-male clothing-optional resorts," hotels, retreats, cruises, or circuit parties. As collective sex moves further into the twenty-first century, truly public places of sex become fewer and we see more private sex venues that are expensive and exclusionary, making collective intimacy accessible only among those from higher socioeconomic status.

Private sex clubs such as those in NYC foster collective intimacy among their attendees, but they may contribute to a fragmentation of communities who engage in collective sex by catering to sometimes highly specialized "niches" of gay men. Many scholars have commented on the liberating potential of public sex, group sex, or sexy community to initiate connections across social divides (Dean 2009; Delany 1999; Orne 2017). However, with privatization, collective sex venues can restrict access to some individuals based on their age, body type, race/ethnicity, or sexual preference. These exclusionary practices might facilitate collective intimacy among a restricted group (i.e., it might be easier for some to share collective intimacy among a group of relatively similar people). However, the fragmentation of communities engaged in collective sex undermines the political potential of the practice. Though group sex remains, its potential for "interclass contact" and for social justice, most eloquently described by Samuel Delany (1999), might fade away.

The exclusionary aspect of gay collective sex is nothing new. The creation of parties that cater exclusively to black and Latino men underscores the racialized dynamics that have long existed in the gay male community (Blotcher 1996). Moreover, private sex clubs in NYC have also mostly catered to gay and bisexual men while lesbian women and transgender people have had much fewer available spaces for collective sex. Increasingly, some events that used to be restricted to cisgender men are now opening their doors to people of any sex and gender identity, but not without some resistance from parts of the clientele. Heterosexual collective sex has also mostly existed in complete separation from gay collective sex. As inclusion and diversity remain important issues within LGBTQ communities, finding ways to foster collective intimacy in spaces that are less exclusionary will be a challenge for collective sex communities.

Besides tracing the trajectory of collective sex in NYC, this chapter has looked at how the significance of collective sex has changed for gay men and other sexual minorities since the late 1800s. Prior to gay liberation, collective intimacy might have been the only possible form of intimacy for gay men as they could only find parcels of sexual privacy within public places. Between the Stonewall riot and the onset of AIDS, collective intimacy was a means for political affirmation and way for LGBTQ communities to assert their place in public life. Through the AIDS epidemic, collective intimacy has been a source of resilience and social solidarity. As we enter a post-AIDS era in which sexual minority individuals increasingly have access to traditional, normative forms of intimacy, the relevance of collective intimacy and of the spaces where it takes shape remain to be fully actualized.

REFERENCES

Baker, Al, and Mick Meenan. 2011. "Sudden Inspection at Gay Bar Mars Victory Celebration for Some." *New York Times; City Room.* Retrieved February 25, 2014 (http://cityroom.blogs.nytimes.com/2011/06/25/sudden-inspection-at-gay-bar-mars-victory-celebration-for-some/).

Berlant, Lauren, and Michael Warner. 1998. "Sex in Public." *Critical Inquiry* 24(2):547–566.

Bernstein, Elizabeth. 2007. *Temporarily Yours : Intimacy, Authenticity, and the Commerce of Sex.* Chicago: University of Chicago Press.

Bersani, Leo. 2002. "Sociability and Cruising." *Umbr(a)* 9–23.

Bérubé, Allan. 2003. "The History of Gay Bathhouses." *Journal of Homosexuality* 44(3–4):33–53.

Blotcher, Jay. 1996. "Sex Club Owners." in *Policing Public Sex: Queer Politics and the future of AIDS activism*, edited by E. G. Colter, W. Hoffman, E. Pendleton, A. Redick, and D. Serlin (pp. 25–44). Boston: South End Press.

Brodsky, Joel I. 1993. "The Mineshaft: A Restrospective Ethnography." *Journal of Homosexuality* 24(3–4):233–252.

Brown, Stephen Rex. 2019. "NYC Regulations of Strip Clubs, Adult Bookstores Belong to 'Bygone Era,' Infringe on Free Speech, Judge Rules." *Nydailynews.Com.* Retrieved January 17, 2020 (https://www.nydailynews.com/new-york/ny-xxx-zoning-ruling-20191001-3axwpfimh5c6bawah5op4gfs3y-story.html).

Califia, Pat. 2000. *Public Sex: The Culture of Radical Sex*, 2nd edition. Cleis Press.

Chauncey, George. 1994. *Gay New York: Gender, Urban Culture, and the Making of the Gay Male World, 1890–1940.* New York: Basic Books.

City of New York: Department of City Planning. 2012. *Zoning Resolution.* Vol. Chapter 2 – Use Regulations.

Colter, Ephen Glenn, Wayne Hoffman, Eva Pendleton, Alison Redick, and David Serlin, eds. 1996. *Policing Public Sex: Queer Politics and the Future of AIDS Activism.* Boston: South End Press.

Corzine, Jay, and Richard Kirby. 1977. "Cruising the Truckers: Sexual Encounters in a Highway Rest Area." *Urban Life* (6):171–192.

Crossley, Michele L. 2004. "Making Sense of 'Barebacking': Gay Men's Narratives, Unsafe Sex and the 'Resistance Habitus.'" *British Journal of Social Psychology* 43(2):225–244.

Dean, Tim. 2009. *Unlimited Intimacy: Reflections on the Subculture of Barebacking.* Chicago/London: University of Chicago Press.

Delany, Samuel R. 1999. *Times Square Red, Times Square Blue.* New York: New York University Press.

Delph, Edward William. 1978. *The Silent Community: Public Homosexual Encounters.* London: Sage Publications.

D'Emilio, John. 1998. *Sexual Politics, Sexual Communities.* Chicago: University of Chicago Press.

Duggan, Lisa. 2004. *The Twilight of Equality?: Neoliberalism, Cultural Politics, and the Attack on Democracy*. Boston: Beacon Press.

Elovitz, Marc E., and And P. J. Edwards. 1996. "The D.O.H. Papers: Regulating Public Sex in New York City." in *Policing Public Sex: Queer Politics and the Future of AIDS Activism*, edited by E. G. Colter, W. Hoffman, E. Pendleton, A. Redick, and D. Serlin (pp. 295–316). Boston: South End Press.

Epstein, Steven. 1996. *Impure Science: AIDS, Activism, and the Politics of Knowledge*. Berkeley: University of California Press.

Escoffier, Jeffrey. 1998a. *American Homo: Community and Perversity*, 1st edition. University of California Press.

Escoffier, Jeffrey. 1998b. "The Invention of Safer Sex: Vernacular Knowledge, Gay Politics, and HIV Prevention" *Berkeley Journal of Sociology* 43(1):1–30.

Escoffier, Jeffrey, ed. 2003. *Sexual Revolution*. New York: Running Press.

Escoffier, Jeffrey. 2017. "Sex in the Seventies: Gay Porn Cinema as an Archive for the History of American Sexuality." *Journal of the History of Sexuality* 26(1):88–113.

Foucault, Michel. 1982. "Sexual Choice, Sexual Act: An Interview with Michel Foucault." *Salmagundi* (58/59):10–24.

Franke, Katherine M. 2004. "The Domesticated Liberty of *Lawrence v. Texas*." *Columbia Law Review* (5):1399–1426.

Gagnon, John H., and William Simon. 2011. *Sexual Conduct : The Social Sources of Human Sexuality*, 2nd edition. New Brunswick, NJ: AldineTransaction.

Gendin, Stephen. 1996. "I Was a Teenage HIV Prevention Activist." in *Policing Public Sex: Queer Politics and the future of AIDS activism*, edited by E. G. Colter, W. Hoffman, E. Pendleton, A. Redick, and D. Serlin (pp. 105–114). Boston: South End Press.

Gilfoyle, Timothy J. 1994. *City of Eros: New York City, Prostitution, and the Commercialization of Sex, 1790–1920*. W. W. Norton & Company.

Gove, Ben. 2000. *Cruising Culture: Promiscuity, Desire and American Gay Literature*, 1st edition. Edinburgh: Edinburgh University Press.

Groff, David, and Robin Hardy. 1999. *The Crisis of Desire: AIDS and the Fate of Gay Brotherhood*, 1st edition. Boston: Houghton Mifflin Harcourt.

Heap, Chad. 2003. "The City as a Sexual Laboratory: The Queer Heritage of the Chicago School." *Qualitative Sociology* 26(4):457–487.

Humphreys, Laud. 1975. *Tearoom Trade: Impersonal Sex in Public Places*, 2nd edition. New Brunswick, NJ: Aldine Transaction.

Jamieson, Lynn. 1998. *Intimacy: Personal Relationships in Modern Societies*. Cambridge, UK/Malden, MA: Polity Press/Blackwell.

Levine, Martin. 1998. *Gay Macho: The Life and Death of the Homosexual Clone*. New York: New York University Press.

Meunier, Étienne. 2014a. "No Attitude, No Standing Around: The Organization of Social and Sexual Interaction at a Gay Male Private Sex Party in New York City." *Archives of Sexual Behavior* 43(4):685–695.

Meunier, Étienne. 2014b. "'No guys with attitude': Sociabilité et hiérarchie sexuelle dans une sex party gaie de New York." *Genre, sexualité & société* (11).

Meunier, Étienne. 2016. "Organizing Collective Intimacy: An Ethnography of New York City's Clandestine Sex Clubs." Rutgers University - Graduate School - New Brunswick.

Meunier, Étienne. 2018. "Social Interaction and Safer Sex at Sex Parties: Collective and Individual Norms at Gay Group Sex Venues in NYC." *Sexuality Research and Social Policy* 15(3):329–341.

Mitchell, Christopher Adam. Forthcoming. Gay Ghetto to Free Market: Entrepreneurship and the Transofrmation of Queer Life in New York City. University of Pennsylvania Press.

Moore, Patrick. 2004. *Beyond Shame: Reclaiming the Abandoned History of Radical Gay Sexuality*. Boston: Beacon Press.

Mumford, Kevin. 1997. *Interzones: Black/White Sex Districts in Chicago and New York in the Early Twentieth Century*. Columbia University Press.

New York State. 2000. *Public Health Law*.

Newton, Esther. 1995. *Cherry Grove Fire Island: Sixty Years in America's First Gay and Lesbian Town*. Beacon Press.

Orne, Jason. 2017. *Boystown: Sex and Community in Chicago*, 1st edition. Chicago/London: University of Chicago Press.

Ponte, Meredith R. 1974. "Life in a Parking Lot: An Ethnography of a Homosexual Drive-In." in *Deviance: Field studies and self-disclosures*, edited by J. Jacobs (pp. 7–29). Palo Alto: National Press Books.

Puar, Jasbir. 2007. *Terrorist Assemblages: Homonationalism in Queer Times*. Duke University Press.

Rechy, John. 1963. *City of Night*, Anniversary edition. Grove Press.

Reeve, C. D. C. 2006. *Plato on Love: Lysis, Symposium, Phaedrus, Alcibiades, with Selections from Republic and Laws: Lysis Symposium, Phaedrus, Alcibiades, with Selections from Republic and Laws*, edited by C. D. C. Reeve. Hackett Publishing Co.

Rocke, Michael. 1998. *Forbidden Friendships: Homosexuality and Male Culture in Renaissance Florence*, new edition. New York: Oxford University Press USA.

Rofes, Eric E. 1996. *Reviving the Tribe : Regenerating Gay Men's Sexuality and Culture in the Ongoing Epidemic*. New York: Haworth Press.

Rubin, Gayle. 1991. "The Catacombs: A Temple of the Butthole." in *Leatherfolk: radical sex, people, politics, and practice*, edited by M. Thompson (pp. 110–141). Boston: Alyson Publications.

Rubin, Gayle. 1997. "Elegy for the Valley of Kings: AIDS and the Leather Community in San Francisco, 1981–1996." in *changing Times*, edited by M. P. Levine, P. M. Nardi, and J. H. Gagnon (pp. 101–144). Chicago: University Of Chicago Press.

Rubin, Gayle. 1998. "The Miracle Mile: South of Market and Gay Male Leather 1962–1997." in *Reclaiming San Francisco: History, Politics, Culture: A City Lights Anthology*, edited by J. Brook, C. Carlsson, and Nancy J. Peters (pp. 247–272). San Francisco: City Lights.

Rubin, Gayle. 2002. "Studying Sexual Subcultures: Excavating the Ethnography of Gay Communities in Urban North America." in *Out in Theory: The Emergence of Lesbian and Gay Anthropology* (pp. 17–68). Chicago: University of Chicago Press.

Seidman, Steven. 1988. "Transfiguring Sexual Identity: AIDS & the Contemporary Construction of Homosexuality." *Social Text* (19/20):187–205.

Tewksbury, Richard. 2002. "Bathhouse Intercourse: Structural and Behavioral Aspects of an Erotic Oasis." *Deviant Behavior* 23(1):75–112.

Thornton, Sarah. 1996. *Club Cultures: Music, Media and Subcultural Capital*, 1st U.S. edition. Hanover: Published by University Press of New England.

Troiden, Richard R. 1974. "Homosexual Encounters in a Highway Rest Stop." in *Sexual deviance and sexual deviants*, edited by E. Goode and R. R. Troiden (pp. 211–228). New York: William Morrow.

Turner, Mark. 2003. *Backward Glances: Cruising Queer Streets in London and New York*. Reaktion Books.

Warner, Michael. 1999. *The Trouble with Normal: Sex, Politics, and the Ethics of Queer Life*. New York: Free Press.

Weinberg, Jonathan. 2019. *Pier Groups: Art and Sex Along the New York Waterfront*, 1st edition. University Park: Penn State University Press.

Weinberg, Martin S., and Colin J. Williams. 1974. *Male Homosexuals, Their Problems and Adaptations*. London: Oxford University Press.

Weinberg, Martin S., and Colin J. Williams. 1975. "Gay Baths and the Social Organization of Impersonal Sex." *Social Problems* 23(2):124–136.

Woods, William J., Daniel Tracy, and Diane Binson. 2003. "Number and Distribution of Gay Bathhouses in the United States and Canada." *Journal of Homosexuality* 44(3–4):55–70.

Chapter 5

Disappearing

The Gay Singleton in Gay Spaces

Aliraza Javaid

The music soars, I can hear the echoes of the music run through my body. I dance to the music on the dance floor of one of Birmingham's popular gay bars. Alone, I see couples and become conscious of my identity. I fade into the background, watching people dance, share a kiss, and, walking past the smoking terrace, I see some of the same people again, with others. Walking, walk, walked upon, my body is unnoticed. Walking, I walk alone. Others walk together. When I encounter others in the midst of this music, I am reminded of my own social location as a gay singleton.[1]

This chapter is inspired by my own dark experiences as a gay singleton, which I have extended upon from elsewhere (see Javaid, 2019b). I am not claiming that my own unique experience as the gay singleton is the same as all other gay singletons; rather, I offer a theoretical insight into the life of one. Scott (2019a) acknowledges that we cannot memorialize something that never surfaced, but we can wonder about a life that could have been. I call this notion imaginings of things that could have been, a life that could have become visible and material. What I mean by this is that the gay singleton, when on the gay scene, is surrounded by missed opportunities or missed lives with potential romantic others. This present piece closely inspects, in a theoretical manner, the social position of the gay singleton on the gay scene and the particular responses that he receives. Drawing on Goffman (1963), I connect the gay singleton's position to the idea of stigma in a relational manner. He writes that the stigmatized person "is . . . reduced in our minds from a whole and usual person to a tainted, discounted one" (p. 3). The gay single is polluted in the social arena of the gay scene since to be single is to appear incomplete, discounted, and as not quite "normal." To be a singleton, I argue, is to be a stigmatized other. Stigma reminds us all too often about whom can actually be accepted in social circles and whom cannot. Goffman goes on to write:

> When normals and stigmatized do in fact enter one another's immediate presence, especially when they there attempt to sustain a joint conversational encounter, there occurs one of the primal scenes of sociology; for, in many cases, these moments will be the ones when the causes and effects of stigma must be directly confronted by both sides. The stigmatized individual may find that he feels unsure of how we [*sic*] normals will identify him and receive him. (1963:13)

I situate coupled gays with their "dating" partners as "normal" and the gay singletons as "stigmatized." This disparity between "normal" and "non-normal"/stigmatized creates an antithesis between who gets counted as owning value and worth on the gay scene. I am not claiming that values are fixed projects but are contingent upon social and cultural capital (Bourdieu, 1993). As a gay Muslim singleton, my own social position reflects the social reality that I am less likely to own symbolic and cultural value in relation to white gay men because of the standards of beauty prevalent within such gay spaces. For example, non-white bodies pose a trouble for gay spaces, in that their bodies are not quite fitting within the paradigms of such spaces since white bodies exude an erotic display (Johnson, 2016). Gay scenes are racialized spaces in which race and sexuality are tied, founded upon power relations. Similarly, a gay couple is likely to sustain more value than a gay singleton because the former mirror a heteronormative structure of unity and togetherness that can fully contribute to society (e.g., getting married and raising children as similar to a nuclear family structure). It is, therefore, important to examine heteronormativity and how it is interwoven with the construction of the gay singleton.

Can heteronormativity hinder the confession of queer love? If so, how? While the term "heteronormativity" was developed long after Goffman's writing, he did anticipate the impact of gay identity upon one's social identity. According to Goffman (1963),

> There is only one complete unblushing male . . . a young, married, white, urban, northern, *heterosexual* Protestant father of college education, fully employed, of good complexion, weight, and height, and a recent record in sports. Every . . . male tends to look out upon the world from this perspective, this constituting one sense in which one can speak of a common value system . . . Any male who fails to qualify in any of these ways is likely to view himself—during moments at least—as unworthy, incomplete, and inferior (p. 128; emphasis mine).

Thus, as the paragraph illustrates, heterosexuality is deemed as culturally normal and those whom are non-heterosexual are likely to view himself, and others will see him in this way, as *unworthy, incomplete and inferior*. There are different power registers with the heterosexual singleton in comparison to the homosexual single; heterosexuality as superior and homosexuality as inferior. Thereby, the gay singleton is positioned as near the bottom tier of a sexual hierarchy of significance. Goffman elucidates that all men view the world through a heteronormative lens by which heterosexuality is deemed "normal" and normative in the sense of assuming that social life is structured around heterosexuality; to be a homosexual, especially a homosexual single, is to deviate from this structure of normalcy. This piece critically unravels the relational dynamics associated with the gay singleton and with gay non-singletons.

WHAT IS THE GAY SINGLETON?

While contemporary scholars of LGBT identity have discussed what I unpack here as a relatively new phenomenon, the tendency to view singles as stigmatized others was first discussed by scholars, such as Ken Plummer (1978). The gay singleton is one that is inconspicuous, on the fringes of society. He denotes an identity that is made questionable, a question mark is hanging over him. Where does he fit in society? Where is his social place in the marginalization of many gays? According to Plummer (1978), the gay single is suspicious if he is alone, without a companion to act as a "shield" against interrogative questions or concerns. Alone, single, and invisible, that is the gay single. Plummer goes on to argue that "those homosexuals who do meet a partner, settle down, and isolate themselves from effective involvement in the homosexual world" (p. 177) are deemed as non-gay singles, which may afford them with particular cultural privileges, such as the "ordinary" status or the position of normalcy. That is not to say that the cultural privileges are permanent since the gay couple can become un-done at any particular historical moment. Conversely, the gay single lacks this cultural privilege, and so potentially losing the ordinary/normality status, which, in turn, can create an uncomfortable social encounter. I previously wrote that, "gay . . . men's confession of love, speaking about love, and embodying it is discouraged and vulnerable to repression, or at least the thought of it is" (Javaid, 2018a:13), meaning speaking about the gay couple, longing to be un-single, is open to gay public scrutiny. How does one respond to a gay single? Many gay singles are dehumanized as objects with which to be "used" in and through social interaction because of their sexual identity as homosexual. I am using "used" here to denote a gay body as one that is extracted for personal gain during social interactions. This may include being used for sexual purposes; for information that may benefit the user in some way; and for creating a stubborn dichotomy between heterosexuality ("normal") and homosexuality ("abnormal"). The gay body can also be used for acquiring a queer friend via technological apps, such as Grindr, which is a mobile app to enable homosexual men to link up with others in their proximity (Conner, 2019). Gay men's body typing, for example, can shape gay encounters online, bleeding into the offline world (Conner, 2019).

The gay single embodies the sexual identity of homosexuality. The gay single, as suggested by Brennan (2016), is also subject to particular discourses containing homophobic and hypersexualized references (e.g., dirt, disgust, contaminated, slag, whore, and more). Drawing on Tom Daley (an openly gay British diver) as a case study focus in order to try to make sense of gay stereotyping on online platforms, Brennan (2016:854) concludes, "Daley is objectified within . . . dedicated homosexual forum[s] via the anonymous comments made about his profession, his body and mannerisms, and his personal life." Daley, like many gay singles, is often objectified like a prop in a play. Thus, singletons, like Daley, face public scrutiny and objectification as inferences are made about their personal character. What distinguishes Daley from other gay singletons is his class position and social status as an athlete. Objectification functions to deem the object as not possessing any authoritarian value; rather, the object is constructed as a way of enabling the objector to momentarily have "ownership" over the object and, by that, I mean assuming that the object is under power and tied into a web of power relations. The homosexual identity, for others, brings about unhappiness and discontentment in that it disrupts the status quo of heterosexuality (Holt and Griffin, 2003; Javaid, 2019a, 2020). Heterosexuality, the "leading" and "superior" form of sexuality, reproduces dichotomies between gay and straight, between normal and abnormal, between deviant and non-deviant. Many heterosexuals, for instance, reproduce such dichotomies through discourses, such as the disease, bottom/slut, and the sex-symbol discourses (Brennan, 2016). Due to such stubborn dichotomies, the queer Muslim single signifies abnormality, deviancy and is judged much more harshly than non-queer Muslim singles:

> [The] gay Muslim single deviating from an arranged marriage to sustain heteronormativity and from fulfilling the cultural expectations of him in the Muslim community to which he belongs could be seen as questionable, inducing dishonor to the family and their Muslim community while also becoming stigmatized in relation to their nonsingle counterparts. He becomes socially excluded, cast as an outsider by his own community. (Javaid, 2019b: 26)

There can be tensions for the gay Muslim single. His family expects him to have an arranged/forced marriage. To say no is to say no to a life of hetero-sexuality, with heterosexual values, and to a world in which heterosexuality is enforced. Saying no means to call out a problem when doing so might define us as problems (Ahmed, 2017). When we become a problem, we are hindered from speaking, looking, and critically interrogating. The gay Muslim single, thereby, is destabilizing the cultural expectations ingrained in South Asian communities. Becoming an outcast means to reverse heterosexuality as culturally "normal." The implication is that he becomes excluded not only from his South Asian community, but also from the gay scene because he occupies the role of the "other." That is, the "other within the other," meaning he divorces from both heteronormativity and white supremacy. The result is that the gay Muslim single lacks cultural privileges of romance, love, and intimacy. Weeks (2008) talks about ethnic cleansing as still being a salient feature in current society, based on unequal racial/ethnic relations. We can extend this to argue that "ethnic cleansing" can be seen among gays whereby non-white gays are pushed to the borders of popularity and desire, excluded, no longer wanted especially during the decisions made surrounding Brexit.[2] The brown gay single is super-subordinate in that he is sexually degraded. However, I am not denying that there have been some changes for the gay single to attain rights based upon sexual equality:

> There have been enormous strides in the toleration of difference, the different ways of being human, and in the recognition of human rights in general and sexual rights in particular. But to say that does not mean I believe change to be either automatic or inevitable. There are too many people who have given their all to the cause of human – including sexual and intimate – freedom to believe that the paths were easy to follow or the struggles cost-free. (Weeks, 2008: 28)

Important changes include the legalization of gay marriages in some parts of the world. Gay parents can adopt, a gay family can be "born." Homosexuality is legal in some parts of the world, though under Sharia law, it is punishable by death. For example, homosexual persons can be stoned to death in Brunei. Despite there being some changes with regard to attitudes in relation to sexual diversity, notably homosexuality, the gay single is unlikely to publicly confess his love for another man for fear of backlash, exclusion, and isolation from others; in some cases, the fear of death and violence propels many gay singles to remain just that: single. The gay single is further reinforced because of the fragility of human bonds in societies and the commodification of sexuality, in that sex sells and is required to sell in order to survive in an economically competitive world (Bauman, 2003). Love, romance, and intimacy are in great decline; the transaction of love and sex have sharply risen in neoliberal times: "the awful state of the present—the broken families, the high rate of divorce . . . the incidence of mindless sexual promiscuity, the commercialization of love . . . the decline of values . . . the rise of sexual diseases" (Weeks, 2008:29) are fracturing close human bonds. The gay single navigates through these issues, occupying the role of survival, living, and breathing in a gay community that echoes current times of selfish competitiveness.

THE SOCIAL LANDSCAPE OF GAY SPACES: EXCLUSIONARY LOCATIONS?

The gay scene, or "gayborhoods" (see Ghaziani, 2016), is one of the only social spaces in which some LGBT+ persons can openly express themselves. They are spaces wherein such persons find gay friends, partners, and lovers, alongside the facilitation of LGBTQ identity politics. Gay spaces are not disappearing; rather, they are multifarious in their persona (Ghaziani, 2016). As Orne (2017) points out, these spaces contain their own cultural logic. As a site in which gay men come to learn about themselves, it also plays an important role in creating and establishing a sense of "community":

> [Gay scenes] may be the only social spaces in which local . . . gay men can openly express their sexual identities, and the limited area of the scene may come to be imbued with special significance as a kind of home and focus for the dispersed . . . gay "community." (Holt and Griffin, 2003: 409)

Is inequality ingrained in gay spaces[3]/scenes? How are gay spaces used? Gay spaces are often characterized as social spaces in which gender is created and reinforced. For example, "the sexualized muscular body is not only an ideal within gay social and cultural settings, but also carries a certain 'gay pride discourse'" (Brennan, 2016:856). Gay spaces are spaces, then, wherein gay men's bodies are judged, where facial appearances are compared, and where racial and ethnic identities are judged upon (Javaid, 2019b). The "gay pride discourse" on the gay scene is one that creates dichotomies: "straight-acting"/"camp";[4] muscular/twink;[5] and white/non-white.[6] These different dichotomies reproduce hierarchical relations in the gay scene, founded upon unequal gender and social relations (Javaid, 2018a). The gay single navigates through this confusing terrain insofar that he is battling for an ordinary status. Depending on his social identity, whether he is camp or not, straight enough or not, has a "gay voice" or not, he will have to negotiate the "rewards" of cultural privileges: sex, intimacy, acceptance, love, romance, and friendship. Not all rewards are distributed equally and fairly; social relations are not equal in and through gay spaces since we are judged upon our appearances, manners, styles, the way we talk, act, and behave. Brennan (2016: 853) writes that "the pressures gay men feel to conform, and the consequences of non-conformity, of being a 'failed representation' (also known as a 'stereotype')" shapes social interactions between and among gay men. In gay scenes, the pressure to conform to a "glamorous" gay—so that one is not placed on the margins—is constant; gay spaces create an ideal gay, but if one deviates from this idealization, one becomes less glamorous, less attractive, or, to put it simply, "deviant."

For example, in "Alienation, Ambivalence, Agency: Middle-Aged Gay Men and Ageism in Manchester's Gay Village," having conducted twenty-seven interviews with men aged thirty-nine to sixty-one and twenty observation sessions, Simpson (2013) found that middle-aged gay men are susceptible to ongoing surveillance in gay scenes because of their age. Ageism, in other words, is present in gay scenes that alienate such men. They are "dead" on the scene, no longer desired, no longer wanted. Middle-aged gay men lack glam and cultural worth. In relation to younger gay men on the gay scene, middle-aged gay men are rejected on the grounds of age (Simpson, 2013). Simpson (2013) forms the notion "ageing capital" to mean "something valuable about the ageing process and that middle-aged gay men might be freer from the discursive pressures of gay/consumer cultures whilst contradicting stereotypes of them as obsessed with preserving youth and sexual marketability" (p. 286).

On the gay scene, while middle-aged gay men might be excluded from the younger gay men, they can develop their own "subculture" comprising their own set of norms, values, cultures, and privileges to make themselves glamorous *within* their subculture. By cultivating this set of culture, middle-aged gay men can still be relevant on the gay scene. Without relevance, we lose status; without glam, we lose privileges. Although single middle-aged gay men can benefit from this close-knit subculture, they still occupy the role of the gay singleton. The gay scene can be a space in which to unite and feel safer; for example, in Sydney, an online survey was carried out with 572 young lesbians and gay men and concluded that they value the gay scene for it is a space wherein sex, intimacy, and affection can be found, without fearing prejudice (Lea et al., 2015). Holt and Griffin (2003) establish that—after having researched Birmingham, United Kingdom, gay bars and clubs—the gay scene is seen as a geographical space that allows gay persons to be their "true" selves, an authentic version of themselves. In contrast, heterosexual spaces are "closed off" for gay persons to enact their "true," authentic selves given the notion of compulsory heterosexuality as governing not only spaces, but also bodies and that includes the bodies of gay people. The bodies become dehumanized since the persons behind the bodies are overlooked, unnoticeable; bodies are regarded as mere objects.

At the same time, gay scenes do not positively accommodate gay Muslim singles because of their being antithetical to white supremacy; however, some may wear white make-up to "blend in" as much as possible to ward off threats of stigma (Javaid, 2019b). Whiteness always guarantees a set of privileges for gay men on the gay scene, whereas brownness does not. Jaspal (2017) argues that British ethnic minority (BEM) gay men suffer long-lasting discrimination to do with their perceived ethnic and racial identities on gay scenes. He interviewed twelve young British South Asian gay men, finding that BEM gay men suffer not only racism on the scene, but also homophobia from the wider population. The racism largely comes from White British gay men while the homophobic responses stem from the ethno-religious communities, such as the South Asian community in which their immediate family reside. The privileging of white gay men over brown gay men is strikingly noticeable across gay scenes in Britain since to be white is to represent a history of whiteness during the slavery era, where whiteness prevailed, and non-whiteness savagely perished. Brown gay men, in current society, are treated as "slaves"—not in the traditional sense, but as in to be looked at, gazed over, treated in social interactions as if they are not there. Consequently, gay scenes are characterized by racist violence with which to legitimate unequal gender and racial relations between and among gay men (Javaid, 2019a). Sexual violence against men on the gay scene is also rife for concern. For instance, 72,000 men in England and Wales are victims of sexual violence each year (Javaid, 2018c). The gay victim becomes feminized and subordinate—positioned in a non-masculine position so that the rapist is momentarily hierarchically superior and hegemonic—to legitimate unequal gender and power relations between men (Javaid, 2018b).

Heteronormativity is pervasive on gay scenes. It erects boundaries between "us" and "them," which shapes whether gay singletons become un-single given the notion of homonormativity, developed by Duggan (2002), whereby gay singles want to mirror a heterosexual lifestyle by way of becoming a couple and seemingly "contributing" to society (e.g., raising children, paying tax, and creating a gendered division of labor in the household). Heteronormativity is a useful theoretical capsule with which to make sense of the social relations between heterosexuals and homosexuals on the gay scene. For example, the former are taking over gay scenes to search for clandestine sex with women because of the presumption that gay men have "fit" female friends with them, while socializing in gay bars/clubs even though heterosexual "women may appreciate escaping the unwanted attentions of heterosexual men on the scene" (Holt and Griffin, 2003:414). Gay bodies, then, become used—dehumanized—as objects by heterosexuals. Heterosexuals usually and violently target gay men on gay scenes in order to legitimate unequal gender and sexual relations, positioning gay men as subordinate and feminine (Javaid, 2019a). In turn, violent, bloody as it may be, heteronormativity becomes reinforced through antigay violence to enforce the dichotomy between "straight" and gay, "normal" and "abnormal." Not only may heterosexuals exercise antigay violence against innocent gay victims, but also they can discursively feminize and emasculate gay men as weak and inferior through antigay words, speeches, and comments. Discursive or symbolic violence is not always literal but rather functions to socially exclude the "other"—notably gay men—through derogatory epithets, such as "puff," "faggot," "sissy," and more on gay scenes, so that heterosexuality can remain as the leading and superior form of sexuality. It is assumed that everyone is heterosexual until shown otherwise; heterosexuality as "normal," heterosexuality as barring all other sexualities from their special significance. For Holt and Griffin (2003:406), "Heterosexual norms continue to be problematic for . . . gay men (particularly in terms of families, relationships and sex)." Gay scenes, therefore, are not places of hope, safety, or even solely for gay people; instead, they are violent spaces in which to "do" gender and wherein to reproduce the divide between heterosexuality and homosexuality. They are spaces where to, ironically, "chip away" at homosexuality: chip, chipping, chipped. Although gay scenes are encountered by numerous folks for fun and enjoyment, the gay singleton signifies a particularly unique social position on the scene; and I will theorize his social location in the next section, drawing on the important writings of Goffman.

THE DEVIANT, THE STRANGER:
THE "INVISIBLE" GAY ON THE GAY SCENE

The gay singleton walks into a gay bar, finding that other gays are there: some are single; some are not. He is mindful of his social location. He worries that others will be judging him, developing judgments based upon who he is, what he looks like, and what he does. Other gays will judge in order to make an assessment about how to respond to him at the chosen gay bar/club. Is he fuckable? Is he dateable? Is he kissable? Have they already kissed the gay singleton? All of these questions may be erecting in others' minds on the gay scene, so as to think through how to respond to the gay singleton: some responses might be positive, others negative. According to Goffman (1956):

> When an individual enters the presence of others, they commonly seek to acquire information about him or to bring into play information about him already possessed. They will be interested in his general socio-economic status, his conception of self, his attitude toward them, his competence, his trustworthiness, etc. Although some of this information seems to be sought almost

as an end in itself, there are usually quite practical reasons for acquiring it. Information about the individual helps to define the situation, enabling others to know in advance what he will expect of them and what they may expect of him. Informed in these ways, the others will know how best to act in order to call forth a desired response from him. (p. 1)

Positive responses to the gay singleton might include offering to buy him a drink—a glass of red wine?—inviting him to the smoking terrace wherein to have a smoke, or encouraging him to have a dance together, and more. These positive responses indicate one's sexual interest in the gay singleton. If successfully performed, the gay single may become unsingle. If the performance is broken, the gay single remains as such. That said, negative responses to the gay single might consist of dirty stares or looks, verbal insults, or violent threats, coupled with interrogative questions like, "Why are you single?" "Why are you alone?" All of which indicate others' refusal for a romantic relationship with the gay singleton. These responses are unpredictable and we cannot be certain when, if and how they will surface. The negative responses, in particular, haunt our waking lives in that they remind us of what could have been: unlived lives with others that are lost, but they act like ghosts for they haunt us and reminding us of potential futures (Scott, 2019b). I illustrate, "Gay singles are like ghosts; only their shadows leave a subtle presence" (Javaid, 2019b:26).

Another negative response to the gay singleton on the gay scene is known as what Goffman (1971) calls the non-person treatment. The gay singleton on the gay scene is afforded the non-person treatment; that is, in social interactions, they are treated as if they are not there, inconspicuous, in the background, hidden from plain sight. For Scott (2019a:14), the non-person treatment is when "an individual . . . declines to recognize another, rendering them non-present" in a performance. Goffman (1971) writes that those who receive the non-person treatment "can be anywhere in public places and be of little interest . . . mere background figures who function within a different frame of reference from co-users of the streets" (p. 307–8). Gay singles are users of "the street" (in other words, gay scenes), but some co-users of gay scenes are also those whom are romantically with others, showing emotion and intimacy for one another. The gay single stands in the background and looks on as a singleton, looking at the gay non-singletons. Envious he may be, lonely he becomes. The gay non-singletons might be just mere one-night stands: Who knows? For the gay singles, they appear to be situationally "un-single," together in a sexual or romantic manner. They surround the gay single, in that the non-singles flaunt their social position in front of the gay single; he longs for a romantic partner. Flaunting here suggests that they are there in the front stage region, performing the role of a non-single at that particular context and time. In *The Presentation of Self in Everyday Life*, Goffman (1956) makes a distinction between the front stage and backstage regions. The former refers to the idea that there is a place in which performers are enacting a particular role (I take this to mean that a gay couple or gay non-singletons on the gay scene are publicly performing their roles as these, and the gay single enacts his role as a gay singleton). The latter indicates that the performers' guard can come down, but while they are at rest, it is not as if there is a solid, fixed identity; in other words, at the back stage region, the gay couple or the gay non-singletons can go their separate ways when they go back home, perhaps the relationship has ran its course or, after a one night stand, the two performers go their separate ways and do not exchange numbers to see each other again. The performance of the gay non-singletons can break at the front stage region. For example, on the same night, one or both of them may find somebody else on the gay scene in which to "get with" (i.e., to kiss, to hold, to have sex with). Performances do not always come off the way we want because "someone steps out of line . . . members . . . may momentarily forget their appropriate places with respect to one another" (Goffman, 1956:129). While the gay singleton is "floating" around the gay scene, notably in gay bars/clubs, and whilst he presents himself to others as a singleton, sources of information are seemingly being performed without the gay singleton realizing it. For instance, he is unaccompanied by a significant other or another gay singleton on the gay scene, as if to suggest he is a singleton himself. Goffman (1956:1) writes:

> If unacquainted with [an] individual, observers can glean clues from his conduct and appearance which allow them to apply their previous experience [of him] . . . more important, to apply untested stereotypes to him . . . . They can rely on what the individual says about himself . . . as to who and what he is.

Others on the gay scene will see the gay singleton as alone during their prior interactions or non-interactions with him. They will make remarks as, "He is alone again," "he has no friends," "he has no boyfriend," or "he is single." Prior experiences and judgments will be surfaced to the fore when they re-encounter the gay singleton, which is likely to formulate negative responses and reactions. Symbolic violence, consequently, follows since the gay singleton becomes rendered invisible. Scott (2019a:170) writes, "Some-bodies make themselves *conspicuously absent*, by intending the very event of their disappearance to be witnessed and acknowledged. In a performative display of non-presence, they aim to be seen as not being there." For Plummer (2019:68), "A dominant story frames the strategies that work to exclude: to silence and shame, discriminate and displace, stigmatize and scapegoat. Symbolic violence is committed." That is to say that the gay singleton suffers symbolic violence since he is socially excluded, and this exclusion manifests from a dominant narrative about him; notably, others will form this dominant story about him that includes a negative story—one that describes him as not belonging on the gay scene; one that stresses his "out of place" existence from white supremacy that is ingrained in gay scenes; and one that emphasizes his non-access to social and cultural privileges (lack of friends, lack of glam, lack of popularity, and prestige on the gay scene). Others on the gay scene will enforce stereotypes onto the gay singleton, such as "the spinster," "the old maid," or the "crazy cat lady," all of which can be male stereotypical versions for the gay single-ton. Others on the scene, if they interact with him, will interrogate the gay singleton but he can control the type of information he discloses to them in order to dilute or avoid exclusion. He can tell a story to others to protect himself. Stories are, according to Plummer (2019), contextual though they can be lifesaving; every story has a consequence. As an example of the gay singleton protecting himself, when faced with interrogative questions, such as "who are you here with" or, in a concerning manner, "where are your friends?" or "are you here alone?," the gay singleton can make up a fictitious story. He can say that, "I'm with someone," as if to signal to the observer that he is not alone and that he is, momentarily, "unsingle." Goffman (1956) calls this "sign-vehicle," which is a clue or an indication to another about one's own self presentation. Protecting oneself is necessary to avoid social exclusion. The excluded is to become an object of scrutiny, one founded on sheer objectification and one of pure use; that is to indicate that the excluded is only useful, or of use, when it serves a purpose for one's own agenda. The voice, heart, and soul remain invisible and hidden, though the humble body can only be seen when needed—not loved.

The gay singleton, however, may not always be successful at conveying a successful presentation of self to others, one that is accepted, respected, and admired. When a performance breaks, or when we do not appear to others how others want us to appear, the end result is stigma. The gay singleton on gay scenes becomes stigmatized in a relational manner; stigma finds him, resulting in him becoming disqualified from full social acceptance (Goffman, 1963). Those who embody stigma are classified as deviants, as not quite normal, as not quite belonging—unusual: "He is thus reduced in our minds from a whole and usual person to a tainted, discounted one . . . an attribute is a stigma . . . when its discrediting effect is very extensive . . . it is also called a failing, a shortcoming, a handicap" (Goffman, 1963:3). The gay singleton is constructed as incomplete for he has no one to bring with him to the party. Alone, single, he is discounted from the rest of the gay persons on the scene as failing to comply with ordinariness. Not being ordinary or seen as such can disqualify him from being accepted from full social acceptance:

stigma, he encounters, so exclusion he receives. Goffman (1963:3) goes on to write that, "An attribute that stigmatizes one type of possessor can confirm the usualness of another." For example, on the scene, gay couples in relation to gay singletons reinforce their usualness; by doing so, a dichotomy becomes materialized in that one is defined as "normal" and the other as "abnormal," a deficit, a shortcoming. As Goffman (1963:5) articulates, "we believe the person with a stigma is not quite human. On this assumption we exercise varieties of discrimination, through which we effectively, if often unthinkingly, reduce his life chances." Gay singles become regarded as not quite human on the scene, an abnormality becomes infused with their identity as lacking someone, a romantic other or a dating partner. However, I argue that stigma is so effective that it can create "sound waves," meaning one's stigma is known to the rest of the gay community and gay scene, making it difficult to acquire a romantic other or a boyfriend. In gay circles, gay people become aware of the singleton's stigma. Nobody would want to come near to the stigmatized for fear of being stigmatized themselves, a process Goffman (1963) calls stigma by association ("courtesy stigma"[7]). Stigma spreads.

When the gay singleton is in the midst of stigma, acting as "waves" that he cannot avoid but can negotiate, Goffman (1963:9) poses the question and offers us a solution, "How does the stigmatized person respond to his situation? In some cases it will be possible for him to make a direct attempt to correct what he sees as the objective basis of his failing." This is correct; in fact, the gay singleton negotiates his stigma by way of information concealment. He may tell a lie: "I'm with someone, he's just gone to the toilet." He may conjure a misleading performance by pretending to others that whom he has met on the night out are his "friends" or potential "dating partners." He may also avoid stigma by avoiding answering interrogative questions on the scene—such as "are you alone?"—by simply walking away or remaining silent. Silence can perform the illusion of stability, in that the actor performs a script of silence by solely focusing on his bodily gestures and movements. No sound: actions speak louder than words. However, silence can make us deviant (Scott, 2019a,b). These mechanisms for avoiding stigma can sometimes be successful; at other times, they can make a performance seem unconvincing. The mechanisms needed to avoid stigma remind us of not possessing a romantic other: "non-possession . . . shapes identity. I know who I am by what I do not have, can never have, or will not have again" (Scott, 2019a:17). The actor is always on stage, in front of others, which is terribly hard work but a necessity for the gay singleton since to perform without a significant other is to perform in the midst of past reminders of what could have been: imaginings of things that could have been.

CONCLUSION

In this piece, I have attempted to theorize the social location of the gay singleton in the social context of gay scenes by which the gay singleton dances, drinks, and socializes. However, there are barriers erected when he tries to socialize in this space. He becomes a phantom, in that he lurks in the background whilst others are partying away given that the gay singleton is unaccompanied by a romantic partner and/or dating partners. Consequently, the shadow of the gay singleton leaves a subtle presence in that other gay folks do not pay much attention to him, other than when necessary to mock, degrade and to humiliate with stares and interrogative questions, such as "Are you alone?" When the gay single is surrounded by others on the gay scene, they are ghosts through which they remind the singleton of what could have been. In other words, they are lost lives or unlived lives; we imagine a life with that other person with whom we previously interacted and/or thought about—but the imaginations we have of those persons do not materialize. The unlived lives are all that we have left to hold onto. Instead of grasping onto these lost dreams, we can find hope in them as a way of configuring self-love so as to treat our wounds with compassion, love and care (Scott, 2019a, b).

On the scene, heteronormativity is pervasive; it structures the lives of gay singles. A sexual hierarchy can be noticeable on the scene, wherein homosexuality is made inferior in contrast to heterosexuality as superior. This can not only hinder the confession of gay love, but also keep it a secret. As a consequence, some gay singles will not publicly confess their love for another man because of their fearing exclusion, backlash, isolation from others, notably from heterosexuals; the fear of death and violence propels many gay singles to remain single. In neoliberal times—where casual fleeting sexual encounters are prioritized over romantic love—love, romance, and intimacy are in great decline. These emotions do not always serve a purpose, or they act as a set of hindrance to survive in a competitive economic market (Javaid, 2018a). Where does love belong, then? What good can love serve us? Are we doomed for a life of loneliness?

In this chapter, I extended Goffman's writings by understanding how the process of stigmatization occurs among gay single men. I drew on Goffman's words as a theoretical lens through which to make sense of the social location of the gay singleton. His work on stigma proved necessary since it helped to bridge the gap between the construction of gay singlehood and stigma. There is a dichotomy between what Goffman calls "normals" (e.g., gays who are coupled with a boyfriend or dating partners) and "non-normals" (e.g., stigmatized gay singletons). On the scene, the latter possess less cultural value and worth in relation to the former. There can also be layers of value in and through gay singletons, such as the gay Muslim single who owns less cultural privileges than a white gay single (Jaspal, 2017; Javaid, 2019b). Both "normals" and "non-normals" are always together in the spaces of gay scenes: "stigmatized and normal are in the same 'social situation,' that is, in one another's immediate physical presence, whether in a conversation-like encounter or in the mere co-presence of an unfocused gathering" (Goffman, 1963:12). Unfocused gathering is also known as interaction that is unfocused or giving off civil inattention, which refers to gestures and bodily movements as signs by which gay social actors communicate with one another on the scene. They are co-present but do not necessarily always verbally communicate with each other. Gay singletons enact a performance to navigate the mucky terrain of stigma on the scene and, by doing so, they may be able to present a convincing performance of normality. For example, some gay singles, especially if they are dark skinned, will wear white make up to "blend in" as much as possible to dilute their stigma that relates to their stigmatized skin color. They may meet others on a night out and signal to others, such as through words or bodily gestures, that they are "with someone" as a cue through which to suggest that they are momentarily un-single. These cues might be tiresome, or even hard work, but they may successfully work to ward of threats of stigma that could socially exclude the gay singleton from finding love.

NOTES

1. At the time of this writing, I have been single for over seven years.
2. Brexit is the scheduled withdrawal of the UK from the European Union.
3. When I am referring to gay spaces, I am indicating gay scenes in which gay bars and clubs are located.
4. "Straight-acting" gay men resemble traditional masculinity, control, and rationality, while "camp" gay men denote femininity, emasculation, and emotion.
5. The muscular male body guarantees social status, whereas the body of the twink lacks cultural value and worth in gay spaces/scenes.
6. White gay persons on the gay scene are afforded cultural privileges more so than non-whites because of white supremacy that reproduces unequal racial/ethnic relations.
7. This is the notion that, when we get close to a stigmatized entity (e.g., a person), we ourselves become stigmatized: stigma as spreading jam on toast. That stigma will also affect us insofar that we become socially excluded, discarded, and potentially binned away like the original entity that is stigmatized.

REFERENCES

Ahmed, S. (2017). *Living a Feminist Life*. Durham, NC/London: Duke University Press.

Bauman, Z. (2003). *Liquid Love: On the Frailty of Human Bonds*. Cambridge: Polity Press.

Brennan, J. (2016). "'Shouldn't Tom Daley be a bottom?': Homosexual Stereotyping Online." *Sexualities*, 19(7):853–868.

Bourdieu, P. (1993). *Sociology in Question* (1st edition). London: Sage.

Conner, C. T. (2019). "The Gay Gayze: Expressions of Inequality on Grindr." *The Sociological Quarterly*, 60(3):397–419.

Duggan, L. (2002). "The New Homonormativity: The Sexual Politics of Neoliberalism." In *Materializing Democracy: Toward a Revitalized Cultural Politics* (eds.). R. Castronova and D.D. Nelson. Durham, NC: Duke University Press, pp. 175–194.

Holt, M., and Griffin, C. (2003). "Being gay, Being Straight and Being Yourself: Local and Global Reflections on Identity, Authenticity and the Lesbian and Gay Scene." *European Journal of Cultural Studies*, 6(3):404–425.

Ghaziani, A. (2014). *There Goes the Gayborhood?* Princeton, NJ: Princeton University Press.

Goffman, E. (1956). *The Presentation of Self in Everyday Life*. Edinburgh: University of Edinburgh.

Goffman, E. (1963). *Stigma: Notes on the management of Spoiled Identity*. Englewood Cliffs, NJ: Prentice-Hall, Inc.

Goffman, E. (1971). *Relations in Public*. New York: Basic Books.

Jaspal, R. (2017). "Coping with Perceived Ethnic Prejudice on the Gay Scene." *Journal of LGBT Youth*, 14(2):172–190.

Javaid, A. (2018a). *Masculinities, Sexualities and Love*. London: Routledge.

Javaid, A. (2018b). *Male Rape, Masculinities, and Sexualities: Understanding, Policing, and Overcoming Male Sexual Victimisation*. Hampshire: Palgrave.

Javaid, A. (2018c). "The Unheard Victims: gender, policing and Sexual Violence." *Policing and Society*, 1–17.

Javaid, A. (2019a). "Hear My Screams: An Auto-Ethnographic Account of the police." *Methodological Innovations*, 12(3):1–16.

Javaid, A. (2019b). "The Haunting of Shame: Autoethnography and the Multivalent Stigma of Being Queer, Muslim, and Single." *Symbolic Interaction*, 43(1):72–101.

Javaid, A. (2020). *Violence in Everyday Life: Power, Gender and Sexuality*. London: Zed Books.

Johnson, P. E. (2016). *No Tea, No Shade: New Writings in Black Queer Studies*. Durham, NC: Duke University Press.

Lea, T., Wit, J. D., and Reynolds, R. (2015). "'Post-Gay' Yet? The Relevance of the Lesbian and Gay Scene to Same-Sex Attracted Young People in Contemporary Australia." *Journal of Homosexuality*, 62(9):1264–1285.

Orne, J. (2017). *Boystown: Sex and Community in Chicago*. Chicago, IL: University of Chicago Press.

Plummer, K. (1978). "Men in Love: Observations on Male Homosexual Couples." In M. Corbin (ed.), *The Couple*. Middlesex: Penguin Books, pp. 173–200.

Plummer, K. (2019). *Narrative Power*. Cambridge: Polity.

Simpson, P. (2013). "Alienation, Ambivalence, Agency: Middle-Aged Gay Men and ageism in Manchester's Gay Village." *Sexualities*, 16(3/4):283–299.

Scott, S. (2019a). "The Unlived Life Is Worth Examining: Nothings and Nobodies behind the Scenes." *Symbolic Interaction* 43(1):1–25.

Scott, S. (2019b). *The Social Life of Nothing: Silence, Invisibility and emptiness in tales of Lost Experience.* New York: Routledge, Abingdon.

Weeks, J. (2008). "Traps We Set Ourselves." *Sexualities*, 11(1–2):27–33.

Chapter 6

Erotic Capital and Queer Men of Color

Omar Ali Mushtaq

The notion of erotic capital (see Green 2008) suggests that individuals leverage embodied forms of cultural resources (erotic capital) within institutions (erotic fields) in order to maximize access to sexual partners and other benefits within these cultural fields. According to Green (2008), race is a key component that gay men of color must navigate when situating themselves within existing sexual stereotypes, racism, and other forms of discrimination within predominantly white spaces. However, Green's theoretical conception of the field presents a unilateral macro-level understanding of this phenomenon. We know very little about how gay men of color resolve these conflicts in situ, especially since LGBTQ spaces constitute an amalgam of institutions (Warren 1974). This chapter seeks to present a more nuanced argument about how gay men of color construct their bodies within the contexts of racism and marginalization in the predominantly white institutions of the gay life world.

LITERATURE REVIEW

Posited by Crenshaw (1989) and Patricia Hill Collins (2002) intersectionality proposes that realities are shaped by a "matrix of oppression." In other words, one's experiences are not simply shaped by one's status position (e.g., being a man) but rather by an interplay of multiple status positions (e.g., a white man or a Latina woman). As a result, different groups experience reality differently depending on their status positions. This then lends itself to understanding how different groups have different experiences in the social arena of sexuality. While the concept of intersectionality has become en vogue within sociology (see Hill Collins 2002), "doing intersectionality" requires us to conduct more empirical research on the lived experiences of persons from marginalized (and non-marginalized) backgrounds. Moreover, we cannot just explore individual aspects of people's lives but must also consider the everyday lived experiences and intimate worlds they reside in (see Orne 2017 for a more detailed argument). Namely, we need an intersectional understanding of gender, sex, and sexuality. Moreover, the promise of sociology lies in its ability to facilitate cross-group communication (see Blumer 1954) to foster cross-group understanding to understand where marginalization exists.

Erotic Capital and Sexuality

In order to understand how race, sexuality, and subculture intersect, I utilize Bourdieu's concept of cultural capital and examine its effects within sexual subcultures. The notion of cultural capital suggests that individuals deploying cultural resources within a cultural field (social institution) develop an internal sense of self from repeated interactions and involvement within a particular cultural field (Bourdieu 1984). Thornton (1996) highlights the notion that individuals deploy cultural capital in various subcultures, especially within nightlife.

However, Green (2008a) deploys Bourdieu's concept of habitus to examine sexual spaces with a particular emphasis of how cultural capital is embodied to produce sexual desirability within a particular sexual field. Green argues that sexual fields are arenas "of institutionalized relations . . . (which) materialize in physical and virtual sites that commonly include bars, nightclubs, and, more recently, erotic Internet chat rooms" (34) Thus, any institutions that center on sexual relations are sexual fields and, within LGBT spaces, these sexual fields often have histories of racial discrimination where "black men [people of color] . . . encounter race-based exclusionary practices in commercial gay venues, such as racially targeted dress codes and 'triple carding' at the entrance of bars and nightclubs" (34). While institutionally queer bars have often discriminated against people of color, they have created environments with a "structure of desire that reflects the fantasies of middle-class, white gay men." (35). As a result, "Race [within these fields] introduces a structure of probabilities for sexual partnership, right of sexual choice, and the establishment of sexual status organized, in part, around racial difference and the meanings white (and, on occasion, black) men attach to this historical distinction" (35). In other words, all sexual fields within queer communities are created with anti-people of color bias, may they be institutional or through the sexual desires themselves.

Importantly, individuals of color, particularly black men in Green's sample, engage in "tailoring their self-presentations to correspond with their perceptions of the field's structure of desire and prevailing erotic currency" (Green 2008:36). Thus, when navigating sexual fields, they conform to the dominant tastes of white gay men and their "image" of racial minorities and, through conforming to these tastes, they deploy particular practices that culminate in their erotic habitus, or how they perceive these sexual fields. Thus, because queer men of color "tailor their self-presentations" to match the dominant values of the cultural field, their bodies are simultaneously less desirable, fetishized, and objectified.

These dominant values within these spaces reproduce sexual racism rooted in racial prejudice and discrimination (Callander, Newman, and Holt 2015), including stereotypes that include how various social institutions hypersexualize black men (McBride 2005) and hyposexualize Asian men, especially within the arena of pornography (Fung 2005). hooks (1992) and West (1993) describe how slavery produced stereotypes of black men in an effort to prevent miscegenation and to control black men's bodies. These stereotypes exaggerated and hypersexualized black men's sexuality depicting them as primitive, animalistic, and uncivilized (hooks 1992; West 1993). These stereotypes disproportionately target black men, thereby reinforcing racial hierarchies (Mercer 1994). Furthermore, black queer communities often have to navigate racial, gendered, and sexual inequalities (Johnson 2016) where, for example, gay black men's sexual behaviors are surveilled through public health efforts (Bailey 2016). Likewise, gay Asian male communities are often feminized and subordinated (Han 2015). There is also research that examines how gay men of color are subordinated on gay dating apps (Connor 2019), urban spaces (Ghazani 2015), and other arenas. Thus, within these spaces, marginalized individuals play into dominant cultural tropes surrounding race (Daroya 2017).

However, literature on sexual fields is sparse. For example, the fetishization of transwomen's bodies results in a sexual field that requires transwomen to embody hyper-feminine gender performances (Weinburg and Williams 2013). Likewise, when living in China, white men often eroticize Chinese women (Farrer and Dale 2013) by sexualizing Chinese women as sexually submissive. However, when white women immigrate to China, their erotic capital decreases as their economic mobility increases (Farrer and Dale 2013). In other words, social actors often compensate for a deficit in social capital in one area by offsetting it with other traits deemed desirable in the setting.

METHODS

To address the limits in how gay men of color deploy erotic capital such as fitness practices and performing masculinity in gay subcultural settings, I conducted in-depth interviews with twenty-two men of color, all of whom were employed as go-go dancers in nightclubs that cater primarily to a gay or bisexual male clientele. I recruited respondents from two gyms in San Francisco, California, and I interviewed them in informal settings of their choice. The data presented here is a subset of a larger dataset that focused on bodybuilding and fitness. I analyzed all such data using a grounded theory strategy (Charmaz 2014).

The average age of my respondents was thirty-seven years, and ranged between twenty-five and forty-nine. My final sample consisted of five black men, seven Latinx men, six Asian men, and four respondents who identified as being of Middle Eastern descent. The sample was also highly educated with only ten having less than a bachelor's degree. Finally, eighteen respondents identified themselves as being non-heterosexual.

RACE, GYM BODIES, AND THE LGBTQ COMMUNITY

The men in this study talked about the importance of having a healthy, muscular, or fit body. In LGBT communities, masculinity is often intertwined with having a lean muscular body (Monaghan 2005; Moskowitz et al. 2013). However, even though they attain the muscular ideal, non-white bodies are often stigmatized. As one of the participants in my sample, Markus explained how this stigmatization occurs:

> I would just think that there is different communities that LGBTQ communities split up, and we all know which one is more favored. That's pretty much White men of course, and those are the mainstream images that you see on all types of television shows. All types of things all over like the whole LGBTQ community. The LGBTQ community is pretty much seen as Whitish. That's why a lot of times people actually come in conflict is when we have to make choices sometimes about being hold on to our blackness, or our gayness, or lesbians, whatever because still those things exists for us. (34, Black, communications director)

Here, Markus described how LGBTQ communities are "split up," and how LGBTQ media and other "images" are constructed through whiteness, where, Green (2008) argues that "structures of desire are reflected in the 'settings'" (30) and, in this argument, these structures are the very institutions that Markus inhabits. In these spaces, he even questioned his own choices, especially since they are contextualized within this racialized purview. Likewise, he acknowledged the relationship between these social institutions and his own agency and, in doing so, he echos Green's argument that "sexual actors may learn to like an erotic world as they develop its habitus through a process of deliberate inculcation" (30). Thus, in describing how Markus's conflicted attitude toward his sexual choices (his "habitus") within a white-dominated sexual field, Green suggests that Markus's socialization makes him aware of how these norms pivot him at odds with his racial identity.

Furthermore, echoing Icard (1986) and Peterson (1992), racial and sexual minorities experience conflicts between their ethnic identity and their sexual identity. Researchers suggest that black LGBTQ members must constantly address homophobia within their own communities but defer to remain there because of their racial ties (Moore 2010). For example, Mignon Moore argues, "Relative to Whites, Black homosexuals perceive themselves as facing more disapproval from their families and from heterosexual Blacks, and have greater difficulty finding alternative sources of acceptance and support through predominantly White LGBTQ-oriented social groups" (2010:3). Markus describes the duality as follows:

Clearly, the White, close-to-heteronormative, homosexual male body is the one that is favored, particularly granted economical privilege, in some instances. But there are some black gay people that are able to, you know, infiltrate that type of arena—usually if they're mixed or they're light skinned.

While Markus draws parallels to heteronormativity, Markus suggests that gay men also develop sexual preferences, but these preferences are rooted in whiteness, especially since he mentions that light-skinned individuals are able to "infiltrate" a white-dominant arena, similar to how the respondents in Green's study described how they "infiltrate" white-dominant spaces (Green 2008:35). Green's respondents also mirrored Markus's perception of how some men with lighter skin tone are able to leverage their skin tone to negotiate the cultural field more effectively than their darker skinned counterparts, where "having 'caramel colored skin'—an attribute that, combined with his hair, eyes and fashion, allow him [Green's respondent] to pass (Goffman 1963) as Latino, thereby increasing his erotic capital." Thus, Markus experiences the notion of how his sexual institutions are constructed through whiteness because he has an implicit understanding that lighter skin tone increases his access to the LGBTQ community.

In addition, Markus' experiences, as well as those of other respondents, highlight an important theoretical implication: that people of color are rooted in "other" cultures that have different notions of health, fitness, and muscularity than do whites. These particular examples are significant because these respondents are non-white individuals calling attention to how expectations are constructed differently among different communities and then interpreted with different racially ascribed meanings in separate fields. As a result, they lead to different practices that facilitate both the development and the perception of bodies that do not concord with dominant constructions of race. Therefore, gay men of color face a double bind when they develop their bodies in accordance with their ethnic identities. In addition, to negotiate their agency in the production of their bodies while they also negotiate their ethnic identities, non-white people are read in particular ways that reproduce normative judgments about the body. These judgments involve having a body that does not meet the cultural ideal of masculinity of being muscular. This is just one way by which their ethnic backgrounds are at odds with their membership within sexual communities.

Furthermore, gay men of color not only are separated from mainstream gay institutions but they must also navigate racialized bodily demands. For example, gay bars are structured so that ethnic nights explicitly separate racial ethnic minorities from their white counterparts. For example, Rodrigo, a nurse, mentioned specific clubs that cater to Asian men and specific nights that cater to Latinx men. One way in which bars did this was by playing music that would cater to specific communities. For example, if a person were into "urban" music, they might end up at Magnum on Thursdays, which serves a predominantly black clientele. Green's (2008) respondents mention this as they discuss how these theme nights create spaces where black skin is leveraged as erotic capital. Thus, in addition to being racially stigmatized within social media, men of color are also physically separated within LGBT spaces.

HYPERSEXUALITY, MUSCULARITY, AND LEANING OUT

Ethnic "theme nights" designate a particular cultural field that ostensibly caters to the needs of their specific clientele. Implicitly, this creates a distinction between white and ethnic nights. However, ethnic nights are constructed within the purview of the desires of white, gay, middle-class men because these nights are part of Green's (2008) "structure of desires" as they cater to racially specific "fantasies" (35). Consequently, within Green's framework, minorities constructed their bodies within racially charged stereotypes in order to fit the theme of the bar. Thus, the respondents reported how they viewed "getting bigger" in relation to stereotypes of black men. For example, Nick discussed, as a black go-go dancer, the sets of expectations thrust upon him. He explained,

> There are definite stereotypes of Black men that people have. If you [a Black man] don't [look like] them, people look at you weird, like a big butt or if you weren't showing enough in the front. It was as if you weren't Black. Almost

like, they have this thing for Black guys . . . People have this preconceived notion that if you don't have it, they're like, "What? You must be mixed." Then, I was like, "No, I'm Black." I don't have the hugest butt in the world . I don't have the biggest [genitalia]. It's not down to my knee. So it's very sad, but it's true. It's the world that we live in. When I started dancing, it was hard. It's like a wake up call. People are like, "Is that all you have?" . . . but I am happy with it. I was go-go dancing early on when I was 21/22, and I thought I was big, and so I kind of went almost anorexic, where I didn't eat a lot. I work out heavy and I went back to the guy who said I couldn't work for him until I look good. I said, "Look at me now," and he goes, "Finally." I thought I was ok, but it's not healthy, but people have these images to let you know what you are supposed to look like. (32, Black, trainer/go-go dancer)

Here, the respondent describes how there are stereotypes that characterize black communities as having large butts, and how having large genitals is often conflated with blackness, especially when the respondents noted that others have mistaken them for being "mixed" or not black. In this case, Nick described how others have made him aware that he did not fit the stereotypical definition of being a black man because he did not have genitalia "down to his knee" and, as a result, he characterizes the advent of his go-go dancing experience as "hard." In addition to his genitalia, he also noted how he thought he was physically "small" (in reference to thinking he was "big") so he modified his work out practices ("lifting heavy") and even his diet ("almost going anorexic") in accordance to how the "guy" thought how he should appear, especially as it came at the expense of his health. This notion of how he modified his body aligns with how Green suggests that people of color navigate white dominated spaces: they align their bodies with white cultural tastes. Similar to Green's (2008) respondents, Nick discussed how men of color are stereotyped. He noted that Asian, Latino, and black men are stereotyped in the gay community and specifically mentioned that if black men do not have a "big butt" or "weren't showing enough in the front," Nick essentially violates racialized expectations of how the broader gay community perceives his body (Icard 1986, Green 2008), even though they exist in an environment that is supposed to be separate from whiteness. Again, for Green (2008), the LGBTQ community is created within the purview of whiteness in that LGBTQ institutions reflect a "structure of desire" (35) in which whiteness reproduces itself, so that these "ethnic nights" represent sites where sexual racism and inequality are reproduced, especially as Nick describes how he did not match the stereotypical conception of a black man. Thus, these ethnic nights are rooted in cultural stereotypes that reproduce social inequality.

These expectations are rooted in stereotypes that have hypersexualized black male bodies and larger stereotypes of black sexuality (Icard 1986;

hooks 1992; West 1993; Best 1993; Mercer 1994). Black men and women have long been stereotyped as being hypersexual (hooks 2006; Icard 1986). One such stereotype, the "buck," dates back to slavery. The buck was characterized as a hypersexual black man. Part of the buck's hypersexuality would be characterized not only by a desire to rape white women, but also having exaggerated forms of genitalia (hooks, 2006), that is, a large rear end (especially for black women) or penis. Thus, in this particular context, Nick notes that this stereotype has an iteration in the gay community—in this case, having a "big butt" and large penis. Thus, Nick was aware of the expectations, and he noted that when he did not fit this stereotype, he was excluded from working as a go-go dancer until he embodied the appropriate features. These stereotypes, then, are codified institutionally because these go-go dancers are judged through racist stereotypes, and that these stereotypes uphold racial discrimination, especially since there were gatekeeping mechanisms (the "guy" that told Nick he was not "big" enough) that enforced cultural stereotypes among the dancers.

Another go-go dancer, John, elaborated on the success of his body when it matched the "thicker" ideal of the stereotype:

> There are times, when I was thicker, not leaned out, when I had the bigger butt and everything else looks good in and people were just throwing money at me. When I got skinny, they're kind of like, "Oh, here's a dollar." There is no way of predicting what people are expecting. I got out of it (go-go dancing) because it was just too demanding on my body that people weren't happy with. I was like, "it's my body and I'm happy with it. If you're not, then (trails off)." . . . One of my best friends is an Asian guy, and he has a huge butt, and people go, "He must be half this. He must be half that." It's like he can't just be an Asian man with a big butt. People are just stuck within the ways of thinking. It's the world we live in. (37, Black, sales associate and go-go dancer)

John noted that, before he "leaned out," his body received praise because he matched the stereotype for a black man. In fact, John noticed people were paying him more because he was physically "thicker." However, when he leaned out, people did not give him the same reinforcement. Based on Monaghan's (1996) notion of gym vernacular, the respondents interpret their bodies and images of masculinity through the language they acquire at the gym. However, this language is contextualized within racialized discourses of masculinity about how black men must adjust their presentation of themselves in order to navigate and survive white-dominated sexual fields (Green 2008; Best 2003; Jackson 2001). John even described how others are read, especially Asian men. If they do not fit the stereotype of having smaller bodies (Choi & Lew 1995; Han 2007; Fung, 2005), Asian men are presumed as "mixed." In addition, John noted that this process of fitting in is "demanding on my [his] body." In other words, as these men are exoticized, they are not only subordinated in the gay community, but they also pay a physical and psychological price. John explains:

> We all work out in the go-go world, and we try to be fit. Sometimes, though, we overdo it. It's demanding. If you don't have what they're going for, they're going to go to someone else. You're constantly getting new stuff. You are constantly on the go. You're constantly trying to find new tricks to do because if there is someone better than you, they're going to be like, "Next!" It's very demanding, emotional, physically and psychologically, and it does some damage. We are constantly comparing ourselves. (37, Black)

Nick then described how dancers alter their physique in order to match a standard of masculinity:

> When I'm dancing with someone and they're getting tipped, the first thing in my head is, What is wrong with my body? I don't have that. My body is not as hard as that. My legs aren't in bad shape. My chest is not big. We constantly compare ourselves to the next person, especially when we think we have an off night. Was it because that I ate that thing last night? There are so many superstitions out there. There are people who don't eat before going on stage because they are going to get a gut. They'll clean out beforehand because that'll keep them thin and flat. (37, Black)

Nick described the demands that go-go dancing imposes on practitioners. Dancers not only learn new repertoire; they also learn to compete with one another. This could be the case for all go-go dancers, especially outside gay bear communities where being physically heavy might require less monitoring. For Nick, as a black go-go dancer, there were also physical demands of trying to meet a hypersexualized stereotype, given that he also felt the need to conform to a racialized image of having a "big butt." These standards conflicted with and compounded the bodily monitoring he subjected himself to in order to make sure his body was "hard enough" to compete with his co-workers. Again, by emphasizing his legs, Nick consciously recognizes the stereotype of black men within the gay community and competes with others in order to match that stereotype. He even mentioned how he adjusted his eating practices to suit the occupation. In the gay community, men of color not only navigate stereotypes but must reconcile the creation of their bodies with(in) the purview of racialized stereotypes.

Both John and Nick highlight aspects of the go-go dancer experience as they deploy erotic capital, especially as they describe how they self-regulated their bodies and felt particular body parts were not "big" enough and Green's (2008) framework would suggest that erotic capital encapsulates behaviors and practices within particular field, especially as the respondents engaged in this self-regulation. However, a key feature within Green's framework is that his notion of the erotic habitus (or how individuals perceive their preferences) is very much situated within both structural and historical realities, and these behaviors occur within the context of whiteness, in particular, in LGBTQ institutions that have a history of racial discrimination (Boykin 1996). As a result, Nick, John, and the other respondents engage in these surveillance behaviors within the context of racial discrimination and, as such, are cognizant of the "fantasies of the gay, white middle class" (Green 2008:35) because they express awareness of racialized stereotypes and their influence on their bodies.

A similar principle applies to how toward how black masculinities are arranged within these erotic spaces. Nick mentioned earlier that if one does not conform to the stereotypes, he is labeled "not tough." In addition to reinterpreting the notion of leaned out (Monaghan 2005), the respondents are also reinterpreting the notion of being "hard" (Alexander 2004) and "tough." While both Monaghan and Alexander suggest that these notions of masculinity encompass dominant constructions of masculinity, nevertheless, while the language of "being tough" is also centered around masculinity, in this case, being "tough" is very much situated within a racialized context. For example, hooks (2006) highlights how racism not only hypersexualizes black men, for instance, with the stereotype that black men are sexually aggressive against white women, but that, also through these stereotypes, black men are often portrayed as more aggressive than their white counterparts, especially in relation to the construction of their sexualities. According to Green (2008), historical discrimination produced these hypersexualized stereotypes, and, as a result, marginalized individuals develop their bodies, sexual practices, and identities within this context. Thus, Nick and other respondents engage being "tough" differently than their white counterparts, and highlight this aspect of "toughness" because they situate their bodies within the purview of White-dominant expectations.

Black Masculinity, Being Tough, and Getting Bigger

Leaning out was part of how men of color learned to navigate gay cultural fields. However, getting bigger was a body project for others as well. Black respondents reported that getting "bigger" was centered around constructions of racialized masculinities. Markus elaborated:

I think the idealized masculinity for a Black man, in particular, is to be very brutish, strong, very assertive and dominant. When it comes to working out, building muscle and stuff becomes a necessity to hold [one's self] to that image of masculinity. To physically look muscular adds a level of attraction that people like . . . over feminine qualities. A major part is that typical images applies to Black men's bodies when it comes to working out and stuff. It gets your foot in the door when it comes to relational partners.

Markus also described these stereotypical images of black masculinity:

Being very muscular and strong is like, very overpowering and dominating and stuff, but you know, if you're able to at least physically look that way even if your personality or mannerisms aren't like that, it still gives you some credit. It's not universal or across the board but it's really permanent.

Similar to Nick's discussion of being sanctioned for not being "tough," Markus described how black men's bodies are situated in the context of a particular construction of a "dominant" masculinity. He noted that black men are supposed to seem "strong," "dominant," and "assertive." These traits helped "overlook" one's gender performance, especially visible in Markus's comment about "mannerisms." He associated these qualities with a muscular body type; for him, these are "attractive" and socially desirable qualities. However, just as Markus noted that the muscular body type gets his "foot in the door," he also notes that his skin color and muscularity are at odds with one another.

Northern California, particularly, is very anti-Black. There is a system of racism set upon not favoring or degrading black bodies. So, you're kind of at a disadvantage on social [media] apps. However, being muscular, there are a lot of guys that will make it through [the anti-Blackness], even though they don't like Black people. But, if you have muscle, they find you attractive. Some people even list on their profiles, "Only into Whites or Latinos." Then I would say, "Why are you hitting me up?" They would say "Oh, you look pretty good." So, it's clearly based off of something other than your face.

Markus acknowledged that he lived in a context of "anti-blackness." Within this context, as documented by Callander et al. (2015), mainstream LGBTQ social media applications, such as Grindr (an application used primarily by gay/bisexual men in order to engage in sexual intercourse with one another), often reproduce racial inequality through its users, especially as they express racial prejudice through discriminatory phrases such as "no Blacks, no Asians" on their social media profiles. As a black man, Markus is very much aware of this racialized context (his mention of anti-blackness), and one way he negotiates this context is through developing his body by mentioning that regardless of how men post these discriminatory statements, his body enables conversation. Furthermore, as he described the racism he endures on social media, he mentions that his body type gets him social validation and, in order to achieve this sense of validation, it involves conforming to a stereotype. While the stereotype of black men created certain expectations of body type, black men must also rely on their bodies in order to market themselves to the broader community. This then complicates the bind that men of color face when having to navigate the development of their bodies.

Green (2008) suggests that white-dominated LGBTQ institutions (which could also include social media), deploy a racialized, hierarchical logic in which power is exercised and that enables a systematic form of discrimination of people of color. However, even while Markus is discriminated against, the sheer exoticism of his body creates an avenue through which his body remains palpable and tangible within these structures because he mentions that people talk to him, even when they actively discriminate against him. Thus, stereotypes heavily impact men of color's sociality within these institutions, as they not only have to meet stereotypes about their bodies but also must navigate their skin color. This then created a complex understanding of the respondents' bodies in relation to their racial identity.

This complexity is nuanced because black men not only navigate the bind of racial discrimination, they must also navigate rigid standards of masculinity imposed by dominant cultural standards with the LGBTQ community. Just like the other black respondents, Markus discussed how he feels pressured to fit a particular body type:

> I want to try to look like the people at the club at Castro. I sense the idea of being muscular was getting the most attention. You want to replicate sometimes, kind of like the Adonis Complex things. That's what you want to replicate: the bigger you get, the better. I don't try to get monstrous but it makes you more appealing.

By referencing the Adonis Complex, Markus references both gay culture's emphasis on muscular bodies, as well as the deleterious psychological effects this culture has on individual gay men. Like the other black respondents, Markus acknowledges that he engages in behaviors to meet the stereotypical image of black men but again, the community's standards of masculinity (Monaghan 2005; Moskowitz et al. 2013) provide parameters through which Markus and other respondents survive. Green (2008a) argued that people of color survive in white-dominated environments by using their bodies as a mechanism to attain some kind of social status. Similarly, Markus could work to attain a body in keeping with the particular standards of masculinity set forth by his community. He also used "bigness" to refer to being muscular because it conforms to Western and white standards of masculinity. This is similar to Monaghan's (1995) conception of bigness. Becoming big, or muscular, allows Markus to conform to dominant beauty ideals. He explained how individuals overlook his race because of his racial identity:

> I think that it does [provide a situational release from anti-Blackness]. We live in an anti-Black world and there is gratuitous violence that occurs to Black people regardless if it is physical or mental or emotional. When there are certain temporal events that allow it to be overlooked, that conflict is suspended for a little bit. You get that temporary release regardless of how temporary that release may be.

He further explained:

> You get guys that say, "I'm only attracted to Latino guys but, you know, you're really attractive." You know, that type of tone, even putting in there is like they're not really attracted to Black people except for this occasion or this event. That's really ignorant and fucked up in a sense, but that's just one. That's one way that you're temporarily kind of relieved from Blackness, but it's not a lot of occasion where it happens.

Markus attempted to separate his body from his blackness using his muscularity. To have a muscular body in the gay community, one must subscribe to dominant ideas of muscularity. However, it also meant subscribing to values established by the dominant white culture. Markus noted that since he was able to meet certain definitions of masculinity, he is able to temporarily leave the stigma of his skin color. Thus, there is a separation between his skin color and his body. The muscular body is placed within the purview of whiteness. To be "big" is a form of erotic capital. This stands in sharp contrast to Green's (2008) work in which he assumes skin color is the only means through which capital is deployed. Rather, it is the interpreted notion of "bigness" that provides access to sexual partners.

CONCLUSION

Literature on erotic capital describes how black men navigate white-dominated spaces. Green (2008) describes that skin color, especially lighter skin, is used as a mechanism to stratify black men. He suggests that whites have dominated cultural spaces, including those within queer communities, and subordinate men of color's experiences. As part of this process, he finds that lighter skinned men have more privilege within these spaces, and queer black communities engage in behaviors that ultimately reproduce white dominant spaces. Other literature details further processes of how black bodies constructed through sexual stereotypes. However, the literature does not describe how cultural spaces that are designed for ethnic minorities also reproduce the whiteness that structures the experiences of people of color.

In this study, I addressed this gap by exploring the lived experience of gay men of color, particularly black men, as they engage in a process of learning the norms of erotic capital within the gay male community—that is, that hypermasculinity and whiteness are seen as important characteristics. The respondents explained how queer communities are largely white-dominated. This domination did not solely present itself as individual actors abusing individual men of color. Instead, whiteness was enacted systematically in that it was codified within LGBTQ institutions, where, for example, the respondents described how gay bars, media, and social networking sites were structured within the purview of anti-blackness. Furthermore, this codification meant that gay men of color inhabited spaces (both digital and physical) where, in turn, they engaged in behaviors that conformed to the "logic" of these spaces.

Respondents explained how sexual stereotypes, buttressed by whiteness, influence how they navigate these spaces. These men then engage in hyperconforming practices of masculinity to offset their skin color and adhere to stereotypical images of black masculinity in order to leverage their erotic capital. As a result, through conforming to these sexual stereotypes, the respondents described how whiteness continues to structure queer men of color and their experiences in these spaces. Given that black men are hypersexualized, the respondents spoke about their insecurities of having "smaller" body parts—due to the perceptions of clientele and other institutional gatekeepers, which validated my respondents when they embodied "larger bodies." However, in conforming to racialized stereotypes of black hypersexuality, they ultimately reproduced existing power structures found elsewhere. Future research should examine the link that I found here, which seems to suggest that queer cultural practices reinforce racial stereotypes and reproduce existing power structures within the confines of the gayborhood.

REFERENCES

Alexander, S. M. 2003. Stylish hard bodies: Branded masculinity in Men's Health magazine. *Sociological Perspectives, 46*(4), 535–554.
Bailey, M. M. (2016). Black gay (raw) sex. *No Tea, No Shade: New Writings in Black Queer Studies,* 239–261.

Best, A. 2003. "Doing race in the context of feminist interviewing: constructing whiteness through talk." *Qualitative Inquiry, 9*(6):895–914.

Best, C. (1987). Experience and career length in professional football: The effect of positional segregation. *Sociology of Sport Journal, 4*(4), 410–420.

Blumer, H. (1954). What is wrong with social theory?. *American Sociological Review, 19*(1), 3–10.

Bouclin, S. (2006). Dancers empowering (some) dancers: The intersection of race, class, and gender in organizing erotic labourers. *Race, Gender & Class*, 98–129.

Bourdieu, P. (1984). *Distinction: A Social Critique of the judgement of taste.* Harvard University Press.

Boykin, K. (1996). *One More River to cross. Black & gay in america.* New York: Anchor Books

Brooks, S. (2010). Hypersexualization and the dark body: Race and inequality among black and latina women in the exotic dance Industry. *Sexuality Research and Social Policy, 7*(2), 70–80.

Callander, D., Holt, M., & Newman, C. E. (2016). "Not everyone's gonna like me": Accounting for race and racism in sex and dating web services for gay and bisexual men. *Ethnicities, 16*(1), 3–21.

Charmaz, K. (2014). *Constructing Grounded Theory.* Sage.

Choi, K. H., & Lew, S. (1995). AIDS risk, dual identity, and community response among gay Asian. *AIDS, Identity, and Community 2*, 115.

Crenshaw, K. (1989). Demarginalizing the intersection of race and sex: A black feminist critique of antidiscrimination doctrine, feminist theory and antiracist politics. *University of Chicago Legal Forum, 1989*(1), article 8. Retrieved from: http://chicagounbound.uchicago.edu/uclf/vol1989/iss1/8

Collins, P. H. (2002). *Black feminist thought: Knowledge, consciousness, and the politics of empowerment.* Routledge.

Daroya, E. (2017). Erotic capital and the psychic life of racism on grindr. *The Psychic Life of Racism in Gay Men's Communities*, 67.

DeMarco, J. R. (2007). Power and control in gay strip clubs. *Journal of homosexuality, 53*(1–2), 111–127.

Farrer, J., & Dale, S. (2014). Sexless in Shanghai: Gendered mobility strategies in a transnational sexual field. *Sexual fields: Toward a sociology of Collective Sexual Life*, 143–170.

Frey, J. H., & Eitzen, D. S. (1991). Sport and society. *Annual Review of Sociology*, 503–522.

Fung, R. (2005). Looking for my penis: The eroticized Asian in gay video porn. *A companion to Asian American studies*, 235–253.

Fusco, C. (1998). Lesbians and locker rooms: The subjective experiences of lesbians in sport. *Sport and Postmodern Times*, 87–116.

Ghaziani, A. (2015). *There goes the gayborhood?* vol. 63. Princeton University Press.

Green, Adam Isiah. 2008a. The social organization of desire: The sexual fields approach. *Sociological Theory, 26*(1):25–50.

Green, Adam Isiah. 2008b. Mental health and stratification in an Urban gay enclave: An application of the stress process model. *Journal of Health and Social Behavior*, *49*(4): 436–451.

Han, C. S. (2006a). Geisha of a different kind: Gay Asian men and the gendering of sexual identity. *Sexuality and Culture*, *10*(3), 3–28.

Han, C. S. (2006b). Being an oriental, I could never be completely a man: Gay Asian men and the intersection of race, gender, sexuality, and class. *Race, Gender & Class*, 82–97.

Han, C. W. (2015). *Geisha of a Different Kind: Race and sexuality in gaysian America*. NYU Press.

Hakim, C. (2010). Erotic capital. *European Sociological Review*, *26*(5), 499–518.

Hebdige, D. (2012). *Subculture: The meaning of style*. Routledge.

Hooks, B. (1992). *Black looks: Race and representation*. Boston: South End Press.

Hooks, B. (2004). *We Real Cool: Black men and masculinity*. Psychology Press.

Icard, L. D. (1986). Black gay men and conflicting social identities: Sexual orientation versus racial identity. *Journal of Social Work & Human Sexuality*, *4*(1–2), 83–93.

Jackson, C. (1999). Men's work, masculinities and gender divisions of labour. *The Journal of Development Studies*, *36*(1), 89–108.

Jackson, J. L. 2001. *Harlemworld: Doing race and class in Contemporary Black America*. Chicago: University of Chicago Press.

Johnson, E. P. (ed.). (2016). *No tea, No Shade: New writings in Black Queer Studies*. Duke University Press.

Liu, H. (2016). Sensuality as subversion: Doing masculinity with Chinese Australian professionals. *Gender, Work & Organization*, *24*(2), 194–212.

McBride, D. (2005). *Why I hate Abercrombie & Fitch: Essays on race and sexuality*. NYU Press.

Mercer, K. (1994). *Welcome to the jungle: New positions in Black Cultural Studies*. New York: Routledge.

Monaghan, L. F. (2002). Vocabularies of motive for illicit steroid use among bodybuilders. *Social science & medicine*, *55*(5), 695–708.

Moskowitz, D. A., Turrubiates, J., Lozano, H., & Hajek, C. (2013). Physical, behavioral, and psychological traits of gay men identifying as bears. *Archives of Sexual Behavior*, *42*(5), 775–784.

Orne, J. (2017). *Boystown: Sex and community in Chicago*. University of Chicago Press.

Parry, D. C. (2016). "Skankalicious": Erotic capital in women's flat track roller Derby. *Leisure Sciences*, *38*(4), 295–314.

Peterson, J. (1992). "Black men and their same-sex desires and behaviors." in *Gay Culture in America: Essays from the Field*, edited by G. Herdt (pp. 147–164). Boston: Beacon Press.

Thornton, S. (1996). *Club cultures: Music, media, and Subcultural Capital*. Wesleyan University Press.

Warren, C. A. (1974). *Identity and community in the gay world*. New York: John Wiley & Sons,

Wahab, S., Baker, L. M., Smith, J. M., Cooper, K., & Lerum, K. (2011). Exotic dance research: A review of the literature from 1970 to 2008. *Sexuality & Culture, 15*(1), 56–79.

West, C. 1993. *Race Matters*. Boston: Beacon Press.

Weinberg, M. S., & Williams, C. J. (2013). Sexual field, erotic habitus, and embodiment at a transgender bar. *Sexual fields: Toward a sociology of Collective Sexual Life*, 57–71.

Chapter 7

The Whiteness of Queer Urban Placemaking

Theodore Greene

In June 2018, a journalist from *The Washington Post* interviewed me about the closing of Town Danceboutique in Washington, D.C.'s Shaw/U Street neighborhood. Opened in 2008, Town quickly developed a reputation as the city's preeminent LGBTQ nightclub, filling the void left as one nightclub after another closed in the city. Its open floor plan offered a canvas for diverse LGBTQ subcultures to carve distinct, yet ephemeral places around their subcultural traditions and practices.[1] Like clockwork, Friday Bear Happy Hours morphed into nightly drag shows and dance parties that attracted younger Twinks and their straight, female companions.[2] Charities hosted fundraisers and event after-parties, at times becoming the backdrop of LGBTQ history, both locally and nationwide. Patrons converged there to celebrate the historic election and re-election of President Barack Obama in 2008 in 2012 and gathered to mourn the victims of the Pulse Nightclub shootings in 2016. Commemorating the first anniversary of the 2016 Orlando shootings, Latinx Pride hosted its annual celebration at Town, interrupting the dancing and performances pay homage to the tragedy's victims. Despite its enormous success, Town could not fight the gentrification that its presence precipitated in the historically black neighborhood. When news broke in 2016 that the developer who purchased the building intended to convert the space into luxury housing, many lamented the enormous void that Town's shutdown would represent, especially for the eighteen-and-over crowd who now have no public place to go.

The journalist asked multiple questions about the club's closing, including its impact on the community and the city's changing queer landscape. Toward the end of our conversation, he asked me how the club had shaped Shaw's reputation as a gay neighborhood. "It seems that with the opening of clubs like Town and Nellie's along the Ninth Street corridor," he started, "gay

men have begun to move into and gentrify Shaw," he said. "To what extent
has Shaw replaced Dupont Circle as the city's gay neighborhood?"

To this day, I do not believe the journalist had adequately prepared for
what followed.

"Let me school you on something," I responded, attempting to maintain
my composure. "It is a mistake to say that Shaw is *now* a gay neighborhood.
Black queer people have always lived in Shaw. In the face of discrimination from the white gay community, residents managed to create and sustain
vibrant worlds there. They hosted house parties and developed their own
club scenes, at times alongside their straight counterparts. They developed
strategies for finding each other in churches and movie theaters, even when
they were not entirely accepted. Black Pride has taken place there for nearly
30 years. It doesn't become a gayborhood simply because white gay men
colonized it." By then, I discovered myself shouting at the poor journalist.

"SHAW HAS *ALWAYS* BEEN A GAYBORHOOD TO SOMEONE!"

My invective to that poor journalist motivates this chapter. In many ways,
the journalist asked a perfectly innocent question, reflecting popular understandings of gay neighborhoods and queer placemaking in cities (Anderson
2003; Castells 1983; Ghaziani 2014; Greene 2014, 2019b; Levine 1979;
Murray 1979). Growing scholarly and popular interest in queer placemaking within cities continues to privilege the cultures and practices fostered
by white, cis-gender, gay men. Participation by queer communities of color
is often misrecognized either as threats to public safety or as destructive to
white queer space production in iconic gay neighborhoods. Consequently, the
common perception of gay white men as harbingers of gentrification in black
neighborhoods like Shaw (Goode Bryant and Poitras 2003; Greene 2014;
Knopp 1990; Lauria and Knopp 1985; Vargas 2006; Volin 2006) often erases
a history of placemaking and community building by black LGBTQ men and
women, whose practices partly grew out of the broader patterns of racial and
economic segregation in cities.

Focusing on the diverse expressions of placemaking by queer communities of color in Washington, D.C., and Chicago, this chapter highlights the
theoretical blind spots created by refracting the spatial production and maintenance of queer communities through white queer subjectivities. I extend on
scholarship that reclaims black urban placemaking as creative forces within
cities (Hunter et al. 2016; Hunter and Robinson 2018) by reimagining and
legitimating otherwise deviant, "oppressive geographies" within the gayborhood as "sites or play, pleasure, celebration, and politics" (Hunter et al. 2016,
4). Additionally, this chapter further challenges the imbalanced scholarly perception of urban communities of color as bounded, isolated, and pathological.
As queer communities of color transport practices traditionally associated
with "iconic ghettos" (Anderson 2012) and ethnic enclaves to iconic gay

neighborhoods, they also reinforce the significance of iconic gay neighbor-hoods, despite evidence signaling their cultural and demographic decline. Often ephemeral, these spatial expressions represent intentional strategies for making gay neighborhoods and queer spaces within cities accessible for the safe exploration of sexual and gender identities.

QUEER URBANISM AS A WAY OF (WHITE) LIFE

While cities have always contained diverse expressions of queer life, much of the scholarship on queer BIPOC[3] communities in the United States has centered around white interest in them. Epitomized by George Chauncey's (1994) *Gay New York*, landmark histories of LGBT geographies offer an impression of black queer communities often refracted through white gay men's experiences. Recounting the vibrant drag balls, black and tans, and rent parties that anchored black queer life in the early twentieth century, Chauncey's interlocutors emphasized how the black gay world of Harlem exceeded its white gay counterparts in Greenwich Village and the Bowery (Chauncey 1994:244). However, the absence of black queer perspectives in the study reveals the limitations of queer placemaking in Harlem. Chauncey mentions nothing about Gay Harlem once Prohibition ends. As white gay men lose interest, Chauncey assumes that black Queer New Yorkers endured the public restrictions of "the closet" similarly to white gay men downtown. Subsequent LGBT histories that engage black queer geographies mainly focus on spaces that resemble white gay spaces. Emphasizing the role of segregation in shaping distinct LGBT geographies in Washington, D.C., Genny Beemyn (2015) primarily shows how black spatial practices paralleled whites. As a result, despite their exclusion from white establishments down-town, black movie theaters and black Young Men's Christian Associations (YMCAs) functioned similarly for black gay men.

As the Stonewall Riots and the burgeoning Gay Liberation Movement accelerated the emergence of iconic gay neighborhoods throughout the United States, scholars aimed to sociologically legitimate gay neighborhoods by comparing them to other established ecological frameworks. Challenging the prevailing assumptions of homosexuality as "deviant," scholars like Martin Levine (1979), Stephen Murray (1979, 1992, 1992), and Manuel Castells (1983; 1982) compared the qualities of gay neighborhoods to Jewish ghettos and ethnic enclaves, respectively. The hallmarks they established—residential concentration, institutional completeness, and a visible gay culture all circumscribed within a bounded area—erased alternate LGBTQ geog-raphies created by communities of color, who because of racially and eco-nomically segregated housing markets, precluded the participation of many

LGBT communities of color (Greene 2019a; Nero 2005). As studies shifted from gay neighborhoods as political projects to create and foster community (Castells 1983) to gay men as economic actors who transform economically depressed urban spaces into fashionable neighborhoods for hip, trendy, urban cosmopolitans interested in consuming diversity (Florida 2003; Ghaziani 2014; Knopp 1990; Lauria and Knopp 1985), queer placemaking became further defined as a phenomenon driven by cisgender, white, middle-class gay men.

Amid evidence suggesting the declining salience of the gayborhood in the post-gay era (Ghaziani 2011, 2014), scholars shift the focus from a central gayborhood to a growing plurality of LGBTQ residential settlements, which Amin Ghaziani (2019) refers to as queer "cultural archipelagos." Hailing cultural archipelagos as a "new direction" in the study of gay spatial communities, Ghaziani's discussion includes the "surprising" finding of "emerging" clusters of queer communities of color in black neighborhoods and ethnic enclaves. Their "emergence" coincides with the deployment of demographic and analytic tools that rendered these communities legible to urban scholars. That these settlements now have the interest of mainstream LGBT scholars does not erase their longstanding legacy for communities who have relied upon them.

Despite popular perceptions of black homophobia in the "iconic ghetto" (Anderson 2012), black sexual minorities have developed vibrant and variably visible communities throughout the twentieth century. While the pressures of "the closet" often forced white gay men to explore their sexual and gender identities in "scattered gay places" throughout the city (Chauncey 1994; Forsyth 1997; Ghaziani 2014), black gay men and lesbians lived out their sexual lives within proximity of their families and friends (Beemyn 2015; Cabello 2012; Drexel 1997; Heap 2009). Private parties, nightclubs, cookouts, and drag balls have always represented integral spaces for developing and maintaining queer black communities. Black nightlife accommodated same-sex couples who often cuddled and necked alongside their straight counterparts (Beemyn 2015; Cabello 2012; Drexel 1997; Holmes 2011). And in a time where the formation of the "closet" forced much of gay life underground, drag balls like "Finnie's Ball" on Chicago's South Side proved so popular among straight black audiences that they received extensive coverage in mainstream black publications like *Ebony* and *Jet* magazines (Drexel 1997).

Economic and political disinvestment of inner-city black neighborhoods altered but did not erase the black queer imagination. Experiencing racial and sexual exclusion in iconic gay neighborhoods and establishments (Boykin 1996; Greene 2018, 2019b), many black sexual minorities navigated a terrain where their sexuality may be known but never discussed. They occupied prominent positions in black churches, enduring preachers who sermonized homosexuality as a sin (Bennett and Battle 2001; Boykin 1996; Monroe 1999). These communities mobilized the resources at their disposal to create ephemeral places to find each other and foster community. Where a gay ball occupying a single night at a straight venue, or a festival occupying a week-end in a public park, black queer geographies represent important spaces that allowed participants to leverage economic opportunities that mitigated the effects of social and economic isolation characteristic of the iconic ghetto (Hunter 2010).

Recognizing the legacies of segregation and exclusion, which have marked iconic gay neighborhoods as white spaces (Anderson 2015), schol-ars have drawn increased attention to the distinctive spatialized practices of queer BIPOC communities. Much of this research relies on a deficit fram-ing (Hunter and Robinson 2018), positioning queer BIPOC geographies as products of institutional forces like racism. As a result, studies exploring the growing visibility of queer BIPOC youth in iconic gay neighborhoods represent forms of resistance against hegemonic forms of queer and post-gay placemaking (Daniel-McCarter 2012; Rosenberg 2016). Yet, a growing strand of research emphasizes these geographies as creative forces within cities. Queer BIPOC communities write themselves into community through practices misrecognized by whites as "pathological" (Bailey 2013; Greene 2019a,b; Hunter 2010; Stillwagon and Ghaziani 2019). Whites may mis-recognize the very presence of people of color as threats to public safety in spaces like iconic gay neighborhoods. However, many of the practices constituting queer BIPOC geographies highlight how gay and queer spaces within cities persist as significant sites for the safe exploration of gender and sexual identities.

Although black queer geographies may not fully represent the experiences of other queer communities of color, they certainly gesture to the array of cultural traditions that subcultures infuse into their placemaking. Drawing on ten years of ethnographic fieldwork conducted in and around iconic gay neighborhoods in Washington, D.C., and Chicago, the following case stud-ies illuminate various expressions of placemaking by LGBTQ communities of color. The next section explores how black LGBTQ residents in D.C.'s Shaw/U Street neighborhood respond to white queer residents' increased presence. The neighborhood's increasingly visible queer culture does not change the spatial logics and practices Black LGBTQ residents use to find each other and facilitate communities. From there, we move to Chicago's Boystown neighborhood, where I describe how queer youth of color draw on "street corner practices" to make the white space of the gayborhood accessible to them. While local residents and business leaders may find large groups of black and Latinx queer youth on street corners a threat to public safety, I suggest that these practices represent a creative force that reaffirms the value of gay neighborhoods as safe spaces to explore gender and sexual identities safely. Finally, I will return to Washington, D.C., to explore how queer Latinx and Muslim groups attempted to rewrite themselves into the collective mourning that took place in the days following the 2016 Pulse Nightclub tragedy.

THE SUBTLETY OF QUEER PLACE MAKING

Keith (fifty, black, gay) has lived in Shaw his entire life. Still living in his family home, Keith has witnessed quite a few changes in the neighborhood. As he observed gay white couples move into the homes of the "mothers" who helped raise and discipline him, Keith sees himself as a "middleman" between the newcomers and the Black old-timers who are "still holding Black Shaw down." Coming out in college, Keith defines his sexuality as "non-secret." He answers questions honestly about his sexuality, believing that his neighbors know (or suspect), based on his perpetual bachelorhood, his perpetual roommates, and the occasional "bachelor" parties that he throws, which now include his new gay and lesbian neighbors. However, despite Shaw's increased gay visibility, Keith remains reluctant to openly live as his white gay neighbors. When not entertaining guests in his home, Keith prefers to spend his time in gay spaces far removed from his community. When asked why he eschews participating in the neighborhood's burgeoning queer culture, he answered: "Oh no. You never shit where you eat."

Keith's succinctness reveals a paradox often invisible by students of sexuality and space. Scholars often champion the "growing" demographic and institutional visibility of LGBTQ communities in cultural archipelagos (Ghaziani 2019), signaling by flags flanking residential streets and HRC "Equality" stickers plastered on minivan bumpers as new indicators of safety and acceptance for LGBTQ communities. However, these practices also ignore LGBTQ communities of color's longstanding existence in neighborhoods like Shaw, where queer residents developed vibrant and visible communities in terrain where family and community members know their sexuality yet never discuss it. Growing out of the homophobia proliferating in certain public cultures and anchoring institutions like the black church (Bennett and Battle 2001; Boykin 1996; Monroe 1999), queer communities of color continue to rely on "interaction and meaning to transform spaces into places, however ephemeral they may be" (Hunter et al. 2016:2). Their white neighbors might misrecognize these spatial logics as "closeted." However, being "invisible in plain sight" represents strategies of resilience, belonging, and resistance for queer communities of color, particularly as the growing residential and institutional presence of white queer residents threatens their displacement.

Many respondents challenged the perception of their lives as "closeted" on the basis that they did not follow hegemonic queer cultural scripts. Some, like Giancarlo (32, gay, Latino), equated acts of coming out by "announcing one's sexuality" as a bit too dramatic. Like Brandi and Keith, Giancarlo believes that he signals to others by keeping "it chill." "I don't need to draw unnecessary attention to myself by explaining to people who I want to fuck," he explained. "That's [what] white people do. My man comes around, and those who don't like it can lick rocks." Brandi (twenty-five, queer, black) described that she never "came out" to her family by explaining her sexuality. "They knew I was a tomboy," she explained. "I wear my hair short, [and] I feel more comfortable in a suit and tie than I do in a dress. I bring my girlfriends around the family all the time. They ask no questions, but they know the deal. And they usually embrace them like one of their own."

This "low-key" visibility does not prevent LGBTQ people from finding each other within public spaces. Sometimes, a look could sufficiently signal sexual or romantic interest. In white gay bars, I have observed two black men glancing at each other from across the dance floor, only within minutes approaching each other and making out without saying a word. While working in a café along U Street one morning, a tall, muscular man walked in wearing a Howard sweatshirt. He ordered his coffee, at times glancing over at my table. When I finally made eye contact, he grabbed his coffee and walked over to me. During our small talk, he asked about my day, what I ordered, and my reason for sitting in the café. After a few minutes of casual conversation, he then asked where I lived. Pointing in the direction without explicitly mentioning the street name, I explained that I lived a few blocks away. He indicated that he was walking in that direction and asked when I expected to finish my work. As I began explaining that I might be a while, it suddenly hit me. Without explicit overtures, he expressed sexual interest, inviting himself to my place for an afternoon interlude. "I might actually be here all evening," I hedged. "I have a deadline, and I have not made much progress today." Realizing my lack of interest, he simply responded, "Cool. See you around," and headed out the door.

Many of the placemaking practices that define queer communities of color prove ephemeral. In addition to private house parties, festivals in local parks, or "gay nights" in local straight bars, queer communities of color might also transform singular nights in mainstream gay bars and nightclubs as spaces for communion. On Sundays, large groups of queer black men walk along U Street to patronize gay white bars like Dirty Goose or Nellie's, which quickly return to white spaces by Monday's Happy Hour. Although these nights are often not advertised as "Black gay nights," establishments respond spatially to accommodate the critical masses of black queer patrons. They incorporated R&B/hip-hop or Latinx music heavily into their rotation, cleared the tables and chairs to create a dance area, and ensured their staff reflected the diversity of their patrons. These spatial forms of accommodation also reveal the prejudices of bar management. The hypercriminalization of black and Latinx queer bodies often results in additional security measures. When Cobalt was still open on 17th Street, police cars sat outside of the club on Saturday nights in anticipation of unruly patrons and potentially violent altercations. "Oh yeah, the police were only there when the Black people took over," Darius (twenty-four, black gay) explained. "A bouncer will tell a patron entering to take off a durag or pull up their pants, and they're looking over their shoulder [at the police], just waiting for someone to get out of line. But we won't give them the satisfaction, because we know that means no more hip-hop nights." Patrons do not see the extra police surveillance on "hip-hop" nights as mere coincidence. Yet, in refusing to give the police or the patrons the "satisfaction" of intervening against them, these patrons also wage subtle forms of resistance that protect the spaces many rely on for creating and fostering community.

DEVIANCE AS QUEER PLACE MAKING

One afternoon, while enjoying coffee on an outdoor patio along Halsted, I observed a group of approximately ten black and Latinx queer youth standing along the corner, gossiping, playing music, and dancing along the sidewalk across the street. Although obstructing pedestrian traffic, they attempted to clear a path when pedestrians approached (several decided to walk in the street or cross entirely to avoid the group). While practicing dance moves, a tall, burly white bear in his late forties, walking northbound on Halsted, barreled through the group of youths, nearly kicking one of the dancers in the head.

"Hey!" one of the youths yelled. "Watch where you're going!" The man stopped, turned around, and approached the gang of youths. "What did you say to me?" The altercation escalated, culminating in the white man screaming an epithet and spitting on the transwoman. That was enough for the crowd to begin swinging wildly. The man punched the transwoman, grabbing her wig off her head before going down. The group started punching and kicking the man while shouting obscenities at him. A couple of gay white men began yelling at the youths to stop, with a few trying to pull them off the man. A woman pulled out her cellphone and called 9-1-1 when a patrol car pulled up on the corner. Two cops got out and began pulling people away, asking what happened. The man started telling the police a tale about how the youths provoked him. As the transwoman began objecting, the officer threatened to arrest her and the rest of the group. Feeling that these youths would not get an opportunity to tell their side of the story, I took a big gulp of coffee and walked across the street toward them.

As back-up arrived, I made my way through the crowd. One of the officers took the man's story, while a second officer chastised the group for interrupting the man. Amid the chaos, I approached the second officer, introducing myself as a researcher observing street life for a project while handing over my business card. While the officer inspected my card, I explained that I had witnessed the altercation from across the street and that the white man started it by behaving aggressively toward the youths.

"But it's their fault," the man interrupted, waving the transwoman's wig he removed during the fight. "They shouldn't have been here in the first place. They are obstructing the sidewalk, making it hard for decent, law-abiding residents like myself to feel safe."

"If you started it, then you had it coming," the officer responded. The teens broke out in laughter, taunting the man for being chastised by the officer. But as quickly as the laughter began, the officer turned his attention toward the group. "And you really shouldn't be obstructing the sidewalk. If I catch you again, creating a disturbance, I'll take you all in." The officer demanded the group to disperse. Snatching the wig out of her opponent's hand, the transwoman and her friends proceeded south on Halsted. That man, slightly scratched and dirtied by the fight, continued talking with the officer while I waved at the group and returned to my table.

As an ethnographer, I rarely intervene in moments like these. However, realizing the tensions brewing between local residents and the queer youths of color who have made their presence known along the streets of Boystown, I felt obligated to defend them. As scholars attribute sociopolitical acceptance for LGBTQ citizens to the declining salience of gay neighborhoods (Barrett and Pollack 2011; Brown 2007; Ghaziani 2014), these areas have increasingly become popular destinations among LGBTQ queer youths of color. Many teens travel for hours, escaping violence and homophobia in their local neighborhoods to participate in a community they believe will support their gender and sexual identities. However, these youths quickly find themselves excluded from local queer life, enduring racial profiling and discrimination from business owners who find their presence bad for business. Many encounter age-based and economic barriers to patronizing gay bars and restaurants. Some, turned out of their homes, even find themselves participating in the local sexual economy, picking up the same white gay men who publicly label them as menaces to community safety. Nevertheless, these youths defend their right to the neighborhood, combining the symbolic culture of gay neighborhoods with spatial practices mirroring the "codes of the street" (Anderson 1990, 1994) to create and foster community.

During the summer months, some youths appear on the streets early in the day, using business storefronts, parking lots, and coffee shop bathrooms to apply their hair and make-up. Their appearance mirrors the styles typical of teenagers you might find hanging out on the south side of the city, and they take their appearance seriously. One warm Sunday morning, as I was running late to present my research on Queer Youth at the ASA conference, I tripped over a large canvas bag in the middle of the sidewalk. I collided with three transwomen applying their make-up in front of a storefront window, sending their make-up and wigs into the street. As the four of us scrambled to retrieve the make-up, clothes, and jewelry, the three women began berating me for my clumsiness: "Why can't you watch where you're going!" "Have you any idea how expensive this stuff is!" "Can't a girl beat her face without having to worry about someone kicking her shit out into the street!" I stepped on the sidewalk and apologized, depositing a pile of mascara, lipsticks, and tangled hair extensions into the large canvas bag. I offered to replace anything I destroyed. The tallest of the three inspected the items and admonished me to be careful in the future.

Throughout the day, the youths hang out on the streets or in one of the local LGBTQ areas like Center on Halsted or the Broadway Youth Center. In extreme weather, they may find refuge in one of the area's local coffee shops. However, lingering in these establishments, even when they purchase coffee or food, makes them vulnerable to increased staff surveillance. While working in a Boystown café one summer, a tall young black man entered. Surveying the nearly empty coffee shop for a second, he made eye contact with me and then approached me in the corner. "Hey baby," he said to me, kissing me on both cheeks before sitting in the empty chair. "Sorry I'm late, but you would not *believe* the crazy shit I just witnessed on the train. Total shitshow!" As I tried to make sense of what was happening, he gestured his eyes toward the barista at the register and mouthed, *Keep cool.* I glanced over to the barista, who stared at him while adding foam to a cappuccino. Realizing that someone might question his presence in the shop and ask him to leave, I smiled at the barista, offering a thumbs-up. After thanking me, the boy pulled out a charger and plugged his phone into the socket. As we chatted, he described how he liked sitting in the café for some quiet time, but he tries not to draw too much attention to himself, which explained his reason for joining me.

Many of their activities mirrored the forms of play indigenous to black and Latino neighborhoods. One afternoon, a group of queer black and Latino youth hung out outside a 7-Eleven on Broadway when a muscular black man approached them with a Bluetooth speaker playing Beyoncé's "Formation" song. Within seconds, the group transformed the sidewalk into a catwalk, strutting along a stretch of Waveland Avenue to hip-hop music before the entire group held a started dancing. Sometimes, these forms of play can resemble violence. One summer afternoon, a group of black teenagers was standing and chatting on the corner across from the Center on Halsted. One of the members—a tall, slender, effeminate man in a plaid-collar shirt and cut-off jeans—began teasing a short, thickset young woman in a white t-shirt, baggy blue-washed jeans, and a backward-turned White Sox cap. She threatened to "pop him if he didn't cut it out," but he continued, eventually slapping the side of her breast. The woman yelled out in pain, grabbing her breast while the rest of the group erupted in laughter. Within seconds, the youths were sparring, the young man attempting to dodge and weave the young woman's jabs to the group's laughter and egging. Yet, despite the appearance of the activity, they nevertheless respected sidewalk etiquette. When a white couple approached them, the group stopped, lined up along the street, and allowed them to pass. When the area was finally clear, the group resumed their play, and within seconds, the woman had the man in a full nelson.

Thinking back on the incident opening this section, a critical reason for defending the queer youths grew from my understanding of their practices. While conspicuous, many of the cliques found in Boystown socialize among themselves, rarely interacting with others conducting their daily and nightly rounds. As local residents perceive the prominent presence of black and brown bodies on neighborhood street corners late at night as "deviant, risky, threatening, and criminal" (Rios 2011:xiv), I recognized their behavior as one method of making "the gayborhood" (Ghaziani 2014) accessible to them. Their practices resemble the counterpublics that scholars often attribute to queer subjects incapable of accessing their local culture (Gray 2009; Warner 2005). However, these practices also operate as a creative force that ironically reinforces the enduring value of gay neighborhoods as safe spaces for the safe exploration of gender and sexual identity.

PRESENTE! PRESENTE!

In the early morning hours of Sunday, June 12, 2016, a gunman walked into a gay bar in Orlando, Florida. As patrons danced and drank during last call, he opened fire, killing forty-nine and wounding fifty-three in what was then considered the deadliest mass shooting in American history. As the world woke to the news of the shooting in Pulse nightclub, various contingents attempted to co-opt the discourse around the tragedy. Conservative pundits labeled it as an act of "radical Islamic terrorism," eliding the fact that the massacre took place inside a gay bar. "Appreciate the congrats for being right on radical

Islamic terrorism," then-presidential candidate Donald Trump tweeted. "I don't want congrats, I want toughness and vigilance [*sic*]. We must be smart" (Frizell 2016). Gun-control advocates seized the opportunity to condemn the tragedy to call for more comprehensive gun control legislation, while gun-rights organizations went on the defense. "Evil struck in Orlando yesterday morning," tweeted Gun Owners of America. "No matter how tragic, no amount of gun control could've stopped evil" (Kanski 2016).

LGBTQ communities around the world vacillated between rumors about the shooter's internalized homophobia to proclamations about the importance of gay bars for fostering community. That the shooting occurred during Pride month was not lost on older generations of gay white men, who took the podium to challenge younger LGBTQ people to protect the spaces that helped anchor the LGBTQ community. "We built these spaces because we knew the importance of protecting each other," a middle-aged gay white man shouted at one of the Pulse Vigils in Dupont Circle. "We've done our part. Now it's your turn. Take care of each other. Protect what [our generation] built."

Missing from these conversations were the voices of Latinx and Muslim LGBTQ citizens, many of whom found the debates misplaced. "Too many people are dismissing that the shooting took place during Pride month at a Latin night event," explained journalist Alan Pelaez Lopez. "Even friends on social media have said that this shooting has nothing to do with race because, after all, white gay people go clubbing, too. But Sunday's shooting was an attack against a primarily young crowd of Latinx and Black individuals celebrating their existence in a world that has continually tried to silence them" (Pelaez Lopez 2016). In Washington, queer Latinos expressed frustration over mainstream LGBTQ organizations hogging the spotlight on the tragedy. "HRC can't speak for us," José (forty, Latinx, gay) said. "It was so frustrating to see one white cis[gender] face after another trying to convey the weight of this tragedy without making any attempt to engage members of the Latinx community."

Meanwhile, queer Muslims found their shared outrage and sadness completely silenced as mourners attributed the attack to radical Islamic terrorism. "We are mourning," Aabirah (twenty-six, Irani, Muslim, queer) told me. "This shooting impacts queer Muslims around the world . . . just as it does anyone else. And yet, we are being attacked by members of our own [LGBTQ] community. They don't care that we are also mourning." Even though Justin (twenty-three, Indian, gay) does not identify as Muslim, he, too, found himself defending himself against accusations by gay men. "I was waiting in line [in a gay bar] for a drink when someone just walked up to me and told me, 'You've got some nerve being here, you fucking Arab.' I was dumbfounded because he couldn't have been more off. I'm Indian. I was raised Catholic, and I grew up in *New Jersey,* for fuck sake! But he didn't

care. It didn't matter to him that I was devastated and that I came out to be
with my community and mourn like everybody else."

Frustrated by their erasure, both the queer Latinx and Muslim communities began planning community-wide events to write themselves into the
conversation. The first organized vigil, organized by the Muslim American
Women's Policy Forum, took place the Monday following the shooting and
attracted nearly six hundred people. The gathering contained elements that
became standard in many of the events taking place that week. The Gay
Men's Chorus of Washington, D.C. performance of the anthem "We Shall
Overcome" and members of the local LGBTQ community shared their feelings about the tragedy during the Open Mic portion. Yet the organizers made
sure to include elements of their own culture into the event. In one powerful
moment, a member of the Latino LGBT History Project read the 49 victims' names lost in the tragedy. After calling out each name, the audience
responded with *"Presente!"* symbolizing the presence of the dead in spirit.

Throughout the week, *"Presente!"* became a rallying cry for the queer
Latinx community. As residents converged onto the makeshift memorial in
honor of the Pulse victims in Dupont Circle, Latinx queer youth chalked the
victims' names and the words *Presente! Presente! Presente!* in rainbow-
colors along the sidewalk surround the fountain. As more people left colorful beads, Pride flags, and votive candles along the fountain's base, rosaries
surrounded sanctuary candles, with images of Our Lady of Guadalupe, Jesus,
and St. Joseph looking down solemnly at color images of the forty-nine victims. Along the walkways, messages in Spanish appeared, chalked along the
sidewalk surrounding the fountain. *"La determinación orgullo y amor de las
personas LGBT brillará más fuerte [sic],"*[4] written in bold colors, dominated
one side of the fountain. Supportive messages in Arabic also soon appeared
alongside the Spanish, transforming the sidewalk into a colorful mosaic of
tributes. The display at the fountain also included objects from the curbside
memorials I remembered all too well growing up in Los Angeles.

The juxtaposition of Arabic and Spanish embodied the spirit of many
events led by the Latinx and Muslim queer communities that week. While
Latinx organizers hoped to elicit sympathy from audiences for the victims
and survivors, they also wanted to clarify the connection between their collective suffering and the vilification of Muslim LGBTQ people. "We quickly
realized that our mourning was not separate from the violence against queer
Muslims or trans people," Pablo (38, Latinx, gay) told me. "We were not
going to repeat what the white gays did to us. We are going to show them
how to do it right." That Wednesday, as the city prepared for the largest *In
Memoriam* to the Pulse tragedy victims in Dupont Circle, representatives of
D.C.'s Queer Latinx and Muslim communities hosted a community dialogue
on the shooting at a church in Dupont Circle. While the program included

opportunities for the audience to exchange their feelings about the tragedy, the event's main goal centered on the audience hearing stories from those representing the communities silenced in the public grieving. "We recognize that you all feel some personal connection to the tragedy," one of the organizers explained to the audience beginning of the meeting. "But, this is also your time to listen to those who are most affected by what happened at Pulse." Throughout the program, organizers emphasized the costs of the tragedy on the lives of the queer and transgender Latinx communities. In one of the most powerful moments of the evening, one of the speakers, a transgender Latinx woman, expressed how the dominant discourses around the tragedy focused on the safety and preservation of white queer spaces, while "safe spaces" for queer communities of color remain scant. "You all sit there crying about no longer feeling safe in your bars," she said through tears. "Pulse wasn't even a queer Latinx night club. It was only Latinx once a month."

Once the town hall ended, we lined up in front of the church for a candlelight procession to Dupont Circle for the vigil. As we walked along P Street, the organizer shouted the shooting victims' names through a megaphone, after which we replied with *"Presente."* Along the journey, Marchers demonstrated extraordinary acts of kindness to each other. Strangers walked arm-in-arm as the roll call began reducing marchers to tears. As one marcher attempted to hold a candle while balancing on crutches to support his broken leg, a car pulled up alongside the road to offer him a ride to the Circle. "Thanks," he told the caravan. "But this is something I really need to do." As the procession neared Dupont Circle, and the man began feeling pain from his leg, marchers came to his aid. One grabbed his crutches and candle while two men carried him the rest of the way.

The observance in Dupont Circle had already begun by the time we arrived. As a black minister continued a rousing sermon about the power of forgiveness, participants stopped behind the procession leader and continued their call-and-response. Our arrival barely registered among members of the crowd. A few bystanders standing in front of us turned around to see what was going on. Once they realized what we were doing, they returned their attention to the pastor at the stage. Undeterred by the ongoing activity, the leader continued calling out the names until he reached the very end. When the leader finished, the group subsequently disbanded, interspersing among the crowd to participate in the service. In the days that followed, reports on the vigil in Dupont Circle eclipsed the dialogue and funeral-like procession along P Street. Yet, several traditions arose out of the week that became standard in the years that followed. On the anniversary of the tragedy, a representative from the Latino LGBT History Project reads the victims' names during the annual commemoration in Dupont Circle, inviting the audience to respond with *"Presente!"* The events of the week did not necessarily create the kind of attention that mainstream organizations rallied. Nevertheless, enacting familiar subcultural traditions, the Latinx and Muslim LGBTQ communities translated Dupont Circle into a place where queer communities of color could mobilize to mourn, heal, and articulate their anger and grief on their terms.

CONCLUSION

This chapter complicates scholarship that centers queer placemaking around the experiences and subjectivities of white queer communities. Conventional methods for exploring the spatial imagination of LGBTQ citizens in cities tend to erase or marginalize the experiences of queer communities of color, whose subcultural practices and traditions might not align with those familiar among mainstream queer communities. Equally, focusing on cosmetic diversity within LGBTQ spaces eclipse the various strategies mobilized by queer communities of color to write themselves into the queer spatial imagination. Latinx and Muslim queer communities' spatial practices in the wake of the Pulse tragedy barely registered as insurgent placemaking. Mainstream queer communities absorbed many cultural symbols marking Latinx and Muslim queer communities into their collective mourning, using *"Presente!"* when remembering the tragedy's victims and incorporating the Spanish and Arabic at the memorial as part of the local community's diversity. However, queer Latinx and Muslim leaders still relied on familiar cultural practices to create sanctuaries of collective mourning and healing while simultaneously critiquing their erasure from mainstream discourses around the tragedy. In the case of the queer youth in Boystown, the strategies for writing themselves into community seem antithetical to the production of white queer spaces. However, while white residents challenged these youths' presence as a threat to public safety within iconic gay neighborhoods, queer youths of color nevertheless transported local spatial practices to render exclusionary spaces accessible. In doing so, they not only developed their claims to the local area, but they also highlighted the enduring value of gay neighborhoods as affirming spaces for gender and sexual expression.

These expressions of community extend beyond conventional symbols of placemaking within gay communities. They lack the permanence and stability of traditional queer establishments and monuments, usually emerging and disappearing when necessary (Greene 2019b; Stillwagon and Ghaziani 2019). They reflect practices misrecognized as disruptive, criminal, and pathological. And yet, these spatial expressions matter. As scholars rely on bar closures and residential deconcentration to indicate the decline of gay neighborhoods, these strategies reinforce the enduring value of gay neighborhoods for those who need them. They also reveal new claims of local citizenship as the reversing economic fortunes of cities have exacerbated marginalized populations' displacement from the spaces they have long considered home.

NOTES

1. LGBTQ refers to lesbian, gay, bisexual, transgender, and queer communities. Although the acronym has expanded to include explicitly various gender non-conforming, asexual, questioning, two-spirited, and same-gender loving communities, this chapter will use LGBTQ and queer interchangeably, whereby queer functions as an (admittedly imprecise) stand-in for the various diverse communities not included under the LGBT umbrella. Unless otherwise indicated by respondents or communities of color, I will use "LGBTQ" or "queer" for the sake of legibility.

2. Although the question of what constitutes a "bear" remains widely contested, general answers suggest that gay bears reject the stereotypical association of homosexuality to effeminacy in favor of a more natural and rugged masculinity (in contrast to the "self-conscious and exaggerated masculinity" characteristic of the gay leather subculture (Hennen 2005:26). Body type commonly associated to bears includes attributes such as stockiness, burliness, and hairiness (Hennen 2005). "Twinks" traditionally refer to young (late-teens to mid-twenties), slender to lean gay men who fit traditional standards of male beauty.

3. BIPOC refers to Black, Indigenous, and People of Color. This acronym has recently gained traction as an umbrella term in the wake of Black Lives Matter protests and public discourses surrounding antiracism.

4. The sentence is translated, "The determination, pride, and love of LGBT people will shine brighter."

REFERENCES

Anderson, Elijah. 1990. *Streetwise: Race, Class, and Change in an Urban Community.* Chicago, IL: University of Chicago Press.

Anderson, Elijah. 1994. "The Code of the Streets." *Atlantic Monthly* 273:80–94.

Anderson, Elijah. 2003. *A Place on the Corner.* Chicago, IL: University of Chicago Press.

Anderson, Elijah. 2012. "The Iconic Ghetto." *The ANNALS of the American Academy of Political and Social Science* 642:8–24.

Anderson, Elijah. 2015. "The White Space." *Sociology of Race and Ethnicity* 1(1):10–21.

Bailey, Marlon M. 2013. *Butch Queens Up in Pumps: Gender, Performance, and Ballroom Culture in Detroit.* Ann Arbor, mi: University of Michigan Press.

Barrett, Donald C., and Lance M. Pollack. 2011. "Testing a Typology of Adaptations to Same-Sex Sexual Orientation Among Men." *Sociological Perspectives* 54(4):619–640.

Beemyn, Genny. 2015. *A Queer Capital: A History of Gay Life in Washington, DC.* New York: Routledge.

Bennett, Michael, and Juan Battle. 2001. "We Can See Them, But We Can't Hear Them." in *Queer Families, Queer Politics,* edited by M. Bernstein and Renate Remain. New York: Columbia University Press.

Boykin, Keith. 1996. *One More River to Cross: Black and Gay in America*. New York: Doubleday.

Brown, Patricia Leigh. 2007. "Gay Enclaves Face Prospect of Being Passé." *The New York Times*. Retrieved http://www.nytimes.com/2007/10/30/us/30gay.html /ei=5070&en=22520eb6996396dc&ex=1194494400&adxnnl=1&emc=eta1&ad xnnlx=1193889647-Ghee4TP7bC3CeCNjLAgyIw.

Cabello, Tristan. 2012. "The Emergence of African-American Queer Cultures on Chicago's South Side, 1920 - 1940." *Windy City Times*. Retrieved http://www .windycitymediagroup.com/lgbt/Queer-Bronzeville-African-American-LGBTs-on -Chicagos-South-Side-1900-1985/36389.html.

Castells, Manuel. 1983. *The City and the Grassroots*. Berkeley, CA: University of California Press.

Castells, Manuel, and Karen Murphy. 1982. "Cultural Identity and Urban Structure: The Spatial Organization of San Francisco's 'Gay Community.'" in *Urbanism under Capitalism*, edited by N. Fainstein and S. Fainstein (pp. 237–259). Beverly Hills, CA: Sage.

Chauncey, George. 1994. *Gay New York: Gender, Urban Culture, and the Making of the Homosexual*. New York: Basic Books.

Daniel-McCarter, Owen. 2012. "Us vs. Them! Gays and the Criminalization of Queer Youth of Color in Chicago." *Children's Legal Rights Journal* 32(1):5–17.

Drexel, Allen. 1997. "Before Paris Burned: Race, Class, and Male Homosexuality on the Chicago South Side, 1935–1960." in *Creating a Place for Ourselves: Lesbian, Gay, and Bisexual Community Histories*, edited by B. Beemyn (pp. 119–144). New York: Routledge.

Florida, Richard. 2003. "Cities and the Creative Class." *City & Community* 2(1):3–19.

Forsyth, Ann. 1997. "Out in the Valley." *International Journal of Urban and Regional Research* 21(1):38–62.

Ghaziani, Amin. 2011. "Post-Gay Collective Identity Construction." *Social Problems* 58(1):99–125.

Ghaziani, Amin. 2014. *There Goes the Gayborhood?* Princeton, NJ: Princeton University Press.

Ghaziani, Amin. 2019. "Cultural Archipelagos: New Directions in the Study of Sexuality and Space." *City & Community* 18(1):1–19.

Goode Bryant, Linda, and Laura Poitras. 2003. *Flag Wars*. Praxis Films.

Gray, Mary L. 2009. *Out in the Country: Youth, Media, and Queer Visibility in Rural America*. New York: New York University Press.

Greene, Theodore. 2014. "Gay Neighborhoods and the Rights of the Vicarious Citizen." *City & Community* 13(2):99–118.

Greene, Theodore. 2018. "Queer Street Families: Place-Making and Community Among LGBT Youth of Color In Iconic Gay Neighborhoods." in *Queer Families and Relationships After Marriage Equality*, edited by M. Yarborough, A. Jones, and J. N. DeFilippis (pp. 168–181). New York: Routledge.

Greene, Theodore. 2019a. "Aberrations of 'Home': Gay Neighborhoods and the Experiences of Community Among GBQ Men of Color." in *The Handbook of Research for Black Males: Quantitative, Qualitative, and Multidisciplinary*, edited by T. Ransaw, R. Majors, and C. Gause (pp. 189–209). East Lansing, MI: Michigan State University Press.

Greene, Theodore. 2019b. "Queer Cultural Archipelagos Are New to US." *City & Community* 18(1):23–29.

Heap, Chad. 2009. *Slumming: Sexual and Racial Encounters in American Nightlife, 1885–1940*. Chicago, IL: University of Chicago Press.

Hennen, Peter. 2005. "Bear Bodies, Bear Masculinity: Recuperation, Resistance, or Retreat?" *Gender & Society* 19(1): 25–43.

Holmes, Kwame. 2011. "Chocolate to Rainbow City: The Dialectics of Black and Gay Community Formation in Postwar Washington, D.C. 1946–1978." Dissertation, University of Illinois at Urbana- Champaign, Urbana.

Hunter, Marcus Anthony. 2010. "The Nightly Round: Space, Social Capital, and Urban Black Nightlife." *City & Community* 9(2):165–186.

Hunter, Marcus Anthony, Mary Pattillo, Zandria F. Robinson, and Keeanga-Yamahtta Taylor. 2016. "Black Placemaking: Celebration, Play, and Poetry." *Theory, Culture, and Society* 1–26.

Hunter, Marcus Anthony, and Zandria F. Robinson. 2018. *Chocolate Cities: The Black Map of Urban Life*. Berkeley, CA: University of California Press.

Knopp, Lawrence. 1990. "Some Theoretical Implications of Gay Involvement in an Urban Land Market." *Political Geography Quarterly* 9(4):337–352.

Lauria, Mickey, and Lawrence Knopp. 1985. "Toward an Analysis of the Role of Gay Communities in the Urban Renaissance." *Urban Geography* 6(2):152–69.

Levine, Martin P. 1979. "Gay Ghetto." *Journal of Homosexuality* 4(4):363–377.

Monroe, Irene. 1999. "The Garden of Homophobia." *The Advocate*, December 9, 9.

Murray, Stephen O. 1979. "The Institutional Elaboration of a Quasi-Ethnic Community." *International Review of Modern Sociology* 9:165–177.

Murray, Stephen O. 1992. "Components of Gay Community in San Francisco." in *Gay Culture in America: Essays from the Field*, edited by G. Herdt (pp. 107–146). Beacon: Beacon Press.

Nero, Charles I. 2005. "Why Are the Gay Ghettos White?" in *Black Queer Studies: A Critical Anthology*, edited by E. P. Johnson and M. G. Henderson (pp. 228–245). Durham, NC: Duke University Press.

Rosenberg, Rebecca. 2016. "Man Who Bashed Gay Couple With Chair at Dallas BBQ Is Also Gay, Lawyer Says." *New York Post*. Retrieved http://nypost.com/2016/05/17/man-who-bashed-gay-couple-with-chair-at-dallas-bbq-is-also-gay-lawyer-says/.

Stillwagon, Ryan, and Amin Ghaziani. 2019. "Queer Pop-Ups: A Cultural Innovation of Urban Life." *City & Community* 18(3): 874–895.

Vargas, Jose Antonio. 2006. "In Shaw, Pews vs. Stools." *The Washington Post*, April 20, C01.

Volin, Katherine. 2006. "Gay Influx Brings Change to Shaw: Shaw Has Growing Pains as Whites, Gays Move In." *The Washington Blade*. Retrieved http://www.washblade.com/print.cfm?content_id=8173.

Warner, Michael. 2005. *Publics and Counterpublics*. Brooklyn: Zone Books.

Chapter 8

Beyond the Heteronormative Framework

How Two-Mother Families in Poland Deal with Social Invisibility and Related Anxieties

Magdalena Wojciechowska

INTRODUCTORY REMARKS: TWO-MOTHER FAMILIES IN POLAND

"Look, they're those dykes!"

Julia was picking her child up from preschool when she heard one of the fathers say it. She later phoned her partner Anna to discuss it.

Incidents like this are common in Poland,[1] which is made all the worse because same-sex couples here receive no legal recognition. Their circumstances become even more complicated when they raise a child, as Polish law only grants for acquisition of parental rights based on biology and does not allow for adoption by same-sex couples. The implications of these laws have long-term consequences for both the parents and the child of same-sex households.

While motherhood is framed in Poland as an obvious, and even obligatory, stage of life for every woman, in reality, it is a role that is reserved for those individuals who fit heteronormative standards or who otherwise occupy a *normal* identity in the Goffmanian sense (i.e., heterosexual, adherent to traditional, preferably Catholic, values). Thus, while heterosexual mothers are afforded allowances for certain deviations (e.g., their very young age, physical/intellectual disability, being addicted to psychoactive substances, or other biographical issues), the same affordances are not made for lesbian mothers. Lesbian motherhood in Poland is perceived as, at best, inadequate. Such views embrace a patriarchal approach to motherhood—reserved for "normal" women who are thought best equipped to socialize the child. The phenomenon can be seen in terms of a manifestation of social control guarding the traditional order, which effectiveness is exemplified by the fact that when considering enlarging their family, the women under study undertake intense emotional and identity work aimed at answering the question of whether they have a moral right to become mothers at all. Furthermore, being socialized within the same society as heterosexual mothers, same-sex mothers understand that their situation may not be seen as normal. For this reason, to avoid anticipated homophobia, they often try to *conceal* their stigma, which demonstrates that the way they act is shaped by having internalized the normal (heteronormative) rules of the game.

In this chapter, I explore how same-sex mothers manage the stigma that comes from their marginalized status as same-sex parents using an interpretive framework (Blumer 1986; Denzin 1992; Prus 1996). As I show, same-sex mothers employ a variety of strategies to deal with social anxiety and discomfort that arise from structural forms of discrimination produced by the heteronormative culture embedded within the law. Participants in this study used a variety of strategies, like information control (Goffman 1986), hiding the nature of their family in front of certain people and, in certain situations, making their status open-ended. They also used stigma management techniques in anticipation of the possibility of experiencing some form of homophobia, directed toward either them or their child. Thus, while Goffman's (1986) original conceptualization of stigma discusses it as a situational phenomenon, my subjects utilized stigma management techniques *prior to* interactions that they felt would "spoil" their identities. I conclude by considering the challenges faced by those attempting to overcome the stigma of raising children in a same-sex parent household.

SOCIAL CONSTRUCTION OF NORMALITY: THEORETICAL INSIGHTS

Norms, or better yet—*negotiated order* (Strauss 1993)—exemplify the shared and thus legitimized hierarchy of values. In such a sense, they can be seen as a kind of signpost for the individual—offering information about the acceptable scale of normality. At the same time, they can lead to some confusion between individuals when confronted with alternatives from which to choose. For instance, two-mother families in Poland are somehow torn between complying with societal expectations of establishing a family and not quite fitting definitional categories of family life, which exemplifies Goffman's (1959) concept of role strain.

The establishment of societal norms is also a product of "power games" (in the Bourdieusian sense). Bourdieu (2002) highlights the fact that social capital allows some groups to impose the elements of their habitus onto other groups, an act he refers to as symbolic violence.[2] An example of this would be using expert knowledge to frame some LGBT+ identities as "normal" (and thus, acceptable) and others as deviant cases. However, more broadly we can also conceptualize this as part of the heteronormative cultural values that define motherhood. This process reproduces itself in both explicit and implicit ways, such as when individuals "choose to walk away" from potential confrontations (Bourdieu and Passeron 1990).

As Michael Warner argues (1999), being understood as normal depends on something else being pathologized. And when it comes to sexuality, those lower down on the ladder of normalcy are shamed and stigmatized just like the participants in this study who were referred to as "those dykes," and who took no related actions other than walking away. Warner observes that, instead of challenging the society that produces stigma, LGBT+ individuals aim to integrate into that society. They just want to be seen as being normal, which translates into applying diverse strategies of dealing with discomfort that arises when their identities are deemed not normal.

Moreover, awareness of what may be considered normal enables the individual to take specific types of actions, including those aimed at *impression management* (Goffman 1959). Such awareness and self-comparison to heteronormative standards may cause same-sex couples to surveil their own behavior in order to remedy what can be seen as problematic, scrutinizing whatever goes beyond the norm through the system of meanings of expert knowledge (Bauman 1993). Consulting child psychologists as to how two-mother families should raise their kids "to do them no harm" is one example of how expert opinion is used to normalize one's actions. Thus, acting in compliance with the rules proves one's normality, in one way or another. Such a diagnosis of culture is made by Jacek Kochanowski (2004:28 [translation—MW]), who sees heteronormativity as "a dominant in a given culture and socially and institutionally sanctioned way of behaving, thinking, and feeling, which refers to all aspects of life."

The act of signaling normality can be seen as a mechanism aimed at protecting the social actor from being labeled as *deviant*—that is, symbolically stigmatized (Goffman 1986). Referring to the issue of constructing and reproducing normality (Berger and Luckmann 1991; Prus and Grills 2003), Erving Goffman (1986) highlights two mechanisms having an impact on the process at hand: (1) the internalization of specific norms and values in the process of socialization, (2) the normalizing social control aimed at "disciplining" the individual accordingly (also see Foucault 1995). Still, it should not be forgotten that social actors adapt to certain norms of social life, guided by a variety of motives, by aligning their own actions with the guidelines provided by their interactional partners.

In such contexts, striving to be labeled normal (insofar as one's stigma is either not known or not visible, making one discreditable rather than discredited [Goffman 1986]) can be seen as protecting oneself against potential symbolic sanctions. While doing so can free the individual from short-term anticipated consequences of disclosing one's deviation, it also creates internal conflict. Thus, one's participation by "playing the game" contributes to reproducing precisely those norms one finds oppressive in the first place. This is exemplified by situations when participants attempt to *pass* or *cover* the nature of their family—precisely out of fear of symbolic sanctions, but reproducing dominant societal norms in the process.

STRATEGIES FOR DEALING WITH STIGMA

As Goffman (1986) observes, while the social actor does not have to accept or identify with their stigma, they must, nevertheless, learn how to deal with it. Since two-mother families living in Poland have either experienced or anticipate negative reactions from other people, they attempt to control those interactions they cannot avoid (e.g., clinic appointments). This illustrates how stigma plays a central role in the framing of their everyday lives.

Goffman's (1986) concept of stigma embraced three main strategies that individuals use to deal with being stigmatized. The discreditable individual can attempt (1) to pass to establish oneself as normal, (2) to cover stigmatized identity by downplaying it, or (3) to control the narrative by limiting access to biographical information. These strategies correspond with the actions that two-mother families in Poland undertake on a daily basis. As it has been pointed out, women who have decided to enlarge their families often strive to develop specific ways of managing the level of their visibility in social space. As a result, they combine information control strategies to help their families "pass."

One unexpected consequence of dealing with stigma is the creation of informal support groups (see Major and O'Brien 2005), as when participants in my study created safe interactional circles with others in similar situations. It was through such informal networks that I have recruited many of the participants in my project.

Another consequence of being stigmatized and marginalized is that the majority of two-mother families taking part in my study interpreted their participation in the project in terms of an opportunity to increase social awareness, "educating" others about their stigma and thus making their situation more normal (Thoits 2011). To this end, they offered an alternative narrative to common stereotypes. Interestingly, while doing so, they acted as a group who wished to deliver a coherent story, which can be seen as an attempt to make their voice stronger.

METHODS

This is a six-year ethnographic study of two-mother families in Poland. Specifically, I conducted semi-structured interviews and participant-observation of twenty-one same-sex couples who had children or were expecting. The women in this study were between twenty-six and forty years of age and, with the exception of the five couples expecting, the children's ages varied from two months to six years old. The couples in my study enjoyed both cultural and economic capital allowing them, in their opinion, to protect themselves and their children against anticipated emanations of homophobia.

I interviewed both women together and separately about their experiences in child care. In sum, I conducted seventy-six interviews with women whose child had been conceived in the course of their relationship—thirty interviews with both mothers and forty-six individual interviews (twenty-one with biological mothers and twenty-five with social mothers). Individual interviews lasted between one and two hours, and interviews with both partners lasted approximately three to five hours. In order to aid in the triangulation of the data (Denzin 1978) I interviewed couples at different times across the six-year span of the project. This added a longitudinal element to the study, allowing me to see how things had changed over time.

I also conducted overt participant-observation during the everyday life activities of my participants. Three families allowed me to accompany them in their everyday life activities such as going to the park, to the shopping mall, to the zoo, picking their child up from nursery school, or playing with the child in the yard or at the playground. To date I have conducted twenty-eight observations lasting approximately one to three hours and analyzed them utilizing grounded theory (Glaser and Strauss 1967; Konecki 2000).

WE JUST WANT TO BE SEEN AS *NORMAL*

Two-mother families in Poland have developed a strong network of ties with one another. When recruiting for this project, I personally encountered that many of my participants have spoken with one another and talked among themselves about the study. However, these informal networks also were utilized to seek out information and resources, for example, how others deal with not being seen and treated as "normal" (traditional) families.

A reoccurring theme in my interviews was that the participants just "wanted to be seen as normal." As two subjects explained:

> What our society needs to understand is that we're the same. When it comes to raising our children, we have the same problems, the same dilemmas, the same concerns, or . . . I don't know, speaking about raising a child to be a good person . . . What I mean is that we're not different, it's our situation that is, right? But, that [additional issues that make the situation different, resulting from being a lesbian mother in a heteronormative society] doesn't happen in a vacuum. (individual interview with a thirty-one-year-old biological mother of a six-month-old child, 2013)

> I would like, I mean, I wish so much that people would find out, understand that we are no different from other . . . well, more typical families. We know some [heteronormative] families raising children of a similar age, and . . . well, the issues that we face are really the same—those are issues of upbringing or well-being, yes, the well-being of the child. (individual interview with a thirty-five-year-old social mother of a three-year-old child, 2015)

These passages not only reflect a desire to fit in but also express their structural inability to fit in as non-heterosexual parents. Like the participants mentioned above, the women I interviewed all felt that "our society needs understanding." And that is why, I believe, the two-mother families I have recruited for this project consented to tell their stories. They wished to normalize their situation by offering an alternative narrative based on lived experiences.

In a sense, their involvement in the project, as well as discussing the study among their informal network, can be seen in terms of taking on the role of social activists who seek to educate Polish society by raising social awareness of their situation and challenging cultural-specific stereotypes about two-mother families by addressing the issue at hand from their experience-based perspective. Needless to say, they felt that "our society needs understanding" because they all experienced stigmatization and marginalization, despite perceiving themselves as "not different, it's our situation that is."

ACTING AS A GROUP: TELLING ONE STORY

While conducting my research many of the women in my study raised detailed questions about how the data would not only be used but also be analyzed. However, since the mothers in my study had strong social ties with one another, they talked among themselves about how they answered and what questions I asked. The result was that instead of directly answering my questions about issues they encountered in child raising, they instead employed a variety of strategies to make sure that they all told the same story.

The following excerpt from an interview I conducted in 2016 with two women (social and biological mothers) captures the issues at hand.

Social Mother: I recall one such instance when we both went to the clinic with the
  Little One. It was about a follow-up visit as he got better after a nasty illness . . .
Biological Mother: After treatment with another antibiotic . . . .
SM: Precisely . . . That's what it was. And I remember one situation that . . . But,
  in fact, I'm not really sure whether that's what you're looking for 'cause Carol
  [a research participant] told us that you've been asking them about how they
  handle clinic appointments when they [social mothers] go alone. . . .
BM: Joanie, please, tell us what you wanted to say 'cause, you know, it's all about
  us here, right?
SM: Yeah, I hear you, Mandy, but I also mean that it is somehow coherent at the
  end—those clinic appointments . . . Don't let me shift from subject to subject,
  all right? 'Cause I also want to talk about how I am treated when I'm at the
  doctor's office. I mean, when there's only me and David [their son]. After all,
  people will read it, right? [*Laugh*]

The aforementioned quote illustrates how participants reframed their answers based on the perception of some other person who seemed to be constantly present in their minds, who would read their interview—perhaps someone who "needs understanding." Thus, in a sense, it shows how a group that feels stigmatized and marginalized attempts to deliver a coherent story to control information about their situation.

As it has been argued, the women in my study wished to raise social awareness of their everyday lives, and one way of achieving this goal was through acting as a group whose voice is even stronger when they tell a unified story.

REINFORCING DOMINANT SOCIETAL NORMS: SHORT- AND LONG-TERM CONSEQUENCES OF PASSING AND COVERING

One of the analytical categories that emerged from the data at a relatively early stage of the project was the "conceptual invisibility" of two-mother families in Poland—their invisibility at the language, institutional, cultural, and social levels. It is particularly severely experienced by social mothers who, because of the norm of monomaternalism rooted in social consciousness, are rarely socially decoded as "real mothers." Due to experiencing the lack of ready-made role scripts while constructing specific ways of presenting their families, some social mothers—keeping in mind the ontological safety of their child (Giddens 1991; Konecki 2018)—choose "to play the game" according to the internalized rules, which allows them to pass as a "normal family." In short, knowing that a woman with a child will, most likely, be taken for their "real mother," or, at least, a relative, the participants, striving to avoid potentially difficult interactional situations, intentionally let people thusly define their relationship. As one of the participants, a thirty-one-year-old social mother of a fifteen-month-old child, explains:

> Honestly, I've been there so many times on my own, especially when Dorothy returned to work [after maternity leave] . . . Chris [their son] and I often go to the hospital on our own. I show them Dorothy's ID so they can schedule the appointment, register him. I guess nobody really looks at me—they just assume I must be his biological mother.

Such strategies seem logical in the short term. However, they also come with long-term consequences. By choosing to remain invisible, the social mothers learn to frame their desires of being recognized as parents in terms of being selfish—thus complying with yet another cultural norm, that of the "good mother," sacrificing anything for the child's sake (Garncarek 2020). Thus, they not only inadvertently perpetuate the norms they find oppressive but may also engage in behaviors that impede their children's sense of self by concealing the nature of their family. The following excerpt from an interview I conducted in 2015 with a social mother captures the issues at hand.

> I care more about my son than about myself. You see, telling everyone that he's my son can make troubles for him, and I don't even know most of those people we meet, like in the park . . . So, and I believe this is what being a good mother means—to put your child's needs before yours. I mean, disclosing our actual relation would be selfish, like, I know who I am and he knows that, so . . . I simply . . . "manage"—that's the word I've been looking for [*laughs*]. I manage information to protect him.

THE IMPORTANCE OF INFORMAL
NETWORKS AS SUPPORT GROUPS

One way the women in my study responded to laws, which were not in their favor was by creating informal support groups. For the participants in my study, support groups provided a variety of functions including access to vital information, acting as a space where both mothers could openly participate, and as an outlet where they could express feelings and share experiences. These functions were summed up by one couple I interviewed:

BM: Look, it was in the blink of an eye. I just heard one daddy saying to another, "Look, they're those dykes!" and I didn't think much about what to do next. There was nothing to think about! I simply took K [the first letter of the child's name] from there [the preschool which the child attended]. Later, I called Anna to let her know that there was no way that K would go back there ever again. And that was it when it comes to figuring things out—the situation required immediate action!

SM: You know, Magda, the thing is that we didn't have anyone to turn to, because it must be different with people around and different when you're left out there on your own. Unfortunately, we were the second case.

The aforementioned highlights the importance, for my participants, in having support groups while acting within an adverse socio-cultural climate.

As the participants' narrations illustrate, when "acting on their own" two-mother families have few options to choose from when they face the actual emanation of homophobia. One of the things that they can do is to withdraw from a conflictive interaction. However, by doing so they unintentionally contribute to perpetuating the dominant societal norms—by making the oppressor believe that their behavior is impregnable.

CONCLUDING REMARKS

The aim of the chapter was to show how the infringing of the seemingly stable structure of norms and assumptions inscribed in the heteronormative framework has an influence on the everyday lives of two-mother families in Poland. Thus, heteronormativity was here embraced as a certain semantic frame, which—having been internalized and then externalized—demarcates how one gives meaning to everyday phenomena. Jacek Kochanowski (2004) sees the issue at hand in a similar vein. He describes heteronormativity in terms of a normalizing procedure subordinating individuals to a specific axio-normative system, which will "punish" insubordination in this respect with making one act within the context of exclusion and limitations, and with little interactional ropes at their disposal.

As it has been demonstrated throughout this chapter, stigma plays an important role in the framing of same-sex families' everyday lives. Their situation becomes even more complicated when they raise a child. One the one hand, they are boxed in between their desire to be seen as a *normal* family and their inability to fit in structurally as they do not fall within accepted categories of family life. On the other hand, they employ a number of strate-gies aimed at *concealing* their family to protect themselves, as well as their child, against anticipated emanations of homophobia. Having no ready-made role scripts at their disposal while paving their way beyond the heteronorma-tive framework, they create informal networks bonding people in a situation similar to their own. Such support groups are of great importance while acting within an adverse socio-cultural climate. Still, they do not have the power to shield two-mother families when they engage in a variety of interactions out-side their safe interactional circle(s). For this reason, and keeping in mind the ontological safety of their child, they frequently choose "to play the game" according to the internalized rules of heteronormative society, which allows them to *pass* as a family. However, what they often fail to see while acting so is that information management aimed at concealing the nature of their relationship comes with unfavorable long-term consequences. As it turns out, dealing with stigma by employing such strategies not only reinforces the dominant societal norms but also gives them more power by reproducing them.

Seeking diverse ways of dealing with stigma allowed two-mother families in my study to see their participation in the project in terms of an opportunity to raise social awareness of their everyday lives. Thus, they made an attempt to normalize their situation by offering an alternative narration based on lived experiences. In a sense, they wished to "educate" Polish society by making them understand that it is not them who are different, but their situation. While doing so they turned to one of their greatest assets—informal net-works—to, as I believe, make their voice unified and thus stronger and more audible. Still, I do not exclude that such motives could have an impact on the way they constructed their narrations aimed at normalizing their situation.

The reflections draw attention to a number of barriers and challenges that two-mother families living in Poland face on a daily basis while acting within a specific sociocultural context. In a sense, they allow the seeing of how *two mothers of one child* make sense of specific elements of their reality that fall within a broad spectrum of their everyday experiences.

NOTES

1. It is estimated in the introduction to *Rainbow Families in Poland* that "data provided by the media speak about over 50,000 children who are raised in Poland by same-sex parents" (Abramowicz 2010:8 [translation—MW]); still, no informa-tion about the source of this information is provided. Meanwhile a research report drawn up as part of the *Families of Choice in Poland* project refers to the collection of 7,028 questionnaires, of which 3,038 were qualified for the analysis (Mizielińska, Abramowicz, and Stasińska 2014). "Among the respondents 9% declared that they

had a child, more than twice as many women (11.7%) than men (4.6%)" (Mizielińska, Abramowicz, and Stasińska 2014:130 [translation—MW]). In relation to conceiving a child in a same-sex relationship—"[in] 8% of cases [in relation to the aforementioned 9%], the child was conceived during the current relationship with a person of the same sex" (Mizielińska, Abramowicz, and Stasińska 2014:133-134 [translation—MW]). In the second phase of the project, aimed at acquiring qualitative data, narrations exemplifying the experiences of non-heteronormative motherhood were collected from twenty-six women (Mizielińska, Struzik, and Król 2017).

2. Symbolic violence is exemplified, for instance, by the fact that homosexuality was not removed from the Diagnostic and Statistical Manual of Mental Disorders (DSM) until 1973, and it was not until 1991 that it was removed from the International Statistical Classification of Diseases and Related Health Problems (ICD). page no. 171, line no. 10 & 11: Diagnostic and Statistical Manual of Mental Disorders (DSM) International Statistical Classification of Diseases and Related Health Problems (ICD).

REFERENCES

Abramowicz, Marta. 2010. "Wprowadzenie do problematyki raportu [Introduction to the Report]." Pp. 7-11 in *Tęczowe rodziny w Polsce* [*Rainbow Families in Poland*], edited by M. Zima. Warsaw: Kampania Przeciw Homofobii.

Bauman, Zygmunt. 1993. *Modernity and Ambivalence*. Malden, MA: Polity Press.

Berger, Peter and Thomas Luckmann. 1991. *The Social Construction of Reality*. London: Penguin Books.

Blumer, Herbert. 1986. *Symbolic Interactionism*. Berkeley, CA: University of California Press.

Bourdieu, Pierre. 2002. *Masculine Domination*. Stanford, CA: Stanford University Press.

Bourdieu, Pierre and Jean-Claud Passeron. 1990. *Reproduction in Education, Society and Culture*. London/Thousand Oaks, CA/New Delhi: Sage.

Denzin, Norman. 1978. *Sociological Methods: A Sourcebook*. New York: McGraw Hill.

Denzin, Norman. 1992. *Symbolic Interactionism and Cultural Studies*. Oxford/Cambridge: Blackwell.

Foucault, Michel. 1995. *Discipline and Punish*. New York: Vintage Books.

Garncarek, Emilia. 2020. "'Living with Illegal Feelings'—Analysis of the Internet Discourse on Negative Emotions towards Children and Motherhood." *Qualitative Sociology Review* 16(1):78–93.

Giddens, Anthony. 1991. *Modernity and Self-Identity*. Stanford, CA: Stanford University Press.

Glaser, Barney and Anselm Strauss. 1967. *The Discovery of Grounded Theory*. New York: Aldine Publishing.

Goffman, Erving. 1959. *The Presentation of Self in Everyday Life*. New York: Anchor Books.

Goffman, Erving. 1986. *Stigma*. New York: Touchstone.

Kochanowski, Jacek. 2004. *Fanatyzm zróżnicowany* [*Differentiated Fanaticism*]. Cracow: Universitas.

Konecki, Krzysztof. 2000. *Studia z metodologii badań jakościowych. Teoria ugruntowana* [*Grounded Theory Methodology*]. Warsaw: Wydawnictwo Naukowe PWN.

Konecki, Krzysztof. 2018. *Advances in Contemplative Social Research*. Lodz: Wydawnictwo UŁ/Cracow: Wydawnictwo UJ.

Major, Brenda and Laurie O'Brien. 2005. "The Social Psychology of Stigma." *Annual Review of Psychology* 56:393–421.

Mizielińska, Joanna, Marta Abramowicz, and Agata Stasińska. 2014. *Rodziny z wyboru w Polsce* [*Families of Choice in Poland*]. Warsaw: Instytut Psychologii Polskiej Akademii Nauk.

Mizielińska, Joanna, Justyna Struzik, and Agnieszka Król. 2017. *Różnym głosem. Rodziny z wyboru w Polsce* [*In a Different Voice. Families of Choice in Poland*]. Warsaw: Wydawnictwo Naukowe PWN.

Prus, Robert. 1996. *Symbolic Interaction and Ethnographic Research*. Albany, NY: State University of New York Press.

Prus, Robert and Scott Grills. 2003. *The Deviant Mystique*. Westport, CT/London: Praeger Publishers.

Strauss, Anselm. 1993. *Continual Permutations of Actions*. New York: Aldine de Gruyter.

Thoits, Peggy. 2011. "Resisting the Sigma of Mental Illness." *Social Psychology Quarterly* 74(1):6–28.

Warner, Michael. 1999. *The Trouble with Normal*. Cambridge, MA: Harvard University Press.

Chapter 9

When the Gayborhood Isn't Enough

How Trans Youth Utilize the Internet to Make a Digital Trans Neighborhood

Jonathan Jiménez

The past few years have seen a rise in the media coverage and national discourse on transgender (henceforth trans) people and the ongoing fight for trans rights. From the federal court cases of trans youth Gavin Grimm and employment discrimination to the election of trans people to public offices nationwide, never before has the United States seen this level of visibility of trans people and their experiences. Increased visibility has coincided with the political and social gains of LGBT populations at large in the United States. For example, in 2015, the U.S. Supreme Court legalized gay marriage on a federal level, a major victory for gay rights groups in the United States. Further, the repeal of the Defense of Marriage Act and Don't Ask Don't Tell law added to the inclusion of gay populations into the mainstream. The consequence of these legal victories has meant the common inclusion of gay and lesbian people in civic life. The power of these victories can perhaps be best seen in the loss of queer space (Orne 2017). Scholars are now asking about the need for queer neighborhoods, given the "acceptance" of gay people into the mainstream. Yet, while the recent milestone civil rights victories were celebrated by gay groups, many trans activists and scholars argued that trans people were an afterthought in the legislative and legal battles, if they were thought of at all (Weiss 2011). Thus, while queer folks are having conversations about whether they need gayborhood stills, trans folks are arguing that the gay rights movement overlooked them, and they have not received the same civic inclusion queer people have (Sumerau and Mathers 2019).

The goal of this chapter then is to explore the position of trans people in relation to queer people. More specifically I examine how trans people are estranged and even evicted from gay spaces and must therefore craft spaces of their own, as gay spaces often continue the ongoing hierarchy of LGBT groups evident in political gains. Additionally, this chapter examines how the whiteness that dominates mainstream LGBT politics and spaces negatively impacts trans youth of color. As noted earlier, some scholars have noted that, while there have been substantial gains for gay and lesbian populations, those successes have not extended to trans people to similar degrees (Sumerau and Mathers 2019). Thus, we must ask ourselves, if we are questioning the role of queer spaces in contemporary times, where do trans people fit into that equation? In this chapter, I specifically am looking at the experiences of trans youth as they demonstrate how young people (who are coming of age in the "post-gay" United States) navigate the legacy of the gay rights movement. I continue the arguments of trans scholars by emphasizing that the successes of the gay rights movement have not translated equally to trans people, leaving them to fend for themselves outside of the broader LGBT movement.

Transgender youth face increased threats and violence in rates that exceed those of their cisgender counterparts. One such example is homelessness rates. Choi et al. (2015) found that trans youth are more likely to be thrown out of their homes and experience homelessness due to parental rejection of identity. In a quantitative study on teen dating violence, Dank et al. (2014:852) found, "Across the board (of LGBT participants) the few trans-gender youth in the sample reported some of the highest victimization rates of physical dating violence, psychological dating abuse, cyber dating abuse, and sexual coercion." Transgender youth are also at higher risks for suicide attempts than both cisgender heterosexual youth and queer cisgender youth, with rates as high as 41 percent (Grant et al. 2011). Given that the situation for trans youth remains so dire, we must ask ourselves what does this mean in relation to the political success of the mainstream gay rights movement as a whole? The battle for trans rights remains as necessary now as it ever has, even in the wake of the nationwide legalization of major gay rights initiatives.

The fight for trans rights may be seen in many ways as a struggle over who belongs within a space (see Stone 2013), such as controversies over bath-rooms (Davis 2020) or the gendered boundaries drawn in worksites (Schilt 2010). This chapter expands on these conversations by analyzing how young people navigate the landscape of these sites of contestation by building a "trans neighborhood" in digital spaces. In this chapter, I analyze twenty-four interviews I have conducted with trans youth to demonstrate how young peo-ple build spaces for themselves online when they feel that they do not have them in physical world. The youth of this study have experienced transphobia in both queer and non-queer spaces, which, in turn, often leaves them "space-less" when looking for an area of safety, exploration, and comfort. This situa-tion is further exacerbated when we consider the role of race in differentiating experiences. My chapter begins with an overview of what we know about gay spaces, followed by a discussion of the existing literature on trans people. Here, I suggest that placing these two bodies of literature in dialogue with one another will advance our understanding of contemporary LGBT space in general, as well as the gender oppression trans youth face when looking for spaces to learn and explore themselves and their identities. I then present an analysis of my data in the form of two major findings. First, I highlight the "eviction" of trans youth from gay spaces by describing the experiences of trans youth who sought refuge and resources in gay spaces only to be turned down or alienated. Second, I demonstrate how trans youth push beyond their eviction from gay spaces to craft spaces for themselves and their community through digital channels. This research emphasizes how trans youth (and trans people more broadly) have been left out of discourses on the impact of the gayborhood and mainstream acceptance of gay people but, despite this, have managed to build a "trans neighborhood" of their own online.

GAYBORHOODS AND TRANS PEOPLE

Gay neighborhoods have historically provided a sense of safety for gay and lesbian people, as well as spaces to find romantic partners, friendships, and even economic opportunities (Ghaziani 2014). Yet, because of the civil rights gains of mainstream gay rights movements, coupled with a growing acceptance of gay and lesbian people, a conversation has arisen questioning the continued necessity of gay neighborhoods, as the needs and wants of gay people are now commonly available outside of gay neighborhoods.

Gay neighborhoods have seen a shift in demographics in the past thirty years (Ghaziani 2014), in part, marked by their assimilation into mainstream white culture (Orne 2017)—itself shaped by the mainstreaming of gay politics since the 1980s. Yet, for all the safety that has been described in gayborhoods for lesbian and gay residents and community goers, this sense of safety still does not transfer to trans people. In a survey of binary trans people, Doan and Higgins (2011) found that one-third of trans people experienced "hostile stares" with 17 percent experiencing physical harassment within gay neighborhoods.

While conversations concerning trans rights have grown in recent years, trans people are still excluded and relegated to the margins in the larger discussions on LGBT rights, where the homonormative (and binary reaffirming) advancements of gay and lesbian populations has actually proved detrimental to trans people (Mathers et al. 2018). Even among sexuality activists, gay men struggled the most with trans inclusion (Stone 2009), denoting that there are clear gaps in community-building among gay identified people and trans people.

This exclusion has seen a marked shift in recent times, however, as there has been a plethora of recent research focusing on the experiences of trans and gender non-conforming youth and their families (Travers 2018; Meadow 2018; see also Rahilly 2015). The rise of this literature demonstrates that trans youth are situated within a significant site of contention. As this body of literature has grown, so too has the understandings of trans as their own social category separate from LGB folks. Here, trans youth represent an important category of study, as they are active recipients of the larger socialization and life course process (see Jiménez 2020) and, as such, are active participants in the larger social world, deserving of having their experiences understood rather than silenced.

Trans within sociology has undoubtedly been studied as a gendered phenomenon, and rightfully so. Yet, single-identity research is often insufficient to capture the nuances of oppression across intersecting lines (Choo and Ferree 2010). The present work borrows from the feminist intersectional perspectives of women of color scholars. Multiple social structures of oppression exist simultaneously and have varying impact on people, depending on how one's multiple identities relates to them (Crenshaw 1991). As such, we must conceptualize the experiences of all trans people, not just as the result of gendered social interactions, but as being informed by multiple structures as well. Analysis across intersecting lines, or intersectionality (see Crenshaw 1989), can be understood as a framework to understand that oppression occurs through multiple systems of oppression simultaneously. Further, these systems, specifically race and gender, gain definitional meaning in relation to one another (Nakano Glenn 2002). As such, the experiences of trans people will be mediated by multiple intersecting lines of identity.

Scholars have noted that there are privilege and access discrepancies between trans people with differing intersectional identities as these relate to access to transition-related health care (Gehi and Arkles 2007), policing and surveillance (Beauchamp 2009; Stanley and Smith 2015)—even that theories of trans embodiment themselves may perpetuate intersecting discrepancies, by rooting the possibilities of trans embodiment within a white, Western framework (Roen 2001). This scholarship highlights a key point of the experiences of trans people: that different identities will bring about differing experiences and degrees of oppression. Thus, I argue that trans people's social positions have left them unprotected by gay rights gains, unwanted in gay spaces, and without a physical neighborhood and community of their own.

METHODS

My field site is a nonprofit organization (henceforth referred to as the Bullock Center), located in the Southwest part of the United States. The site is in a building complex comprising four, two-story buildings. The buildings are home to various offices of lawyers, travel agents, therapists, and other businesses. The nonprofit organization occupies four of those offices. Two of the offices are in one building and the other two are in a separate building. Although the Bullock Center is spread out amongst four rooms, my field site is located in only two of the offices. One of those rooms is the meeting place of the weekly transgender youth support group. The other room is where the staff meet twice a week to discuss the organization, and how they can best assist the youth as well as other people (sexual violence services, Latinx groups, etc.) for whom they provide services.

The Bullock Center provides outreach for persons who are victim of different forms of gender oppression. Participants for this study were chosen based on their involvement with the services provided to transgender youth. Eligible participants were those who fit in the age group of thirteen to twenty-four years old. This age range is consistent with that of other transgender literature that focuses on youth identity and experiences. Transgender people from all racial identities were eligible to participant in the study. While most scholarship on racial identity focuses solely on people of color, this chapter focuses on race and racial identity as social phenomena that are not unique to bodies of color, but rather something that all bodies experience.

I collected data through semi-structured interviews with twenty-four transgender identified youths and through participant observation. Erving Goffman (1989:125) suggests that "subjecting yourself, your own body and your own personality, and your own social situation to the set of contingencies that play upon a set of individuals, so that you can physically and ecologically penetrate their circle of response to their social situation" is the best method for collecting data when studying any population. Following this approach, I engaged in participant observation at the Bullock Center, which allowed me to build relationships with both the youth and the staff. In addition to spending time with the youth and staff at the Bullock Center, I attended weekly support group meetings and weekly staff meetings. I was invited to attend both groups by the executive director of the Bullock Center but did not attend until I obtained the permission of both the youth and the staff to attend their respective meetings.

The interviews were face-to-face and took place in a private office in the Bullock Center. They ranged in time from forty-five minutes to two hours and were audio recorded, then transcribed. Interview questions primarily focused on how race and gender shaped the youth's identity development and experience. Questions addressed the participants' self-definitions of their race and gender identity, their day-to-day activities and experiences, and whether they feel a sense of empowerment.

About half of the youths identified as persons of color and the other half identified as white. At the time of the interviews, one was in middle school while most of the rest were in high school. One of the interviewees (who was in the tenth grade) had just begun homeschooling, making the decision to leave public school because of intense and constant bullying. The experience of bullying is a common experience for trans youth overall. The Gay, Lesbian, and Straight Education Network reports that 85 percent of transgender students have experienced verbal harassment, while 49 percent have reported experiencing physical harassment (Kosciw 2008). For the youths of this study, school harassment was an all-too-common experience.

A handful of the interviewees had graduated high school and were in the labor force. For these participants, the jobs ranged from those in the service industry, such as working in a coffee shop, to non-service jobs like working for construction companies. For those who have graduated, entering the work force also created numerous challenges and obstacles. Many experienced severe difficulties with having their employers acknowledge their identities, pronouns, and names. Analysis of my data reveals two primary findings: exclusion of trans persons in gay neighborhoods and the role of digital spaces as a source of trans community formation.

ANALYSIS AND DISCUSSION

Exclusion

Transphobia in Adult Spaces

Trans youths in this study experienced a variety of negative experiences while seeking community in gay-oriented spaces, both in more adult-oriented spaces, as well as high school spaces. As the concept of the gay-borhood has evolved, so too have spaces outside of neighborhoods that are oriented for gay people. Grindr, for example, is one of several dating apps designed for men who want to meet up with other men. While these apps have gained in popularity as a means for gay men to bypass physical difficulties in meeting one another, trans men have found these spaces to perpetuate cisnormativity, even as they challenge heteronormativity. Andrew, a twenty-two-year-old white trans man, told me that his friends have found the space to be transphobic. "I have had friends who've gotten like nasty messages on Grindr and guys being like, 'Get the fuck out of here. You are a straight woman. Get out of our space.'" Previous research has noted the image management trans men must perform in order to present a self they believe will be more appealing to cis gay men (Edelman and Zimman 2014). Trans men in this study similarly expressed a need to navigate how to exist in gay spaces that privilege cisgender embodiment. Andrew continued by explaining that, even in physical gay spaces, the idealization of cisgender bodies remained:

> I feel like there is the gay community and the trans community. So I made a bunch of stickers that said that said like trans bodies belong in gay spaces and trans bodies created gay spaces and then I went up to Hollywood and I went down the strip and put them all over the polls. I feel like the trans body is not accepted in those spaces. I mean, there's body issues in those spaces all over the place like, you know, being fit and muscular and blah blah.

Thus, while gay spaces have evolved over time to include phone apps in addition to physical neighborhoods and bars, the privileging of cisgender bodies (and marginalization of trans bodies) remains. Hope, a twenty-six-year-old white trans woman, worked as a hostess in a gay bar located in a gay neighborhood in Southern California. While it might seem that a gayborhood would be supportive of other members of the LGBT community, Hope's experiences demonstrate the stigma that trans people often carry when they are in gayborhoods:

> That bar was a nightmare. Drunk gay guys thinking they can just ask me questions. They were just so disrespectful of my body. I mean, tables of people just dissecting how I look. And I have to just smile. "Can I get you another cocktail?"

While Hope was in the gay bar, she constantly felt eyes on her, attempting to "dissect" her gender identity. Because of the cisnormativity present in gay spaces, gender presentations are subject to additional levels of scrutiny even among marginalized LGBT gayborhood residents and visitors.

LGB Affirmation, Trans Exclusion

Many LGBT youth (and indeed people of all ages) have found refuge in apps, neighborhoods, and bars that allow them to experience a world with some separation from heteronormativity. Young LGBT folks also take refuge in Gay-Straight Alliances (GSA) that operate in their high schools. Many young cis gay people (myself included) have found community, safety, and resources in these spaces. As with Andrew and Hope, one might assume this would be a safe space for all LGBT people, yet the trans people of my study have had vastly different experiences. Schools are often a site of contention for trans youth and their parents (Meadow 2018). For example, Stevie, a sixteen-year-old trans girl, experienced severe bullying from peers, following a public "outing" from school administrators, forcing her to leave school and be home schooled. Yet, while schools generally tend to be transphobic, even spaces geared for LGBT students can be, as well.

Michael, an eighteen-year-old white non-binary person, noted about how focused on gay issues and dismissive of trans issues that his school's GSA was:

> They were making a GSA at my school, but it wasn't until my junior or senior year that it was a thing. And even then, it was very gay central. There weren't very much things about the trans people, and I didn't really know what was going on. Back then, I didn't really know the difference between gender identity and sexual orientation, so it was just a lot of figuring things out with myself.

This trans dismissive attitude is not always limited to a school's GSA but in many cases was present in the entire school. Morgan, a twenty-two-year-old white non-binary person, recalled the attitude of the school they attended toward their LGBT students: "You know the school wanted to focus on an image of being a very gay friendly place, even if that wasn't super the case." Morgan felt that the school went to great lengths to present a very gay friendly façade but, underneath the surface, remained incredibly marginalizing to trans students.

Often trans youth must live in isolation in high schools, navigating their gender identities, often alone. For example, Lily, a nineteen-year-old white woman, recalled her stigmatizing experiences after coming out her senior year by saying that she was singled out because of her identity, effectively becoming "*the* (emphasis added) trans kid on campus." Similar to Michael, Noel, a twenty-eight-year-old gender-fluid person, felt isolated when they began to think about their gender identity in high school:

> I don't know when the word started or when a lot of these terms came into being but, when I was in high school, I definitely identified as both genders at one point or another, but I didn't have a word for it, so I didn't really understand my gender identity at that point too much.

Both Lily and Noel did not have a space in high school to be supported or any resources to help understand their experiences.

Racializing LGBT Spaces

Many of the trans young people described in this section have noted that their high schools often had many resources for gay and lesbian students, including support groups and information. Yet for trans students, the LGB support spaces on their campuses did not prove to be safe for them to find others questioning their gender identity or even reading materials to understand what they were experiencing. This disparity was made even greater when trans students of color searched for resources and community, as existing spaces were often as one participant put it, "white centered." These youths of color did not just have to contend with the transphobia present in gay spaces but also were subjected to the racism that is prevalent in gay spaces (Hunter 2010).

Max, a twenty-two-year-old Filipino trans man, describe his experiences going to a local LGBT community center, specifically to a support group designed for trans people. He expected to find an understanding community looking to engage with the diversity of trans experiences, but soon realized that was not the case.

> It would be often times have mostly white/older MTF (male-to-female) or just MTF in general. And as a trans man I felt a little outcasted and whatnot. In my experiences there has been the lack of people of color representation in any sort of LGBTQ group, which sucks. I felt that everyone was super sensitive and certain topics weren't allowed to be discussed or that we weren't talking about any resources and et cetera.

Max found the LGBT community center to only focus only on issues concerning white trans women. As a trans man, he found it difficult to discuss his own experiences. Further, he felt he was not allowed to discuss racial issues in that space because, when he attempted to bring these up, his concerns were dismissed as "not what the group is for." These youths are well aware of the role that race plays in differentiating their experiences. Lily, a white trans woman, explained the impact she felt that race had on the perception of trans people:

> Well, for starters, I'm not going to be one of those people who says, "I don't see color," because you kind of have to with these issues. Now, as much as I really hate to say this, white privilege is definitely a thing. It's definitely not a great thing. I'm not proud that it's a thing. I feel kind of bad that it's a thing. But it's a thing we'll have to live with, hopefully for not much longer, but I do think it's harder for a lot of dark-skinned folk to be accepted as anything but straight. I don't usually talk about race stuff because I just feel I don't know much about it, but I feel like white people are definitely a lot more accepted as anything but straight compared to like, an African American person or a Latino person.

When discussing trans experiences and LGBT spaces, race must be accounted for as it differentiates the experiences of all LGBT people. As Max pointed out, even when finding a space specifically geared toward trans people, he found no community or resources because of the identity politics at play. This section highlights the difficulties that trans youth face in searching for a sense of self or community. They often go to spaces they believe will be helpful (spaces marketed as LGBT-friendly or -inclusive) only to find that cisgender gay and lesbian identities are privileged while trans identities are relegated to the margins. Yet, while the gayborhoods and other physical spaces may have failed them, they have found a new channel to provide what the physical world could not provide them. As Kevin, an eighteen-year-old Korean trans man, stated, "But now it's the Internet. And that's whatever anyone says, and you choose your own narrative. Now, there's a lot of young kids choosing exactly their own narrative." The Internet thus has provided an opportunity for youth that was previously unavailable, which will be further explored in the next section.

Creating the Trans Neighborhood

Digital Possibilities of a Trans Self

In her work on how contemporary LGBT youth *Grow Up Queer*, Mary Robertson (2019) notes, unlike previous generations, today's youth are growing up during a time of increased space and access to gender nonconformity and exploration, leading many of them complicating the gender binary. Robertson also notes, however, that increased access to gender nonconformity among young people does not necessarily lead to increased acceptance of transgender folks in general. This is why many of the transgender youth in this study have turned to the safety of digital spaces to engage in social communications about being trans. While recognition of gender nonconformity is more common than in previous generations, transphobia remains rampant.

All of the participants of this study spoke about utilizing digital spaces to understand their gender identity as well as finding community there. For previous generations, experiencing their stigmatized identities often meant developing them in relative isolation (Sedgwick 1990), but today's youth utilizes online spaces as an alternative to transphobic physical spaces. In this regard, Andre Cavalcante (2018) argues that access to digital media technologies can move the notion of transgender subjectivity from "the outskirts to the realm of possibility," (Cavalcante 2018) where digital resources provide an opportunity to explore the social understandings of trans to which these youths are denied.

DJ, a white twenty-six-year-old non-binary person, first heard the term "transgender" in person but decided it would be best to learn more about it on the Internet. DJ went to Tumblr to explore the concept of trans identity. This online site was vital to understanding their gender identity—so much so that, during our interview, they remarked, "My identity is from Tumblr. That's where I come from." As such, the use of digital spaces is vital, as it is the path through which many of these youths learn about themselves and the possibilities of living life as a trans person.

While these youths do often search for resources in the physical world, this is often not without consequences. Roy, a nineteen-year-old trans man, noted that going out in public to search for research runs the risk of being outed.

> Yeah, because like, going out in person and asking someone about information or like, going to a library, you're seen and you're traced and like, someone can tell someone else, "Oh, I saw him there," and online, you need a bit of like, technological information to go track someone's online footsteps.

Online spaces thus allow for a sense of anonymity for the youth to explore their sense of self and find others like themselves while maintaining their safety. As noted earlier, many trans youths who went to spaces that they believed to be helpful were often stigmatized. As Roy's story in particular illustrates, these youth are well aware that the physical world holds a number of risks for them in their search for resources, information, and community. Further, even when resources do exist, they often fall short of providing the trans youth with the information or support they need. But digital spaces do provide access to opportunities for community and resources. As Alex, a twenty-four-year-old biracial trans man noted:

> I'm so glad we have the Internet. I may have seen some characters on TV but I didn't really realize that that's like, a real thing that you can do or, you know, I was kind of way amazed, I guess, because I didn't really think it was a real thing. You feel less alone and all that.

Access to digital spaces allowed the youth to see their own experiences unfold in front of them. Dillon, a twenty-six-year-old white trans man, stated that the trans community online (in this case, YouTube) shares their stories so as to make people feel less alone:

> There's a big trans community on YouTube of folks documenting their transition processes. And this one was specific to you like someone going from childhood to now: how they're feeling at all these different stages in their life, and me just realizing that the thing that I thought I was the only person to have ever experienced and I should not talk about it, this person was detailing every step of my feelings and found that I wasn't the only person that was feeling this way.

As Dillon's experience demonstrates, transgender youth not only engage with digital spaces for information but also find a sense of belonging with groups of people who are similar to them. As with gayborhoods, these digital spaces

allowed the youth to overcome the isolation that often accompanies stigmatized identities.

The New Digital Community

The trans youth in this study made connections with people both online and
in person. Yet, at least in the early stages of their transition, it is the digital
connections they made that were the most significant to them. At this critical
stage, the anonymous protections of the Internet were vital for these youths
as they attempted to navigate their early transitions. Lily, a nineteen-year-old-
white trans woman, did have friends that she grew up with, yet she remained
in the closet to her friends for fear of the reaction she might receive. She
remained undecided about whether to disclose her identity to her friends.
However, once she made online friends who were trans affirming and supportive, she decided not to disclose her gender identity to her in-person
friends:

> Before I came out, the main people I would usually talk to were people from
> school or people I knew from childhood. But as time progressed I got more into
> the Internet. I made some friends from other states—sometimes even from other
> countries. After I came out I realized that, maybe, some of those people weren't
> necessarily the best, and it probably wouldn't be very good for me if they found
> out who I really am.

A supportive (and worldwide) online community empowered Lily to consider
her well-being first when making her decisions about disclosing her identity.
The advice and experiences shared in online communities also allowed the
youth not to have to experience their marginalized identities alone. In a similar experience, Kim, a twenty-five-year-old white trans woman, described her
experiences with online support. When asked what role online trans communities played in her experiences, she responded,

> It definitely helps to connect with some people or, you know, we're going
> through similar experiences and that's when I started to like, connect the dots,
> realizing for myself that I felt this way and that I am trapped. So that's it. It
> connected me to my cyber world of support.

Morgan, a twenty-two-year-old non-binary person, responded similarly:

> Yeah, I think it was helpful for me. I mean like, the first time I learned what
> it's like, and then also because the people I met were kind of like my resources
> at first, but then I think I learned more and connected with more people online
> about it.

Access to online spaces, however, is racialized, as the youth of color in this research have noted. Thus, the communities that are built online are often reflective of real-world racial dynamics within trans communities and society at large. In an interview with a twenty-four-year-old Filipino trans masculine person, Max, the racial ideologies that infiltrate trans communities online were all too evident:

> There are some trans white guys who live off of their YouTube videos. But if a person of color does it, they would get less views, less ratings, less com-ments—less of everything because we live in a very white-centered culture. So if it's a white person doing it, it must be important and if it's a person of color, it must not be. If a person of color, trans—anyone—tries to go to a doctor and get hormones, more often than not, they need a therapy letter, or they are rejected because of the color of their skin. Now, if it's a white person, whether they are trans masculine, trans feminine, or even non-binary they're able to get the hor-mones even easier than a trans person of color. So, they're more likely to get the things they need, even surgery, than a trans person of color.

Just as the people of color found it difficult navigating whiteness online, white-ness gave space to the white people of this study to navigate online spaces. Angela, a seventeen-year-old white trans woman, in our interview, noted the power of anonymity that being online provides that the physical world does not. She stated that you can say things online that you are not able to say in person. She used the n-word (which she stated outright) as something that can be said online but not in person. While she was slightly hesitant to say it in front of me, she ultimately felt comfortable enough to. This example highlights how racial ideologies infiltrate trans communities. While members of this community may share in gendered oppression, they are not free from influence from racial ide-ologies (and the oppression/privilege that result) that dominate social relations. While this chapter sheds light on how trans spaces (both digital and physical) can be racialized, it is not the main focus of the chapter. Nevertheless, the work of how spaces are racialized is important to understanding the complexities of trans experiences across racial lines. As such, I call for further research to be conducted to focus exclusively on how race impacts space for trans people.

CONCLUSION

The goal of this chapter is to place trans youth within contemporary discus-sions of the gayborhood and gay spaces at large. While those within the LGBT community are having discussions about the viability and necessity of gay neighborhoods, given the recent civil rights gains of the gay rights movement, I argue that trans people are excluded from these benefits as they have felt stigmatized in a variety of gay spaces, ranging from bars to LGBT student groups. This stigmatization left these individuals isolated in their search for resources to understand themselves and find community.

In lieu of the limited access they found in gay spaces, the trans youth of this study created their own "trans neighborhood" in online spaces that they had access to. This trans neighborhood allowed them to make connections to people who shared their marginalization and to discover a wide range of resources from learning about hormones or other medical transition services, to videos of trans people documenting their social and medical transitions step by step.

While conversations about the gayborhood and gay spaces feature prominently in current discussions, trans people are both metaphorically and literally excluded. For these individuals, the physical world presents challenges to exploring their gender identities regardless of the advances made by gay people in the last decade. Concerns over being outed or being mistreated (even in gay spaces) because of their trans identity led the youth to maintain those identities in secret. Yet the community they were able to form online released them from the "closet" as they were able to communicate openly with others about what they were feeling and experiencing. Taken altogether, the youth in this study found digital spaces to be vital to building community in a virtual trans neighborhood.

REFERENCES

Beauchamp, Toby. 2009. "Artful Concealment and Strategic Sensibility: Transgender Bodies and U.S. State Surveillance After 9/11." *Surveillance & Society.* 6(4):356–366.

Calvalcante, Andre. 2018. *Struggling for Ordinary: Media and Transgender Belonging in Everyday Life.* New York: New York University Press

Choi, S. K., Wilson, B. D. M., Shelton, J., & Gates, G. 2015. "Serving Our Youth 2015: The Needs and Experiences of Lesbian, Gay, Bisexual, Transgender, and Questioning Youth Experiencing Homelessness." Los Angeles: The Williams Institute with the True Colors Fund.

Choo, Hae Yeon & Ferree, Myra Marx. 2010. "Practicing Intersectionality in Sociological Research: A Critical Analysis of Inclusions, Interactions and Institutions in the Study of Inequalities." *Sociological Theory.* 28(2):129–149.

Crenshaw, Kimberlé. 1989. "Demarginalizing the Intersection of Race and Sex: A Black Feminist Critique of Antidiscrimination Doctrine, Feminist Theory, and Antiracist Politics." *University of Chicago Legal Forum.* 139–167

Crenshaw, Kimberlé. 1991. "Mapping the Margins: Intersectionality, Identity Politics, and Violence Against Women of Color." *Stanford Law Review.* 43:1241.

Dank, Meredith, Lachman, Pamela, Zweig, Janine, & Yahner, Jennifer. 2014. "Dating Violence Experiences of Lesbian, Gay, Bisexual, and Transgender Youth. Journal of Youth & Adolescences." *Journal of Youth and Adolescence.* 43:846–857.

Davis, Alexander K. 2020. *Bathroom Battle Grounds: How Public Restrooms Shape the Gender Order.* Berkeley, CA: University of California Press.

Doan, Petra L., & Higgins, Harrison. 2011. "The Demise of Queer Space? Resurgent Gentrification and the Assimilation of LGBT Neighborhoods." *Journal of Planning Education and Research.* 31:6–25.

Edelman, Elijah A., & Zimman, Lal. 2013. "Boycunts and Bonus Holes: Trans Men's Bodies, Neoliberalism, and the Sexual Productivity of Genitals." *Journal of Homosexuality.* 61(5):673–690.

Gehi, Pooja S., & Arkles, Gabriel. 2007. "Unraveling Injustice: Race and Class Impact of Medicaid Exclusions of Eransition-related Health care for Transgender People." *Sexuality Research & Social Policy.* 4(4):7–35.

Ghaziani, Amin. 2014. *There Goes the Gayborhood.* Princeton, Nj: Princeton University Press.

Goffman, Erving. 1989. "On Fieldwork." *Journal of Contemporary Ethnography.* 18(23):123–132.

Grant, J. M., Mottet, L., Tanis, J. E., Harrison, J., Herman, J., & Keisling, M. 2011. "Injustice at Every Turn: A Report of the National Transgender Discrimination Survey." National Center for Transgender Equality.

Hunter, Marcus Anthony. 2010. "All the Gays are White, and All the Blacks are Straight: Black Gay Men, Identity, and Community." *Sexuality Research and Social Policy.* 7(2):81–92.

Jimenez, Jonathan A. 2020. "Becoming Trans Adults: Trans Youth, Parents, and the Path to Adulthood." *Journal of LGBT Youth.* 1–20.

Kosciw, J. G., Diaz, E. M., & Greytak, E. A. 2008. "National School Climate Survey: The Experiences of Lesbian, Gay, Bisexual and Transgender Youth in our Nation's Schools." GLSEN.

Mathers, Lain A. B., Sumerau, J. E., & Crugan, Ryan T. 2018. "The Limits of Homonormativity: Constructions of Bisexual and Transgender people in the Post-Gay Era." *Social Perspectives.* 1–19.

Meadow, Tey. 2018. *Trans Kids: Being Gendered in the Twenty-First Century.* Berkeley: University of California Press.

Nakano, Evelyn Glenn. 2002. *Unequal Freedom: How Race and Gender Shaped American Citizenship and Labor.* Cambridge: Harvard University Press.

Orne, Jason. 2017. *Boystown.* University of Chicago Press.

Rahilly, Elizabeth P. "The Gender Binary meets the Gender-Variant Child: Parents' Negotiation with Childhood Gender Variance." *Gender & Society.* 29(3):338–361.

Robertson, Mary. 2019. *Growing Up Queer: Kids and the Remaking of LGBTQ Identity.* New York: New York University Press.

Roen, Katrina. 2001. "Transgender Theory and Embodiment: The Risk of Racial Marginalization." *Journal of Gender Studies.* 10(3): 253–263.

Schilt, Kristen. 2010. *Just one of the Guys: Transgender Men and the Persistence of Gender Inequality.* Chicago: University of Chicago Press.

Sedgwick, Eve Kosofsky. 2008. *Epistemology of the Closet.* Berkeley: University of California Press.

Stanley, Eric. A., & Smith, Nat. 2015. *Captive Genders: Trans Embodiment and the Prison Industrial Complex.* Chico, CA: AK Press.

Stone, Amy L. 2009. "More than Adding a T: American Lesbian and Gay Activists' Attitudes Towards Transgender Inclusion." *Sexualities.* 12(3):334–354.

Stone, Amy L. 2013. "Flexible Queers, Serious Bodies: Transgender Inclusion in Queer Spaces." *Journal of Homosexuality.* 60(12):1647–1655

Sumerau, J. E., & Mathers, Lain A.B. 2019. *America Through Transgender Eyes.* Rowman & Littlefield.

Travers, Ann. 2018. *The Trans Generation: How Trans Kids (and Their Parents) are Creating a Gender Revolution.* New York: New York University Press.

Weiss, Jillian. 2011. "Reflective Paper: GL versus BT: The Archaeology of Biphobia and Transphobia Within the U.S. Gay and Lesbian Community." *Journal of Homosexuality.* 11(4):498–502.

Chapter 10

Gays under Glass

Gay Dating Apps and the Affection-Image

Tom Penney

Men as a Class are the Fetish, viewable at the National Gallery of Australia website,[1] is a piece of art created through collage by David McDiarmid in 1978. Embedded in his work is the idea, "A sexually exciting fetish may be an inanimate object, a living object, part of a human, an attribute of a human, or a whole human seen as an abstraction" (McDiarmid, 1978). In this piece, McDiarmid cut up an assortment of images relating to homoerotic masculinity—a leather boot, a collar, a torso, a penis, and a face with a moustache, to name a few. All of these objects come to form an image of (white) men themselves as a fetish, or as a "class." This image is jarring, to some, because it reflects the heteronomativity embedded within the formation of "mainstream" gay culture, and also illustrates the ideal images of beauty that make up gay taste cultures (see Becker, 1982).

The images within this piece of art are reproduced within gay online dating apps, such as Grindr, which present users with a grid of images of partial male bodies; a "collage" of digital squares promoting users that seek to be desired and varying degrees of affection. Upon viewing both this original work and the digital collage of Grindr, we might consider McDiarmid's proposition that men as a class are the fetish, and how this is exacerbated by digital interfaces today. Why is it that gay men desire masculinity in its normative, symbolic, and abstracted form? How do dating apps function to reproduce, and reinforce these codes over time through their use? In this chapter, I consider how this is achieved through users' rapid parsing of what I term "affection-images."

Building off of Gilles Deleuze's work on faciality (1986) and further political thought by Felix Guattari (1988), I conceptualize affection-images as those that communicate interiority and from which we attempt to read affection. Such images are "facialized" because the face is the model psychic structure from which humans read affection in objects; literal faces or other-wise (Deleuze, 1986). In analyzing these images I incorporate Sarah Ahmed's *Queer Phenomenology* (2006) as a frame for my enquiry, orienting this work more closely toward affect theory. More specifically, I am interested in the interplay between images and emotion in shaping gay culture and ultimately how users interact.

Finally, I conclude this chapter with a discussion of Deleuze and Guattari's concept of "microfascism" (1988) as a frame for how images, through their use, orient and inscribe internalized rules that govern our acceptance and rejection of such images online. In the process, this transforms users into despotic machines that sort faces using collective, internalized algorithms to judge what passes a "yes/no" binary. By masking taste as preference and allowing users to sort in a somewhat algorithmic process, a system of taste and prejudice emerges that is molded by our habits and orientations. This is not unlike the process described by Ruha Benjamin (2019) when describ-ing how technologies deepen social inequity through automation. Thus, this chapter contributes to the growing scholarly literature that explores how user produced images reproduce heteronormative standards that privilege white hypermasculine bodies, and offers up suggestions for why users in online spaces engage in these practices.

APPROACH

My approach is to offer a novel adaptation of Deleuzoguattarian terms, and use those to explore how we might read and frame affection-images in online dating apps. This involves how users transmit and receive affection on either side of their screen-based flatness. My approach does not seek to solve these issues, but rather offers a different way to perceive the mechanics and poli-tics of affection employed in dating-app imagery. The concepts explored in this chapter are informed by my experiences as a practicing contemporary artist, designer, queer person, and user of apps like Grindr. As an artist, I have already considered how Grindr can be understood through caricature, interactive 3D art, and have explore such representations of bodies in my own creative works (Penney, 2015, 2018).[2]

In this chapter, I explore five themes of the visual narrative that comprise the culture and norms of the Grindr cyberscape. First, I will explore the app's design limits the ways users can express their identities, and how this design promotes superficial interactions. Second, I utilize Deleuze's insights into the role of the face in establishing an affection response from its users. Third, I discuss how other images of body parts (dick pics, torso shots, and selfies) are also used to invoke an affective response—but how these may achieve different ends. Fourth, I discuss how users participation in the Grindr cyber-scape produces a normative orientation through repetitive interaction with affection images (Ahmed, 2006). Finally, I conclude with the idea of micro-facisms as a concept to understand why gay men desire and submit to the normative standards of whiteness and masculinity that Grindr produces. This concept, "microfascism," was developed by Deleuze and Guattari as a term for an internalized algorithm of judgment that has become despotic through the over-application or compounding of a form of subjectivity. They claim that this term provides the answer to the question "why does desire, desire its own repression," which I compare to McDiarmid's proposition, that men as a class are the fetish.

APP DESIGN AND IDENTITY PORTRAYAL

User-experience (UX) and user-interface (UI) designers are attuned and accustomed to reading and designing the movements that users will shift through. They manipulate the visual design, placement of buttons, and sonic and haptic feedback to maximize user engagement. Digital media products must be designed to give meaningful, fluid, and swift feedback to encourage efficient pathways. Organic-feeling animation, satisfying sound, and visual effects all contribute to the feeling that a device is responding to our input and that we are the ones affecting change in the software we are using. Interfaces are expressive and responsive; in a Deleuzian sense they are like abstracted human faces, and designers manipulate them so that we know we are "in conversation" with a device, or another person mediated by one.

On Grindr, users are presented with either facial or bodily images that represent potential intimate others. When users connect with one another, they are experiencing a responsive or conversational response. This feeling of responsive conversation occurs mostly while we are in the chat window, but the user may also feel a closeness due to how Grindr sorts its users. Part of the Grindr experience utilizes a constantly updating array of geo-location-sorted faces that are presented for users to interact with, and orients them to think of themselves in relation to these assorted images of other users. I think of this as "faces-within-a-face," where individual faces become the structure of a larger, digitally produced, geo-location-based gay space, but are organized by many calculations and algorithms fashioned by designers and maintained by machines kept by a corporate server in some unknown place.

The facial grid format for Grindr remains effectively unchanged since its release in 2009, a testament to its efficiency at achieving consistent user engagement through simplicity. The way users present themselves through their profiles is always a simplified representation. We know through keystone thinkers such as Erving Goffman (1959), Judith Butler (1988), and Steve Seidman (2003) that any portrayal or fixity of a "self" is essentially a contrivance; a performance designed with the knowledge that we will be seen by others (see also Nunes, 2013). Grindr requires the participation of a subject[3] who freely enters into this activity of self-fixity through the production of a social mask in the form of a digital profile, which presents as an intelligible and self-contained singular object in Grindr's grid-like interface.

While conventional understandings within digital app design industries still understand the self as a unified manifestation, or require it, such conceptualizations are reductive (Van Zoonen, 2013, p. 44). Selves are not fixed (Deleuze, 1986; Simondon, 1992; Denzin, 2002) and are contextually and situationally (in)dependent—there is no one point in time that we are one "self" ontologically. However, while the self is an ongoing and ever developing self-reflexive concept, our ongoing behaviors throughout our performance of it inscribes meaning on our (future) identities. Jacques Lacan (1949) describes how we come to recognize ourselves as objects that can be compared to others in early childhood when he writes about the "mirror stage" and as such we are aware of how our identity performances impact the environment and communities around us,[4] and we, in turn, adjust our own to increase our social standing, or in the case of Grindr, our number of affectionate responses.

Because such performances are reflexive and produced with a spatial awareness, gay men have come to "average themselves out" in order to collectively perform the hyper-masculinized standards of beauty in an attempt to maximize responses and participate in a "sexual marketplace" (Race, 2018, p. 152) and accrue "sexual capital" (Green, 2013). The performance thus validates itself in a ritual that elicits a response from other viewers in the digital panopticon of Grindr. The result is that users (re)produce their own standards of predominantly white and Eurocentric participation, which exclude difference from within online dating platforms (Robinson, 2015; Conner, 2019). However, Grindr is also reductive in the sense that it requires users to mold themselves into predetermined categories such as "twinks," "bears," "jocks," or "daddies." The implications of this are such that, because the interface relies on users to remain in the app to monetize them, users' presentations of self and sexual capital impact revenue—sexual capital becomes real capital.

While we are afforded the opportunity to "write ourselves into being" (Light et al., 2009), we are still limited, explicitly and internally, to doing so according to shared categories and behaviors and, on Grindr, this is commonly to a white, fit, "masc" standard:

> Individuals write a version of themselves and of this gay community into being.
> However, because of the desire to commodify "the difference" that is gay,

predominantly white men, online and offline, such inscriptions become mono-lithic caricatures that are obdurate and enrol even those who do not participate in such arrangements at all or only by proxy. (Light et al., 2009)

Parsing the many bodies-under-glass[5] on Grindr operates within the tendency of the past decade in interaction design toward "pictures under glass" (Victor, 2011). This tendency in app design allows fingers to command, rub, swipe, and browse others numbly, as if calloused, upon the surface of still images of visual bodies and digital objects. Smartphones are on our bodies, we touch them all the time, and we bring them to bed with us. The smartphone is a kind of surrogate object of affection, being a physical device through which affection is sent and received.[6] Through the prevalence of apps like Grindr, gay people have come to expect that the app and their smartphone will bring them affection and sexual gratification at a steady pace. One is ever-presently checking for a buzz in the pocket that indicates a new message has been received.[7,8] Affection and intimacy, I argue, cannot be perfectly translated, or modulated, into the comparatively discrete packages of representation provided by the app.

THE PRIMACY OF THE FACE

The human face itself is the first interface that we "read" from and gain mean-ingful feedback. The face is, as Deleuze states in *Cinema 1* (1986), an "organ carrying plate of nerves which has sacrificed most of its global mobility and which gathers or expresses in a free way all kinds of tiny local movements which the rest of the body usually keeps hidden" (Deleuze, 1986, p. 98). To summarize, Deleuze discusses how the face communicates what is internal to a body. It is the surface we read to understand what is hidden in others and that communicates and exchanges affection.[9] Brian Massumi describes how affection refers to encounters between two specific bodies; an affected body and an affecting body (Shouse, 2005) and therefore to power relations between individual bodies—our attempts to interact with each other are attempts to also see how we have affected change in what we have interacted with. On Grindr this is very often a desire to affect sexual arousal. An affected body could be a machine ("is this app working") or a person mediated by one ("have I turned this person on by sending my dick pic").

Interfaces that utilize flat surfaces based on grids of pixels and design-grid systems are not dissimilar to human faces, which are also based on grids. Deleuze and Guattari (1988) together note that human faces are measured (by humans, not machines) in terms of a grid and are recognized based on the variation of contrast within such grids. Darkness implies the openings

of the face—eyes, nostrils, mouth, ears—which together form the recognizable organs on a facial surface. These dark spaces are contrasted against
the relative lightness of the surrounding facial structure, and thus a face is
recognized. This is not really any different to how digital facial recognition
systems now recognize human faces; assessing patterns of contrast given a
grid of pixels in a digital image to denote faces. It is important to note that
Deleuze and Guattari in this discussion of dark/light contrasts consciously
highlight the racism of this dominant "white face" model, and are concerned
for how the model of recognizing white faces produces subjects that "tend
toward" white faces. It is implied that the orienting toward white faces in the
consciousness of people globally is a product of white-European globalization and media power. When looking at dating apps, it would appear that
users create a homonormative environment that privileges masculine looking
white-faces, which are standards of beauty that are in fact rooted in heteronormative power structures. This normalization necessarily rejects queerness
and thus limits the potentially liberating aspects of apps like Grindr (Kellner,
2021).

AFFECTION-IMAGES

Affection-Images are any images, including moving images, that attempt
to elicit being read affectionately. To Deleuze, although affection-images
are always "faces" (or "facified"), they do not have to actually be faces. In
his original use of the term, Deleuze describes affection-image through the
device of close-up in film. A close-up on a clock-face in a film is an attempt
at revealing the inner characteristics of the clock. If its hands are moving
(its micro-movements), it tells us this clock is alive, functioning and that
it has internal parts. If it is, still its surface is like the "skin plate" of the
face, merely reflective, symbolic or standing in for something—reflective,
because stillness reflects what we see in it, and withholds its subjective state.
Affection-images have both of these elements because faces have both of
these elements—micro-movements and reflective surfaces.

> Each time we discover these two poles in something—reflecting surface and
> intensive micro-movements we can say that this thing has been treated as a
> face—it has been facified, and in turn it stares at us and looks at us. (Deleuze,
> 1986, p. 98)

This idea, that an affection-image is always facified, even when the object of
affection is not a face, is important when thinking about online dating apps.
This is because on Grindr, we are presented with a wide variety of images

from which to glean affection. To Deleuze, an affection-image implies a body; an image is "read" in such a way that it describes the functions of the body it references through our reading of its micro-movements. As Deleuze (1986, p. 99) suggests such readings raise questions relating to what a subject is sensing or feeling emotionally. These questions seek answers or reciprocity that can transform into action—ranging from dates to sex. Even if our interpretations are wrong or spurned, they tell us something about the interiority of others that we rely on throughout the user experience.

Grindr profiles are read by whatever emotions might be visible on the faces that users present. These could be expressive, but on Grindr, these are often "poker-faces"—images created to mask their interiority, either through stern expression or removal of the face altogether by presenting an alternative image.[10] These "poker faces" are linked to the emotional textures and desirability of masculinity, which I will discuss later. When we cannot read any interiority in a body; each image becomes a close-up, generally cold, and designed to mask anything but the "objective" appearance of the person; this is the person attempting to function reflectively and symbolically, as a "type" or "class," and less so as a messy, complex individual. This is a flattened or averaged-out form of the person designed to attract the greatest number of affective responses, as users are on some level aware that they are an object within this grid that is comparable to others.

Face pics are often stern or "masculine" in this way—attempting not to render themselves too specific in order to illicit a maximum number of responses. This is especially true of what is colloquially known as "bear face," which is a kind of grimace that is posed to make users look more gruff, stern or "masculine." Through "poker-faces" we see not a specific person but a person attempting to function more as a reflective type (or perhaps as a "class" like McDiarmid suggests), in the case of "bear face," this is to fit a standard "masculine bear" type.

What we find here is the Deleuzian distinction between "quality" and "power" in the affection-image, the difference between reading a face as having qualities "common to several different things" (the still, whole, face as a "type"), and the expression of "power which passes from one quality to another" (the ability to read movements in individual features in the face) (Deleuze, 1986, p. 101). We must read other human beings in terms of their "quality" as we do not have enough expressive information. We must fit these self-representations to what we already expect, desire or fetishize in them. Knowing this on some level, as such we find in many, a person who has self-averaged their affection-imagery so as not to offend others' tastes by offering overly specific signals, and capitalize as best as possible in the sexual-facial market. What is ultimately consumed in this market varies (affection, intimacy, hook-ups), but all begin with the affection-image, and an image that may initially represent the opportunities a body can facilize. Even if a user chooses to have no image, they will be represented by a blank automatically generated silhouette of a face in most cases; the ultimate "poker face."

Faces represent bodies (their inner workings, the operation of their organs) and faces are close-ups. Even more "poker-faced" than a stern or blank facial expression is a torso shot as the profile image. When we are faced with a body image as a profile image, we must read close-up bodies as faces because we are trying to glean affection from them. Still or reflective torso shots are exceptionally common on Grindr. A torso online, as an avatar, is to be met as face. It is the first point of contact for an identity and we must guess the identity or interiority of its owner. If it is a healthy-looking torso, then perhaps it describes a sexually abled body that can achieve the purposes of a sexual exchange. Like faces, torsos present a flat plate with a few features upon them; the only "organs" upon their surface are perhaps nipples or a belly button. Different levels of muscularity, ribs, or fat tell us limited information about the lifestyle or personality of the subject.

While Grindr's terms of service will not allow you to use a penis or a bottom as a profile image, they are images that users can trade with one another in the chat feature. The penis-as-close-up or bottom-as-close-up, like torsos, can stand in for identities. The penis-as-input displayed is often used to indicate the dominant sexual role, while an anus close up is often used to indicate one's role as passive receptacle. These are private images that users very commonly reveal to each other if they want to display what sexual assets they have and are core to the affection-economy. A penis as affection-image is more readable in regard to subject interiority or an affected body. It quite clearly states "I'm interested" if erect, as does a bottom-pic often communicate the desire to be penetrated. Movement is more easily imagined here than in the poker-face torso; the rise and fall of arousal. Veins suggest power or the flow of blood—and there is the urethra—the growth of the erection or the folds of the testicles. A flaccid penis is relaxed and confident perhaps, where a bold erection is ready to perform. A penis reveals more than a torso but in many instances is still an affection-image that avoids the presentation of a totally revealing face; it deflects to a simpler symbolic form.

PARTIAL OBJECTS AND OVERCODING

Through the above readings of body parts such as torsos, penises, and bottoms as affection-images (and of course, they are not the only ones, there are infinite others), the term "partial object" is apt as a "post-Freudian" term present in Deleuze that describes the breaking down of an object (here the body) into its component parts. We see these partial objects in the collage of

McDiarmid. Partial objects are those perceived and desired in isolation from the whole body. The classic example from psychoanalyst Melanie Klein is of an infant desiring interaction with the mother's breast (Klein, 1946, p. 1) and not yet seeing the mother as a whole. Often partial objects refer to sex organs, such as lust for penises, feet, or anuses instead of whole, complex bodies. On Grindr isolated images of male body parts become objects of desire in isolation from the whole.

Partial objects are here synonymous to Deleuze's use of close-ups and speak to the history of cut-up bodies and perversion in both film and art (see Žižek, 2006; Mulvey, 1975). Because partial objects are symbolic, they are essentially consumed for what they represent in a system of desire and do not actually fulfill desires. This exacerbates an unending process of desire and consumption as such images are produced in abundance. As users log in and out, the user browses, the geo-location changes, and the illusion of an abundance of symbolic desires in the form of affection-images and partial objects is produced. Divorced from a unified whole, affection-images as partial objects cannot be read or actually confronted, as a person faces another person physically, but will always reflect desires that are projected on or into them. They are reflective affection-images. Their internality becomes false or invented on behalf of the consuming subject, if considered at all. We can also say that these objects have become "overcoded," for they no longer represent physical things but standards for our sexual interests.

> Hand, breast, penis, stomach, penis, vagina, thigh, leg and foot, all come to be facialized . . . an overcoding of all the decoded parts. (Deleuze, 1988, p. 199)

When an object is divorced from its physicality, it becomes clean, symbolic or "overcoded" as a fetish. In *A Thousand Plateaus*, the plateau called "Year Zero: Faciality", Deleuze and Guattari extend their discussion of the face, to "a machine specific to faciality" (1988, p. 200) especially in regard to how the structure of the face organizes our response to other human beings. "Certain assemblages of power require the production of a face, others do not" (Deleuze and Guattari, 1988, p. 205). Normativity on Grindr requires the production of a face. This is the discussion of the face not as a head (where it is part of a body), but as an abstract system of overcoding. The face or faciality to Deleuze and Guattari are really modes of seeing and organizing things, and particularly of measuring deviation to norms. "Overcoding" (Deleuze and Guattari, 1988, p. 71) refers to the use of language to dominate through translation, and refers to the overriding of heterogeneous things existing on their own terms, unifying them in a new way, under a new code. When something is "overcoded," it ceases to be "messy." In terms of capitalism, money is an example of a numeric code that generifies labor and value through translation. The face, when overcoded, becomes a language and a measure of difference, a standard, rather than a "head":

> The face is produced only when the head ceases to be part of the body, when it ceases to be coded by the body, when it ceases to have a multidimensional, polyvocal corporeal code—when the body, head included, has been decoded and has to be overcoded by something we shall call the Face . . . to be facialized. (Deleuze and Guattari, 1988, p. 198)

Deleuze and Guattari's notion of perversity is the ability to constantly manufacture new desires in order to maintain a "plateau of intensity" (Goodchild, 1996). We maintain such a plateau by rapidly parsing and consuming these overcoded desire objects in the app space, without much fixity, pause, or focus. Users of Grindr become accustomed to, or even oriented-toward, a mastery of a perverse facialized surface. This surface is the faces-within-a-face grid, as well as the chat space, where a play of over-coded partial-objects takes place. The purity of the partial object—the promise it offers as an overcoded standard rather than as a physical thing—eclipses the messy reality of situated bodily experiences. Even after hookups, dates or other such experiences, the phone will buzz, the grid, re-opened, and partial objects re-presented. Each object is readily suggesting more idyllic scenarios that seduce users away from pursuing others, or contribute to a short attention span because physical encounters can't fulfill the standards of overcoded objects. Physical affectionate realities become by comparison relatively confronting or laborious outside of the pattern-consumption of fetishized representations online.

ORIENTATIONS THROUGH
AFFECTION-IMAGES AS PARTIAL OBJECTS

> A queer phenomenology might offer an approach to sexual orientation by rethinking how the bodily direction "toward" objects shapes the surfaces of bodily and social space. (Sarah Ahmed, 2006, p. 68)

I have alluded to how the processing of affection-images at the level of the individualist user constitutes the time-based production of a standard of participation on Grindr online that users produce and desire. Deleuze and Guattari point to how normativity enforces itself through overcoding. Sarah Ahmed in *Queer Phenomenology: Orientations, Objects, Others* (2006) sheds light on how situatedness with objects-over-time (sexually) orients us. We know through Judith Butler (1990, p. 192) that identifications such as masculinity rely on the "stylized repetition of acts through time" and that identification is a time-based effect. We can here think about how such behaviors become normative in online settings as the repetitive consumption and parsing of affection-images, the behaviors of sorting; pressing, swiping, blocking, typing, and looking, surely orient, and have a lasting effect on, users of Grindr and similar apps. Here the finger as a body part too plays a role. We use our fingers to access and browse all contents. The finger is an individualist scepter of command, and is the physical manifestation of a user's internal judgment; the point of decisive action. It enacts the decisions toward what external objects are to be included or excluded from the users' world, that is, which objects or individuals "make the cut". Fingers curate, they choose what complements the individual, but the tendency is for users to curate a closed circuit. Buttons are designed for users to perform such judgments efficiently. These are all repetitive orienting actions. Thus, we learn through this repetitive process how sexual performances occur (Ahmed, 2006, p. 57).

Grindr users are thus oriented to engage in cultural practices in which they take for granted norms for engagement in their evaluation of others and themselves (Schutz and Luckmann, 1974, p. 4; Ahmed, 2006, p. 33). However, this is part of a much larger phenomenological process whereby smartphone users engage in repetitive interactions through apps in which the personal handset mediates their communication. "The repetition of the work is what makes the work disappear" writes Ahmed (2006, p. 56); the practice of swiping, gazing, blocking and chatting become invisible forms of labor that shape our tendencies toward consuming affection images and partial objects as "comfortable" inscriptions on our behavior.

Grindr constantly presents other users as "within reach" a certain kind of face; a "poker-face" or a "white face." In the Grindr interface, which relies on the arrangement of bodies in a grid, it is easy to spot bodies that attempt to participate "out of line" with the usual standards of participation. Queer, which is originally "a spatial term" (Ahmed, 2006, p. 67), "does not follow a 'straight line,' a sexuality that is bent or crooked" (Cleto, 2002, p. 13) Because users are generally presented as sexualized bodies next to each other as comparable squares, an awareness of the need to compete or sexualize in a particular way in order to participate is implicit. Users also expect these arrangements from other users. If we are not oriented toward a particular kind of faciality that deviates from a norm, or through expressive movements producing a deviant arrangement of facial organs, we may desire not to continue and eventually seek to turn away from that face over time, or even very rapidly. The fear of different facial arrangements, as Deleuze and Guattari discuss at length, is fundamental to racism. Faces that do not conform to the organization of "nice faces" are a threat to a normative and primal stability. Obscure faces, or obscure (and queer) expressions, (as organizations of the elements of a face) are just too difficult in the face of faces that are easier to digest; symmetrical, clean, and generic.

The critique of Grindr as a space that promotes normativity (or "homonormativity"; see Ferguson, 2005; Binnie, 2004; Bell and Binnie, 2004; Duggan, 2014) among homosexuals is common and topical. Usually this normativity is characterized in terms of white-maleness and its racism toward and exclusion of bodies that deviate from a "gym-fit" white male standard or pressures such as the need to "bear-face." Racism classically manifests on Western Grindr through requests before-the-fact such as "no Asians" (Han, 2008). This defensive normativity extends to the pervasive privileging of masculinity as its own fetish; the demand for "masc only, no fems" or "sane and sorted only"[11] is very common on Grindr profiles. While Grindr is a homosexual space, it isn't necessarily a very queer or feminist one. Users reject (mostly by ignoring the advances of) affection-images that deviate from homonormative ones. Users attempt, by averaging themselves out, to remove or hide the qualities that render them specific racially, sexually, or emotionally. Alternatively, they stop participating altogether. The result is a monocultural grid of bodies that highlights not only the preferences of the individual user, but the preferences of the broader community that users collectively cultivate (see Ahmed, 2006, p. 57) and these preferences create a dynamic feedback loop. The white male body thus structures a "norm" against which judgments are made. Fit, white, masculine male bodies are privileged as something sought out by the majority of users.

Ahmed implicitly claims that the white body is "hard" and emotionally challenged (Ahmed, 2004, p. 4). This is not because it lacks emotions, but because it distances itself from, or turns away from others; it is simply a different kind of emotional orientation. The way the white body deals with complex emotions is to disconnect, to not participate in affective exchanges. On Grindr, ignoring the advances of another, blocking others, or even preemptively saying "no fems" on one's profile constitutes this "turning away from" an undesirable face. The consequences are intense and heavy silences; tense and emotionally charged spaces of time where affection is not being reciprocated. Such waiting games can only be tempered by attempting to contact more and more people, "trying one's luck," and further inscribing repetitive engagement with still faces into the orientation of the user "playing" the game of Grindr (see Woo, 2013).

MICROFASCISMS

What ultimately causes any of us to "turn away from" others, however? Here I conclude by taking into account Deleuze and Guattari's extended concept of "micropolitics" from *A Thousand Plateaus* (1988) in order to propose "microfascism" as a frame that governs the maintenance of, and submission to, powerful and implicit codes accompanying faciality in gay online dating apps. I am not generally discussing fascistic repression at the hands of forces external to homosexuality, but forces of male homosexuality acting upon itself on the level of the individual—"the little fascist in all of us," perhaps. I return to McDiarmid's original proposition that "men as a class are the fetish" and the question of why users of Grindr continue to reproduce or perform models that bind or restrict them into a normative white, masculine, minimal faciality? "Desire is never separable from . . . micro-formations already shaping postures, attitudes, perceptions, expectations" (Deleuze and Guattari, 1988, p. 251). What we desire is what we already want, and the availability of such efficient tools and structures for parsing and judging faces compound what users already desire, rather than necessarily broadening or making their experience more perverse.

When Deleuze and Guattari talk about "micropolitics," they are talking about the propensity for everyone to form in themselves a set of stances or orientations toward power relations around them. This is an internalized politics functioning on the level of the individual. We could say that the forming of micropolitics is part of being oriented over time—it constitutes what we will "accept" or "reject" when we face toward things but is also structured by the things we face toward over time. "Microfascism" is Deleuze and Guattari's term for an internalized algorithm of judgment—a micropolitics— that has become despotic through the over-application of this subjectivity and speaks to the subjective singularity or "sucking-inward" of blackholes. It is our propensity to want others, the external world, to conform to our own predetermined rules and determines what we decide to face-toward, or not.

> Only microfascism provides an answer to the global question: Why does desire desire its own repression? (Deleuze and Guattari, 1988, p. 251)

Enacting a microfascism could be as simple as deciding not to reply, rather than block or react. It is rules behind the sorting mechanism—the yes/ no binary that decides whether we engage. The personal situatedness and immediacy of Grindr on smartphones constructs a thriving environment for microfascism. This is in part because the structure of judgment is very much based on an algorithm—a microfascism of the face. If affection-images represent desire as partial objects do, then a more perverse form of desire is repressed if our consumption of others as desire objects is limited by internalized microfascisms informed by the oriented privileging of white bodies. The face, at least in terms of affection-images, is the structure of this politics. A smartphone full of affection-images is a place for microfascisms to operate and collide. Each face perceived by a microfascist as reflective (symbolic) masks another microfascist. Each body replaced by a partial-object creates a temporal and aesthetic delusion between the two. Every microfascist experiences others in terms of proximity to their own body, as (partial) objects "within reach" of the microfascist. A very literal dialogue for this might go something like this:

> I am here, with myself, and my phone. These subjects are for me, they present themselves to me. I can delete, block, sort, filter, chat, ignore, turn off, engage or not—as I see fit. I am not buffeted by complex faces; faces that respond complexly, faces that I am challenged to assess myself against, to have a discussion with or negotiate. If they turn out to operate through any deviation to what I accept, I can simply "turn-away-from" them. I do not have to learn, develop or change, as the device gives me the tools to sort users based on what I, and this app have taught me to accept.

NOTES

1. McDiarmid, David, 1978. "Men as a class are the fetish." Collage. New South Wales, Australia. National Gallery of Australia. Accessed 3rd December 2020 (https://cs.nga.gov.au/detail.cfm?irn=71511).

2. Also see Norman Denzin's (1991) application of many of these ideas in sociology and especially the use of montage and pastiche as techniques that appear in both art and cinema, but also in the social world.

3. While users are free to create presentations of self that reject pervading norms, doing so carries social sanction and ultimately rejection from the larger Grindr cyberscape.

4. A point that serves as the basis for many studies using a symbolic interactionist framework (Blumer 1969).

5. Smartphone screens are made of glass, thus the digital representations of bodies on Grindr are literally under glass.

6. The epitome of this would be the image of a gay men on their phone while simultaneously engaged in sex.

7. In this way, we could think of a "gay phantom phone syndrome" which is amplified due to the app's role in intimacy (Rosenberger, 2015)

8. Grindr's unique message notification is so unique that several DJs in the circuit party scene have used is as samples in their live performances.

9. This is not unlike Goffman's writings on facework (Goffman 1967)

10. Very often this is just a torso shot.

11. Sane and sorted is a European expression found in many Grindr profiles. It should be understood as meaning the individual seeks only those without sexual hang-ups, and those who reflect a "normal gay lifestyle." However, by using this phrase users essentialize and reify the homonormative world of Grindr.

REFERENCES

Ahmed, S. 2004. *"The Cultural Politics of Emotion."* Edinburgh University Press, Edinburgh.

Ahmed, S. 2006. *"Queer Phenomenology: Orientations, Objects, Others."* Duke University Press, London.

Becker, H. 1982. *Art Worlds.* University of California Press, California.

Benjamin, R. 2019. *Race After Technology.* Polity Press, Cambridge.

Bell, D., and Binnie, J. 2004 "Authenticating Queer Space: Citizenship, Urbanism and Governance." *Urban Studies* 4(9): 1807–1820.

Binnie, J. 2004. *The Globalization of Sexuality.* Sage, London.

Blumer, Herbert. 1969. *Symbolic Interactionism: Perspective and Method.* University of California Press, Los Angeles.

Butler, B 1988, "Performative Acts and Gender Constitution: An Essay in Phenomenology and Feminist Theory," viewed July 14, 2020. http://seas3.elte.hu/coursematerial/TimarAndrea/17a.Butler,performative%5B1%5D.pdf

Cleto, F. 2002. "Introduction: Queering the Camp." in Cleto, F. (ed.), *Queer Aesthetics and the Performing Subject: A Reader.* University of Michigan Press, Michigan.

Conner, C. 2019. "The Gay Gayze: Expressions of Inequality on Grindr." *The Sociological Quarterly* 60(3): 397–419.

Deleuze, G. 1986. *"Cinema 1: The Movement Image."* Bloomsbury Academic, London.

Deleuze, G., and Guattari, F. 1988. *"A Thousand Plateaus."* Bloomsbury Academic, London.

Denzin, Norman K. 1991. *Images of Postmodern Society: Social Theory and Contemporary Cinema.* Sage.

Denzin, Norman K. 2002. "Cowboys and Indians." *Symbolic Interaction* 25(2): 251–261.

Duggan, L. 2014. "The New Homonormativity." In Grzanka, P.R (ed.), *Intersectionality: A Foundations and Frontiers Reader.* Westview Press, Boulder.

Ferguson, Roderick A. 2005. "Race-ing Homonormativity: Citizenship, Sociology, and Gay Identity." In E. Patrick Johnson and Mae G. Henderson (eds.), *Black Queer Studies: A Critical Anthology*, pp. 52–67. Duke University Press, Durham.

Goffman, E. 1959. "The Presentation of Self in Everyday Life." in Newman, DM and O'Brien, J (eds.), *Sociology: Exploring the Architecture of Everyday Life Readings.* Pine Forge Press, Sage Publications, Los Angeles.

Goffman, Erving. 1967. "On Face-Work. An Analysis of Ritual Elements in Social Interaction." In *Ders.: Interaction Ritual.* Doubleday, New York.

Goodchild, P. 1996. *Deleuze and Guattari: An Introduction to the Politics of Desire.* Sage Publications, London.

Green, A. 2013. "'Erotic capital' and the power of desirability: Why 'Honey Money' is a Bad Collective Strategy for Remedying Gender Inequality." in *Sexualities.* Sage Journals.

Han, C.-S. 2008. "No fats, femmes, or Asians: the utility of Critical Race Theory in examining the role of Gay Stock Stories in the marginalization of gay Asian men." *Contemporary Justice Review* 11(1): 11–22.

Kellner, Douglas. 2021. *Toward A Critical Theory of Technology and Technocapitalism*. Springer, Switerzerland.

Light, B., Fletcher, G., and Adam, A. E. 2009. "Gay men, Gaydar and the commodification of difference." *Information Technology and People* 21(3).

McDiarmid, D. 1978. *Men as a Class Are the Fetish*, drawings, collages, collage of printed cut paper on light cardboard mounted on oriental paper, viewable at the National Gallery of Australia. https://cs.nga.gov.au/detail.cfm?irn=71511.

Mulvey, L. 1975. "Visual pleasure and Narrative Cinema." *Screen* 16(3).

Nunes, M. 2013. "Facebook, identity and the Fractal Subject." in MacGregor, J., Koskela, H. (eds.), *New Visualities, New Technologies, the New Ecstasy of Communication*. Ashgate Publishing, Burlington USA.

Penney, T. 2015. "Faceism and Fascism in Gay Online Dating." in *.dpi Feminist Journal of Art and Digital Culture* (32), viewed September 6, 2020, https://dpi.stu dioxx.org/en/no/32-queer-networks/faceism-and-fascism-gay-online-dating%E2% 80%A8.

Penney, T. 2018. "Playing the Subject." in Cermak-Sassenrath, D. (ed.), *Playful Disruption of Digital Media*. SpringerLink, Singapore.

Race, K. 2018. "Speculative Intimacies." in Race, K. (ed.), *The Gay Science: Intimate Experiments with the Problem of HIV*. Routledge, London and New York.

Robinson, B.A. 2015. "'Personal Preference' as the New Racism: Gay Desire and Racial Cleansing in Cyberspace." *Sociology of Race and Ethnicity* 1(2):317–330.

Rosenberger, R. 2015. "An Experiential Account of Phantom Vibration Syndrome." *Computers in Human Behaviour* 52: 124–131.

Seidman, Steven. 2003. *The Social Construction of Sexuality*. WW Norton, New York.

Simondon, G. 1992. "The Genesis of the Individual." *Incorporations* 6: 296–319.

Shouse, E. 2005. "Feeling, Emotion, Affect." *M/C Journal – A Journal of Media and Culture*, 8(6), viewed July 14, 2020. http://journal.media-culture.org.au/0512/03-s house.php

Van Zoonen, L. 2013. "From Identity to Identification: Fixating the Fragmented Self." *Media Culture and Society*, 35(1): 44–51.

Victor, B. 2011. "A Brief Rant on the Future of Interaction Design," viewed July 14, 2020. http://worrydream.com/ABriefRantOnTheFutureOfInteractionDesign/

Woo, J. 2013. *Meet Grindr*. Self-Published, United States.

Zizek, S. 2006. *The Pervert's Guide to Cinema*. Fiennes, S., Rosenbaum, M., Wieser, R., and Misch, G. (producers).

Chapter 11

Gayborhood Change

The Intertwined Sexual and Racial Character of Assimilation in Chicago's Boystown

Jason Orne

"Oh shit, now we're equal to people. Now we're normal. Is that what we fought for?" (Sam, mid-thirties biracial black gay man)

In this chapter,[1] I aim to demonstrate that the assimilation of a minority group contains intertwined sexual and racial assumptions due to what I've called the *intersectional knot* (Orne 2017). The *intersectional knot* refers to a puzzle that I observed within my fieldwork in Boystown, Chicago's gay neighborhood, or gayborhood as they are colloquially called. First, instances of heterosexism between queer men and straight women fed into sexism demonstrated by these men. Second, situations in which a particular community space managed to ameliorate one aspect of inequality (e.g., the sexy communities I studied having less racism) often relied on other forms of inequality to maintain rigid boundaries to create instances of cross-racial interaction (e.g., the sexism and 'no women allowed' policies of these spaces, to continue the example).

Intersectionality (McCall 2005; Collins 2005) argues that systems of inequality and power are mutually reinforcing. A classic dictum is, "Where is the sexism in this racism? Where is the racism in this sexism?" Intersectionality *does not* merely refer to looking at the experiences of those experiencing multiple marginalized statuses, or "accounting" for the effects of multiple marginalized peoples within one's model, but rather that the experience of those at intersecting statuses reveals important aspects of how these systems of inequality interact. The *intersectional knot* (Orne 2017) further argues that these systems are tangled, and that attempts to loosen one strand that do not consider the totality of the systems of power will tighten other strands within the knot, magnifying those forms of inequality as a result.

In this chapter, I examine the intersectional knot by examining the intertwined sexual and racial consequences of assimilation of a minority group into the mainstream. I argue assimilating a cultural group involves acculturating that group into mainstream sexual norms, restructuring sexual fields to discourage marginalized sexual behavior, and whitening that group's cultural heritage to fuse it with the mainstream. I use data from my ethnography of Chicago's Boystown neighborhood (Orne 2017). First, I demonstrate some gay men in Boystown are acculturating, adopting mainstream sexual norms. Next, I show that restructuring Boystown's sexual fields reinforces sexual assimilation through changes to the neighborhood's gay bars as straight white women consume them. Finally, I discuss the racial consequences. As gay men become "ethnically straight" (Hicklin 2012) and integrated into straight society, racial boundaries in the neighborhood harden, whitening the area, and casting gay men of color as violent outsiders. These results demonstrate sexual assimilation involves a racializing component. By extension, I argue that to understand assimilation, we must proceed intersectionally to understand not only how it acculturates ethnic groups to mainstream white values, but also that those values include heteronormative sexual mores.

ASSIMILATION

Assimilation is a core concept of twentieth-century sociology. From Park's 1926 race relations cycle to contemporary articulations (Alba and Nee 1997; Portes and Zhou 1993), scholars examine how racial and ethnic groups integrate into the white American mainstream. Assimilation researchers focus on the spatial assimilation and place stratification of ethnic groups (Pais et al. 2012), the structural assimilation of minority groups (Gordon 1964), and acculturation to majority norms (Zolberg and Woon 1999).

Assimilation theories often privilege ethnic groups' sexuality and family formation demographics. To illustrate, Portes and Zhou discuss the expectations of immigrant Sikh families that female children marry quickly, require parental consent to date, and avoid dancing. They saw successful passing of such norms to second-generation children as evidence these families selectively assimilated, resisting Americanization (Portes and Zhou 1993). Alternatively, problematic depictions of black sexuality and family structure in the 1965 Moynihan Report marked African-Americans as unassimilatable. Park originally placed emphasis on intimate relationships as the method that would break down barriers between racial groups (Park 1914). Therefore, unsurprisingly, scholars use interracial relationships as markers of assimilation, (Bonilla-Silva 200; Zhou 2008; Song 2009). Relationship demographics and family structure are forms of sexuality, more tactfully named.

Surprisingly though, sexuality researchers ignore racial assimilation scholarship when discussing sexual minorities. In the gay context, assimilation refers to integrating gay individuals into heterosexual society and adapting queer sexual cultures to mainstream straight cultures. Homonormativity (Duggan 2012) is the 'new normal' focusing gay political activism on integrating into neoliberal institutions like the military and marriage. With the repeal of "Don't Ask; Don't Tell" and marriage equality across the United States, the political assimilation of gay sexual minorities into the American mainstream is well on its way.

Gayle Rubin's charmed circle is a helpful lens on assimilation diagraming how sexual practices interrelate. The circle's inside wedges are mainstream and hegemonic (e.g., heterosexuality, sex in the home, same-generation, vanilla, procreative, married, monogamous), while those outside are subversive, stigmatized, and, I would say, queer (e.g., homosexuality, sex in public, inter-generational, BDSM, for pleasure, out of wedlock, with multiple partners). As the stigma of homosexuality fades, society expects queer people to follow the other parts of hegemonic sexuality like marriage, monogamy, and procreation (Rubin 1992).

Therefore, society accepts same-sex partners, but only if they look like straight relationships. Political victories like marriage focus on acculturating, not equalizing, a separate queer culture. As such, these social movement victories are markers and drivers of assimilation of queer people. How are these macro changes influencing the micro- and meso-level sexual lives and sexual cultures in gayborhoods?

In December 2012, after winning *Out Magazine*'s Person of the Year, Nate Silver told the magazine, "I'm kind of sexually gay, but ethnically straight" (Hicklin 2012). The white *New York Times* journalist and former Boystown resident does not "want to be Nate Silver, gay statistician." His desire to be "ethnically straight," embracing straight norms while maintaining a nominal gay identity and engaging in same-sex relationships, is evident in his favorite club in Boystown, Chicago's gay neighborhood. He likes Berlin because it is mixed. While it has gay clientele, straight people regularly attend late into the night to enjoy the throbbing house music and two dollar PBR Tuesdays.

Berlin's mixed atmosphere is increasingly common in more traditional male gay bars. Straight people are integrated, both residentially and commercially, across gay neighborhoods (Ghaziani 2014). Queer people's destigmatization strategies (Lamont 2009; Saguy and Ward 2011)—for instance, coming out—mostly worked. Some scholars argue queer people are now "beyond the closet" (Seidman 2002) and "post-gay" (Ghaziani 2014). However, LGBTQ people's lived experience remains mixed (Williams, Giuffre, and Dellinger 2009). They still must employ a strategic outness (Orne 2011) and they continue to use traditional sexual identity labels (Orne 2013). Post-gay theorists contend gay identity is disappearing. Instead, gay people are assimilating, becoming "ethnically straight," gay but not queer (Orne 2017).

"Ethnically straight" or ethnically gay, only people who perceive themselves as raceless (e.g., white people) could think of themselves as such. Queer of color critique emphasizes this distance, one that has been perpetuated by the academy, especially sociological understandings of queer communities (Ferguson 2004). Positioning homosexuality as an ethnic-like cultural group whitens gay identity, rendering queer people of color (QPOC) invisible. Queer people's race is often unmarked, thus raced white. For instance, the mass media in the aftermath of Proposition 8's passage—the California anti-gay marriage amendment—reported the story as the black community versus the gay community, as though QPOC did not exist. As Moore articulates in her book on black lesbian families, QPOC are often "invisible" (Moore 2011).

Because of this invisibility within communities of color presumed to be homophobic (Connell 2014), queer communities presumed to be white, and the academic community itself invested in this monolithic distinction (Ferguson 2004), work on the assimilation of gay people into American society pays inadequate attention to the legacy of work on assimilation in the sociology of race and ethnicity. Assimilation literature provides a wealth of concepts: acculturation, structural assimilation, spatial assimilation, gentrification, and so on. When these encounter the previous ethnographic work on gay neighborhoods that focus on gay identity and social movements (Ghaziani 2014) and the structure of their sexual fields (Green 2011), the fusion reveals the intersectional character of assimilation. The assimilation of sexual groups has racial consequences and, I argue, vice versa.

I would like to stress that, as I discussed in *Boystown* (Orne 2017), the goal here is not to reproduce the argument of queer of color critique (Ferguson 2004). Instead, I seek to demonstrate how our understanding of a central concept within sociology—assimilation—can be deepened through understanding its intersectional knot. To understand the connection, we turn to a classic site in which its effects are often studied.

Enclaves and Gayborhoods

Enclaves are the metropolis's visible marker of assimilation. The presence of an enclave signals the degree of the group's assimilation or separation. The activity occurring within enclaves indicates the resistance or accommodation to assimilation. Gayborhoods are cultural enclaves serving a primarily gay male clientele. Like other cultural enclaves—such as religious enclaves like Chicago's Skokie for Jewish people or racial enclaves like Chicago's historic Brownsville for African-Americans—they insulate stigmatized communities from outsiders and employ members who might be able unemployable outside the enclave (Portes and Jensen 1989). Enclaves might be dissolved through assimilation into mainstream society, moved around the city through gentrification, or remain as a historic neighborhood although the "old-timers" represent only a minority share of residents (Brown-Saracino 2009). The enclave allows a separate lifestyle from the mainstream, often allowing entrepreneurs to setup businesses that would be otherwise impossible and workers to use cultural social networks to secure jobs (Nee et al. 1994). Cultural enclaves are not uniformly helpful to their minority residents, with some evidence that wages, for instance, would be higher if they sought work outside of the enclave (Nee et al. 1994).

Scholars have not examined classic assimilation theories in gay neighborhoods. Instead, they examine sexual identity politics or gay men's sexual networks. The first tact tracks the meaning of gayborhood change to sexual identity social movements and sexual identity politics (Ghaziani 2014). In this vein, scholars trace changes in the need for gayborhoods as queer people move into a "post-gay" era. The rise and fall of gayborhoods is related to other historical forces shaping sexuality and the creation of a homosexual minority group post–World War II (D'Emilio 1983). For instance, some work looks at the vicarious citizenship gay men feel with gayborhoods when not residents (Greene 2012). These studies reveal the context for assimilation, but do not themselves situate the structural integration or segregation within their studies within classic assimilation frameworks.

The second tact maps the sexual networks of gay men. Laumann et al.'s Chicago Health and Social Life survey took special care to include the same-sex sexual networks of gay men and lesbians. Work in this vein looks at gayborhoods as a nexus of sexual activity and relationships for men who have sex with men (MSMs), primarily through a sexual markets lens (Ellingson and Schroeder 2004; Laumann et al. 1993). More recently, scholars like Green draw upon Bourdieuian field theory as an alternative to sexual markets (Martin and George 2006) to trace sexual fields' creation and transformation. Sexual fields are collective social worlds with their "own particular social organization, status hierarchy and regulative principles" regarding sexual activity (Green 2008a, 2008b, 2011, 2012). One sexual field would be the hookup scene at a college's Greek fraternity life, with all the sexual scripts, stratification, and interactional strategies that scene entails. This tact similarly reveals activity within the sexual fields of gayborhoods that is useful for tracing the resistance or accommodation to assimilation but does not itself comment on assimilation.

This chapter examines assimilation on the ground, a meso-level approach synthesizing these two tacts by looking at gayborhood change through the lens of scholarship in the sociology of race and ethnicity. I trace the transformation of the sexual field of Boystown and connect it to the structural assimilation and acculturation of the neighborhood due to the transformation of the meaning of gay people in society. This approach reveals that assimilation has an intertwined sexual and racial character, an intersectional knot (Orne 2017). Examined intersectionally, Rubin's 'charmed circle' is hegemonically white and a group's assimilation into the center racializes that group as white. This article also connects how sexual organization creates and maintains shifts in collective identity. Work in both sexuality and racial scholarship needs to consider the intersectional character of assimilation. Before we examine what this intersectional assimilation looks like in Boystown, I turn to my methods.

METHODS

Starting mid-2011, I conducted an ethnography of the Chicago neighborhood Boystown (Orne 2017), in the style of classic Chicago-style ethnographies like *Black Metropolis* (Drake and Cayton 1993) and *Street Corner Society* (Whyte 1993). Multiple data collection methods triangulated information, giving me a comprehensive picture of the neighborhood. Over three years, I conducted participant-observation at community events, neighborhood bars and clubs, and private social gatherings. I collected twenty-six hours of formal interviews with twenty participants. I also conducted countless informal interviews with bartenders, club patrons, shop clerks, and passersby. On a number of occasions, I conducted non-random establishment surveys and tallies to assess neighborhood consumers using the phenotypic gender, race, and sexual identity as they appeared to me, a longtime resident of the Midwest. I also examined my auto-ethnographic experience of these spaces through a daily journal that I completed in addition to traditional fieldnotes.

Given the digital nature of modern life, I included online components of Boystown. There are a number of print and online publications that follow Chicago's queer life. I comprehensively followed these throughout my fieldwork, with an eye to discussions of race, sexuality, and Boystown. I also examined social media like Facebook and Twitter discussions by participants and others. I collected over 600 of these print and social media accounts. Following the lead of Nakamura, I also analyzed the structural organization of race and sexuality on online dating and hookup websites participants identified (Nakamura 2002), such as Grindr or Adam4Adam, both of which use location data, thereby identifying Boystown.

I selected Boystown for theoretical reasons. The project began with an interest in the interracial dynamics of gay male relationships and communities. Boystown combines Chicago's tumultuous racial history, Fryer's finding that the Midwest has the least interracial relationships (Fryer 2007), and previous studies of gay sexual networks in the city (Ellingson and Schroeder 2004). These findings led me to explore the neighborhood as a possibility during early 2011. The Take Back Boystown event, which I describe later, crystalized the racial issues in the neighborhood. Thus, mid-2011, I began ethnographic fieldwork in the area, ultimately moving to Boystown in January 2012, living there for over a year before following white gay participants' residential patterns north. I did not restrict my fieldwork to Boystown. When participants invited me to other parts of the city, I followed. These other neighborhoods—like "lesbian" Andersonville, latinos in Pilsen, white queers in Edgewater, or gay Black communities on the South side—often were reference points when groups discussed the neighborhood.

I primarily spent my time in Boystown split between six different social groups that crossed racial and class scenes: JJ's Latinx group, Frank's "anti-racist" white queer friends, Darrin and Jon (a pair of QPOC friends), Marcus's racially diverse Leather family, a largely white group of "poz" (HIV positive) friends, and the "Boat People," an upper-class white group known for parties afloat Lake Michigan. My interview sample evolved through theoretical sampling (Charmaz 2006), selecting participants through ongoing analysis, and did not generally overlap with the ethnographic groups. Participants and I co-constructed interviews (Corbin and Morse 2003), conversing about Boystown, queer life, race, and sex. Key informants were in community organizations, bartenders, club promoters, club personnel, journalists, and people that both frequented Boystown and hadn't gone back in years. Analysis using the tools of constructivist grounded theory (Charmaz 2006) led me to several insights about the structure and evolution of queer life and racism. One such follows.

BOYSTOWN AND GENTRIFICATION

Located in Chicago's Lakeview East neighborhood, Boystown is the center of gay male community life. Although tendrils of queerness extend throughout the city, Boystown is the only area Chicago designates as a gay village, the first in the country to have such a designation. During the early eighties, gay men moved up Halsted Street from the Lincoln Park area to what was then called NewTown. The largely Puerto Rican residents began to be displaced as gay men, from a variety of races but mostly white, began to settle in the area. In 1998, Mayor Daley arranged beautification projects—often involving large public art to mark the area—to four neighborhoods in the city: three neighborhoods identified with Chicago's major ethnic groups and Boystown, solidifying the neighborhood's official status as the gay enclave. In the past decade, the neighborhood continues to change. This time, straight white women and heterosexual families are displacing Boystown's gay residents.

Boystown's history is an almost textbook case of gentrification. Brown-Saracino (2009) divides gentrification into two different stages. In early-stage gentrification, white people with high cultural capital, but low economic capital, push people of color out of a neighborhood through a series of "cleanup" projects and rising rent prices. These gentrifiers are often white gay men, due to marginalization from their homosexuality that prevents them from fully accessing their white and male privilege in the housing market. As the neighborhood changes, becomes more fashionable and more hip, "yuppies"—white young professionals with high economic capital—begin to move into the area. This late-stage gentrification is much less analyzed. It involves straight white people, often families, exchanging their greater economic capital to move into the trendy new area. The early-adopters are pushed out and into a new area, starting the cycle again. Boystown is experiencing late-stage gentrification.

As one would expect from a neighborhood that completed early-stage gentrification, a previous study identified the area as almost completely white (Ellingson and Schroeder 2004). However, my fieldwork indicates this claim overly relies on residential status, ignoring the lengthy history of QPOC traveling to the area for entertainment from other parts of the city.

Thus, this chapter concerns itself less with the demographic change in residential status and more with the demographic change in neighborhood consumption my participants believe to be tied to changes in society. Although the residents that have lived in Boystown may have been predominantly white, the consumption of the neighborhood was not. Although they did not live in the neighborhood, QPOC came from across the city to hang out on Boystown's streets and in its gay bars. Similarly, regardless of true residential changes, participants believe the area now is settled and consumed increasingly by straight white women.

Ethnographic observations lent credence to my participants' views that the area is experiencing an influx of straight white women living in the area and consuming its nightlife. As an illustration, table 11.1 describes a tally that I took of people on the streets of Boystown on December 6, 2012. At 7:30 p.m., a few of these people were coming into or out of bars and restaurants, but many of them were walking home, carrying exercise clothing, walking dogs, or pushing strollers. This tally is conceptually representative of the new face of Boystown. For an area purportedly for gay men, the presence of

Table 11.1   Count of Boystown Pedestrians

Thursday, December 6. 2012 7:30 p.m.		
41	(53%)	White women
8	(10%)	Men of color
26	(34%)	White men
2	(3%)	Women of color

an overwhelming majority of white women, I argue, has an influence on the community life of the area.

The area has become a destination for many people, straight and gay, to consume a "gay lifestyle" that includes a kind of nightlife and shopping popularized by media depictions of gay men. As Adam, a gay black man in his forties, put it, "It's a mall. You go to the mall to hang out or to shop, but you don't live at the mall." Many people expressed similar sentiments. Frequently, they referred to the area as a "gay Disneyland." Asked what this meant, Jackson, a late twenties black gay man, described it as "everything that you would want if you were going to visit a gay neighborhood some-where. Fifteen clubs, everyone is adorable, and people are roaming around in groups. It's like, you know, a TV gay neighborhood." The area is now a destination. A place where one does not necessarily live (Ghaziani 2014), but a place they still return to consume. This chapter looks at the change in who and how people come to consume the neighborhood, and what that change indicates about assimilation.

The neighborhood has not followed the typical gentrification cycle, which would involve another area of the city rising up as the new major gay area, just as Boystown moved north transforming NewTown. Although many white gay men have moved north to Buena Park, Edgewater, or Rogers Park, none of these places have displaced Boystown as the gay capital of Chicago. There are three reasons that the neighborhood hasn't moved.

First, the official recognition by the city gave the neighborhood a historical character. The city erected pylons along Halsted St. from Belmont to Grace. These large golden pillars topped with rainbow colors—my participants sometimes referred to them as Boystown's "golden phalluses"—were later supplemented in 2012 by plaques that listed famous LGBT people and their historical significance. Many people referenced these pylons as marking the neighborhood as *the* gay neighborhood. They are literal stakes in the ground.

Second, legal differences exist between the neighborhood when it moved into the area and today. Today, many of the buildings on the block are owned by the backers of the clubs. Those that do not own the building their clubs reside in are more transient, opening and closing regularly. Some of these— like a black and Latino club circuit that briefly closed after arguments over rent with building owners—reopen in another part of the city, only to return later. Others, like Cocktail, frequently open and close, change ownership and even names, but remain in the neighborhood. Both major landmark bars, Sidetrack's and Roscoe's, own the building they are located in. Owning their locations means they are rooted in a way that discourages moving further north to follow white gay male residential movement.

Third, in 2008, a major LGBT community center opened in the neighborhood called the Center on Halsted. The Center, a major target of the Take Back Boystown campaign described later, is a multimillion dollar facility and nonprofit organization. They provide space for community groups to meet, host social events, and provide many social services. For instance, the Center supplies mental health services, HIV testing, a youth program, and job training. Their senior program will expand in the coming years to include a new senior living building close by. The Center is another stake in the ground, identifying this area as *the* gay area of Chicago. That the Center is in Boystown, rather than several smaller community centers across the many areas of Chicago where queer people live (as was originally a proposal), gives Boystown a special emphasis as the gay center of Chicago, a destination to come to consume either the thriving nightlife or the Center's social services.

I asked one new resident, George, a mid-thirties white gay man who returned to the neighborhood after having moved away for nearly ten years, what had changed since he last lived there. He responded, "When I moved back here, I wanted to live in Lakeview [the official city name for the area that includes Boystown] because it's a fun place to fuck and like hang out. And my husband and I were looking and we're like 'Oh my god. It's fucking Lincoln Park.' It's the demographic that I do not want. You know? It's not the neighborhood that it was ten years ago. It's less gay, it's less diverse, it's more of a tourist spot." This transformation of Boystown from a stigmatized gay enclave to a thriving gay Disneyland represents the assimilation of the neighborhood into the fabric of traditional mainstream society.

Assimilation's Intertwined Character

The late-stage gentrification of Boystown and its transformation into a "gay Disneyland" reflects the assimilation of gay men. It has an intertwined sexual and racial character. I first present evidence that some gay men are taking up mainstream straight sexual values. Next, I show how sexual assimilation is reinforced through restructuring sexual fields, changing the ways people find sexual partners. Finally, I document the racial consequences of sexual assimilation: racial boundaries in the neighborhood harden, whitening the area, and, thereby, casting QPOC as outsiders.

Sexual Assimilation

Sexual assimilation is the spatial assimilation, structural integration, and acculturation of a sexual minority to mainstream straight sexual values. Acculturation is the taking up of a belief, attitude, or cultural practice by a minority group. Acculturation is not one-way. It can also occur through the blurring of boundaries between the two groups, transforming a stigmatized practice associated with the group into a commonplace occurrence no longer associated with the group. It need not be totalizing to have occurred.

To understand the queer cultural ethos that some gay men are acculturating from, return to Rubin's charmed circle. Some queer communities have an alternative queer sexual lifestyle and culture (Orne 2017), separate sexual fields from straight culture with their own social organization and interactional rules (Green 2012). Perhaps because gay men are marginalized along one part of the pie (i.e., homosexuality), their sexual field does not stigmatize some of the other parts of the pie (e.g., nonmonogamy and public sex), resulting in acceptance of multiple partners, casual sex, public sexuality, adult toys, and other sexual activities marginalized by mainstream straight culture. Although it was threatened by the AIDS/HIV epidemic, this queer sexual ethos survives today in the plethora of gay hookup websites, some bathhouses, and in niche gay male communities like bears, leather, and the HIV positive "poz" community.

This section discusses how some gay men are acculturating to mainstream straight sexual culture that devalues the outer circle and emphasizes inner circle activities like marriage. Now that the possibility of marriage exists for gay men, a traditional marriage like their parents has become the goal. For example, Frank, a gay mid-twenties white Catholic, wants to get married. He expectantly waits to find the right guy. When asked who the "right guy" looks like, he specifies this means a monogamous relationship, marriage, and a family. He "wants the same things as everyone else," meaning straight people. When he discusses the straight white women in Boystown's gay bars, he only disapproves of bachelorette parties because they "rub my face in it. It's just rude when they have rights I don't have."

In the meantime, he's not going to let that stop him from going on sexual hook up websites, but he feels shameful doing so because "that's not the type of relationship that [he's] looking for." Again, acculturation need not be totalizing to have occurred. In this case, hookups are accepted in some straight cultures, although not to the extent in queer culture, as long as that the eventual goal is marriage and monogamy (Currier 2000). His shame also reflects a change in attitudes toward what is often seen as "normal" gay sexuality, a shift toward the beliefs of the straight sexual majority. The boundary between the alternative sexual culture of queers and straight people has blurred, one kind of acculturation (Zolberg and Woon 1999).

However, many gay men do not wish to participate in the hook up culture associated with queerness. Alexander doesn't want to be involved in the hookup culture and "slut shames" those who do. During several of our conversations, Alexander, a mid-twenties white gay man who immigrated to America as a teenager, talked to me about two different men that he's had sex. His sense of shame was palpable. He stressed that if they only want him for sex, well, "I'm not a slut" and would not continue to see them. Through ethnographic triangulation, I observed Alexander out with one of these two men during fieldwork. The potential boyfriend appeared to genuinely desire a relationship with him. Alexander, however, rejected him, primarily because of the man's history of hooking up and large number of previous sex partners. Men like Alexander have acculturated to straight sexual norms, more closely reflecting their parents' traditional sexual systems.

The neighborhood also reflects acculturation through a change toward valuing the "stroller set," as Sam puts it, over other neighborhood groups. These refer both to queer families and nonqueer families. More straight families are hanging around and moving into the neighborhood, but also queer families now desire the gayborhood to be "more quiet" and less "a party scene." One of the most noticeable consequences has been several complaints about the sex toy shops with open windows on the street. At a doctor's appointment at a neighborhood clinic, my phlebotomist, who looked to be in his early thirties, told me that he sees Boystown's streets as much different than when he first came out: "During the day, it's a family area now, not really a gay one." The shift toward families represents favoring the procreative segment of Rubin's charmed circle over the non-procreative.

These forms of acculturation are not totalizing. Acculturation is not a one-way street, it involves the blurring and, to an extent, the queering of these boundaries. While some men are slut shaming or desiring of marriage, they still participate in casual sex, but in ways consistent with straight culture. Each of these attitude changes represents a shift from the outside of the charmed circle toward a hegemonic inner circle value. Changes to the sexual field of Boystown reinforce these attitudes, making queer sexual culture increasingly hard to actualize regardless of one's sexual ethos.

Sexual Field Restructuring

"NO BACHELORETTE PARTIES," read the sign outside of Cocktail, a gay bar on one of Boystown's most bustling corners. Yet, inside I couldn't tell. For a gay bar, the place probably had as many women as gay men. Surely, a few of these women were lesbian, bisexual, or otherwise queer, but a good many were straight. Near the stage, a male stripper in his underwear—who often tells me he only strips to support his wife and children—caressed a woman in leopard print pants and open-toed strapped high heels, a style of shoe thought to be so alluring to men that the late neosoul diva Amy Winehouse called them "Fuck Me Pumps." He gyrated into her, moving her hands along his body as her two other female friends laughed beside her. Over the next half hour, this routine continued only occasionally punctuated with a quick dollar down his waistband from one of the few gay men standing around.

I've dragged my partner along for the night and he tells me that he's had enough of what has become a strip club for straight women. After quickly taking a few more jottings of the situation on my iPhone, we decided to head across the street to Roscoe's, perhaps the most popular gay bar in the area. After seeing three separate groups of women head out the door, he threw up his hands, "Can we go somewhere gay?"

I relented. We walked toward the Lucky Horseshoe, a gay strip club raunchy and literally dirty enough to resist the changes overtaking Boystown's other bars. Along Halsted St., Boystown's main thoroughfare, I continued taking notes on my phone, categorizing the groups we passed along the street. It was a busy night, a definite girl's night out.

These nights are common in Boystown. It is not just gay men who come to consume "gay Disneyland." The late-stage gentrification of the area has brought more women into the area, most of which my participants believe to be straight. There are consequences of the real and perceived structural assimilation of straight women into the bars and clubs, the community "third spaces" of Boystown. As gay men sexually assimilate to straight norms, the structural assimilation of straight women into gay male bars restructures the sexual field gay men navigate, reinforcing mainstream sexual norms.

The sexual field of Boystown is restructured by the presence of large quantities of straight white women primarily because it breaks down the interactional rules that once governed the space. Sam, a biracial Black gay man, says the result is that gay men in these bars feel objectified, like they exist for straight white women's entertainment:

> It's become this petting zoo where they come and look and gawk at the gays. It's not as much just the gay neighborhood as it is where people go to see the gay people. A lot of people don't like that. I can't stand it when women will come up to me at a bar like, "You're gay, you're my best friend." Just because you've seen a gay on TV doesn't mean I'm going to be your best friend.

This feeling of objectification means that they no longer feel comfortable engaging in the hookup rituals, public sexuality, and other actions the queer sexual field entails. In Sam's words:

> Those days [before straight women were present], you go to the gay bar to be gay. There are a lot of guys who want to go to a gay bar to be free. To like take

off your shirt, be raunchy, and just have at it without this whole table full of straight girls, "Oh, gay men are so safe and pretty and I love you." Bitch, get off of me I'm trying to suck this guy's dick. I'm sorry just being completely open here.

These changes reinforce assimilated straight, inner charmed circle, values. When gay men no longer feel comfortable engaging in the behavior, it reinforces mainstream straight sexual beliefs. In this case, as Rubin's charmed circle shows, sex belongs in the home. The segments of the circle are mutually reinforcing.

I even saw this reinforcement out at some leather events, a raunchier queer subculture. At a Tom of Finland, a gay leather artist known for his hyper-masculine drawings, themed event at Hydrate, Jon and I were astounded to see five young white women come inside off the street. I struck up a conversation with them as they gawked at their surroundings. They didn't know it was a leather themed event, but were walking along the street and thought the venue looked like fun. When Jon and I turned to go to the back "No Shirts Allowed" dance floor—a rule meant to foster a sexually charged atmosphere—they followed us. The bouncer stopped them. "No shirts," he reminded them. While two of the women were reluctant at first, the other two convinced them, negotiating the bouncer down to bras only. As they entered the dance floor clad only in their bras, they gleefully yelled, telling me what a wild time they were having. The men around me on the floor moved away slightly, shooting me dirty looks. While I did see sexually charged dancing, I didn't see any of the making-out or groping I had witnessed at previous themed events. At least, not near us, and, not until the women left the bar a few hours later.

This reinforcement is not just discouraging gay men that might wish to engage in alternative sexual behavior. It also discourages gay men from identifying as a separate culture from the mainstream straight world. Frank, the gay Catholic who's marriage views I describe earlier, for instance, doesn't mind that more women are in the gay clubs he frequents. When I asked him about how he feels about more women in gay clubs, he responded:

What's the difference? We're always bringing our girlfriends with us. At least I do. My two girlfriends are the ones I come to Boystown with. I never come to boystown with gay guys. It's not a big deal. I don't belong to this culture of I can only be around other gay men.

This culture he explains is one that wants to maintain itself as "separate" from the straight world. To Frank, women in the clubs represent the acceptance by the straight world that he mimics in his beliefs about marriage and monogamy. The structural changes to the sexual field blur group boundaries that maintain queerness as a separate cultural group and enclave.

Thus, the sexual assimilation of gay men in Boystown is reinforced on two levels by the structural integration of straight white women into Boystown's night life. First, they restructure the sexual field of the neighborhood, discouraging behavior that is not aligned with mainstream straight values—the hegemonic inside of the charmed circle. Second, the integration demonstrates to people like Frank that gay men are accepted by straight culture, they are not a separate group, and Boystown is a district for a certain consumer.

Racial Consequences

As the neighborhood assimilates, QPOC, because of their racial difference, become the most visible affront to the hegemonic "gay Disneyland" model of the neighborhood. The assimilation of the neighborhood, including its integration into straight society, racializes the neighborhood as a white neighborhood. QPOC in the area are "outsiders" and racial boundaries harden.

"Make sure that when you are writing this book, you write about both the good and the bad changes to the neighborhood," an older affluent white gay man admonished me after I told him about my project. We were drinking whiskey in Buck's, a gay bar on Halsted St. known for its older clientele. The good changes, he explained are "how nice everything is nowadays," evoking the same language others used when referencing Boystown's late-stage gentrification and "gay Disneyland" atmosphere.

The bad changes? "The ghetto trannies and gay kids on the street" who are "loud" and don't realize that they can be "respectable" now. I hear these references frequently toward the young black men, drag queens, and transwomen who come to Boystown, like gay men of other racial groups, for entertainment and social services.

He is not the only one to feel that the presence of QPOC is a change in the neighborhood. In the summer of 2011, a stabbing in the neighborhood was caught on video by the white gay owners of a condo overlooking Halsted St. The video shows two groups of young black men coming together, a short argument, and then a burst of violence as one man stabs another. The owners leaked the video to the mainstream Chicago media, prompting articles and a wave of hysteria to grip the neighborhood about the sudden "crime wave" in Boystown. The accused culprits of this crime wave were clear: young black and latino men hanging out on the street.

The Take Back Boystown event and accompanying Facebook page formed shortly after. Take Back Boystown was meant to be a "community loitering" event, where "residents" of Boystown would band together and hang out on the street to show "those that don't belong here" that the neighborhood would not be intimidated. The event was protested by a queer community group, GenderJUST, calling the event racist and an attempt to prevent QPOC from coming to the neighborhood.

Much of the blame was placed on the Center on Halsted, the multimillion dollar LGBT center that opened in 2008, for attracting "outsiders" to the neighborhood with its social services. In an interview with the *Windy City Times*, the major gay newspaper of Chicago, the Center's Chief Executive Officer (CEO) Modesto Tico Valle similarly expressed his beliefs that the Take Back Boystown event was driven by racism:

WCT: "The Center has been controversial for a lot of Lakeview residents worried about safety, especially last summer with the "Take Back Boystown" Facebook page campaign. Why do you think that is?"

MV: "We are a significant presence on Halsted Street. This is the go-to place . . . I think the issue is a lot more complicated and it involves a lot of the "isms" of our society. Some of it has to do with fear and facing your own prejudices. When you really have the opportunity to speak to some individuals in the community and challenge tone and language, people can pause for a minute and realize "hmm, maybe there is a bit of racism."

WCT: "What were you hearing from youth *[Author: the codeword* for *young black men* in *the area]* in the Center last summer when this was going on?"

MV: "I heard from a lot of young people a roller-coaster of emotions: anger that they were being blamed for something that they had no role in, sadness because they came into a community that they thought was going to embrace them and be safe after being beaten, raped, abused in their neighborhoods, in their families. They kind of saw this as their safe haven and their family. The community—not everyone, but some—slammed the door in their face in a very ugly way" (Sosin 2012).

It should surprise no one in the sociology of race and ethnicity that a belief in rising crime rates was connected to the visibility of QPOC on the streets of Boystown. The perception of crime in a neighborhood is not related to the level of reported crimes in a neighborhood, but to the percentage of African-Americans seen on the street in the area (Quillian and Pager 2001). In fact, Boystown was experiencing some of the lowest crime rates in years (Demarest 2012).

Most importantly, QPOC in the neighborhood are not a new phenomenon. Instead, because of the changing assimilated status of the neighborhood as a "gay Disneyland" to be consumed, QPOC in the neighborhood *began* to be seen as outsiders to the neighborhood. Pauline, a black bisexual woman in her early forties, remembers when she was a young black woman engaging in precisely the same kind of street activity in the early 1990s that Take Back

Boystown suddenly identified as new and the cause of crime. She used to visit the neighborhood from her home on the south side of Chicago—where most of Chicago's black population lives—to hang out with her friends on the Belmont Rocks, a popular destination for people under twenty-one when Boystown first formed. QPOC coming to Boystown is not new.

However, it is now seen as new, or at least noteworthy. The comments on the Take Back Boystown Facebook page vividly show that the neighborhood is now seen as a white space:

"It's the blacks tearing the neighborhood apart. They're a bunch of monsters."

"Most of the drama is caused by black a- holes who live in other neighborhoods who come here and I [*sic*] respect the area."

"I've lived in Chicago for 46 years. These comments arten [*sic*] racist. They are true."

"Go back to your hoods!!!"

Such posts—and the often sixty+ comment threads that followed them debating whether the post was racist—demonstrate the area is now seen as a white area.

While the area did not have an exclusively white reputation earlier, that does not mean that it did not have racism. There is a difference between racism in a space where both white gay men and gay men of color are assumed to be present and the racialization of Boystown as a white area. Boystown, like all of society, has had plenty of interpersonal and structural racism. For example, they did not have a black bartender in the area until 1998.

I argue not that Boystown was a place of racial harmony, but rather that the new vividness of race in the area and the hardening of its racial boundaries is bound up in its new status as an assimilated space, a "gay Disneyland." QPOC, rather than being members of the gay community that have always been present in the space, are newly salient as out of place. The area has been recategorized as being aggressively white.

DISCUSSION AND CONCLUSION

Assimilation has an intertwined sexual and racial character. Through ethnographic fieldwork, interviews, and content analysis, I demonstrated a cultural group assimilates along multiple lines. Assimilation involves acculturation to mainstream sexual norms. Demographic change and structural integration conspire to restructure sexual fields discouraging unassimilated sexual behavior. Concurrently, these changes whiten the area, fusing it with the mainstream.

Specifically, this chapter demonstrates gay men are a cultural group that is assimilating in American society and the consequences are mixed. Some gay men have profoundly conservative sexual attitudes. These gay men engage in "slut shaming," express concern over how to find "good" relationships within gay culture, and look to forward to marriage and children. Neighborhood institutions reflect this as well with increased family programming, concern for children in the neighborhood, and efforts to "clean up" the party atmosphere of the entertainment district. Of course, these are not negative, unless they come at the expense of alternative queer cultures that celebrate non-hegemonic sexual values.

Structural integration and spatial assimilation reinforce this acculturation. The neighborhood has experienced demographic change, with white straight women moving in and increasing their consumption of Boystown's institutions and nightlife. Structural assimilation of this kind changes the way that gay people use the bars and clubs. Previously "raunchy" sexually charged places are de-queered, straightened up, and desexualized. However, these places are still read as gay. It is a more commodified and commercialized form of gayness.

This data also shows that as sexual fields in the neighborhood reshape, the area is not only mainstreamed heterosexually, but also whitened. The Take Back Boystown event is the most vivid example of the policing of the neighborhood's racial boundaries. The neighborhood is cast as a white area. QPOC are outsiders to a neighborhood they had long been a part of. This is of course not a bastion of racial harmony previously, but the area is recast as exclusively white—gay as a white ethnicity—rather than an area in which QPOC were expected albeit under conditions of discrimination. The distinction is important.

This finding goes against the cultural predictions of post-gay theorists, who argue, however unevenly the process occurs that the cultural distinctiveness of gay identity is disappearing (Ghaziani 2014). Rather, I demonstrate that due to assimilation tensions within the gay community that have always been there have begun to rise to salience. The cracks in the foundation binding the assimilationist gay community and separatist queer community have begun to become visible. Separate community spaces supporting gays and queers will continue to diverge. One mainstream, commercialized and supported; one separatist and continually marginalized. Equality has not brought liberation. It has merely separated the few to be lifted up, as long as they act like their former oppressors.

Theoretically, I argue there is an intersectional character to assimilation. As one would expect, scholars of a particular axis of privilege—gender, ability, sexuality, race, class, and so forth—typically focus on assimilation in their area. Throughout this chapter, I have demonstrated assimilation of gay men in Boystown has both a sexual aspect—acculturation to straight sexual norms—but also a racial aspect—whitening of the gayborhood and ethnicizing gay identity.

The most important extension of these findings is that racial assimilation likely also has a sexual character. For instance, immigrants to America often are struck by the radically more liberal sexual norms in mainstream American culture (for a Canadian example, see Uskul 2007). Assimilation of cultural and racial groups erases their family structures and unique sexual cultures as they become acculturated to the mainstream American norm. Research that looks at single motherhood in black-American communities (e.g., Edin and Kefalas 2007) might be illuminated by the possibilities of "queerness" in their participants. These alternative family structures only appear alternative to a heterosexual middle-class white norm. By illuminating the racial character inherent to sexual assimilation, we should be more attentive to the sexual character inherent to racial assimilation.

Furthermore, as I demonstrated in the case of Boystown, the hegemonic forms of sexuality in Rubin's charmed circle also carry with them the whiteness that is inherent to mainstream sexuality in American society. I urge scholars to continue to examine the ways that the charmed circle is both hegemonicly straight, as well as raced and classed.

NOTE

1. This chapter was previously published as Orne, Jason. 2019. "Gayborbood Change: The Intertwined Sexual and Racial Character of Assimilation in Chicago's Boystown" in C. Winter Han and Jesus Gregorio Smith 2019. *Home and Community for Queer Men of Color*. Lanham: Lexington Books.

Acknowledgements: Thanks to Loka Ashwood, Michael Bell, and Amanda Ward for their comments on earlier drafts of this chapter. Some material presented also appears in my book, *Boystown: Sex and Community in Chicago* (2017, University of Chicago Press.)

REFERENCES

Alba, Richard, and Victor Nee. 1997. "Rethinking Assimilation Theory for a New Era of Immigration." *International Migration* Review 31(4): 826–874.

Brown-Saracino, Japonica. 2009. *A Neighborhood that Never Changes*. Chicago, IL: University of Chicago Press.

Charmaz, Kathy. 2006. *Constructing Grounded Theory: A Practical Guide through Qualitative Analysis*. Thousand Oaks, CA: Sage Publications, Inc.

Corbin, Juliet, and Janice M. Morse. 2003. "The Unstructured Interactive Interview: Issues of Reciprocity and Risks when Dealing with Sensitive Topics." *Qualitative Inquiry* 9(3): 335–354.

Collins, Patricia Hill. 2005. *Black Sexual Politics*. Abingdon-on-Thames: Routledge.

Connell, Catherine. 2014. *School's Out: Gay and Lesbian Teachers in the Classroom.* Oakland, CA: University of California Press.

D'Emilio, John. 1983. *Sexual Politics, Sexual Communities: The Making of a Homosexual Minority 1940-1970.* Chicago, IL: University of Chicago Press.

Demarest, Erica. 2012. "Citywide Crime Down in 2011, Slight Decline in Lakeview." *Windy City Times*, April 4, 2012. http://www.windycitymediagroup.com/lgbt/Citywide-crime-down-in-2011-slight-decline-in-Lakeview/37107.html.

Drake, St. Clair, and Horace R. Cayton. 1945. *Black Metropolis.* Chicago, IL: University of Chicago Press.

Duggan, Lisa. 2012. *The Twilight* of *Equality?* Boston, MA: Beacon Press.

Edin, Kathryn, and Maria Kefalas. 2007. *Promises I Can Keep.* Oakland, CA: University of California Press.

Ellingson, Stephen, and Kirby Schroeder. 2004. "Race and the Construction of Same-Sex Sex Markets in Four Chicago Neighborhoods." *The Sexual Organization of the City*: 94–123. Chicago, IL: University of Chicago Press.

Fryer, Roland G. 2007. "Guess Who's Been Coming to Dinner? Trends in Interracial Marriage Over the 20th Century." *The Journal* of *Economic Perspectives* 21(2): 71–90.

Ghaziani, Amin. 2010. "There Goes the Gayborhood?" *Contexts* 9(4): 64–66.

Ghaziani, Amin. 2014. *There Goes the Gayborhood?* Princeton, NJ: Princeton University Press.

Gordon, Milton M. 1964. *Assimilation in American life: The Role of Race, Religion and National Origins.* Oxford: Oxford University Press.

Green, Adam Isaiah. 2008a. "Erotic Habitus: Toward a Sociology of Desire." *Theory and Society* 37: 597–626.

Green, Adam Isaiah. 2008b. "The Social Organization of Desire: The Sexual Fields Approach." *Sociological Theory* 26(1): 25–50.

Green, Adam Isaiah. 2011. "Playing the (Sexual) Field: The Interactional Basis of Systems of Sexual Stratification." *Social Psychology Quarterly* 74(3): 244–266.

Green, Adam Isaiah. 2012. *Sexual Fields: Toward a Sociology of Collective Sexual Life.* Chicago, IL: University of Chicago Press.

Greene, Theodore. 2012. *"Sexual Orientation, Sexual Identity and the Politics of Place."* Evanston, IL: Northwestern University Press.

Hicklin, Aaron. 2012. "Nate Silver: Person of the Year." *Out Magazine*, December 18, 2012, pp. 1–6. http://www.out.com/news-opinion/2012/12/18/nate-silver-person-year.

Lamont, Michèle. 2009. "Responses to Racism, Health, and Social Inclusion as a Dimension of Successful Societies." *Successful Societies: How Institutions and Culture Affect Health.* Cambridge, UK and New York: Cambridge University Press.

Martin, John Levi, and Matt George. 2006. "Theories of Sexual Stratification: Toward an Analytics of the Sexual Field and a Theory of Sexual Capital." *Sociological Theory* 24(2): 107–132.

Moore, Mignon. 2011. *Invisible Families.* Oakland, CA: University of California Press.

Nakamura, Lisa. 2002. *Cybertypes*. Psychology Press. London: Taylor & Francis Group.

Nee, Victor, Jimy M. Sanders, and Scott Sernau. 1994. "Job Transitions in an Immigrant Metropolis: Ethnic Boundaries and the Mixed Economy." *American Sociological Review* 849–872.

Orne, Jason. 2011. "'You Will Always Have to "Out" Yourself'." *Sexualities* 14(6): 681–703.

Orne, Jason. 2013. "Queers in the Line of Fire: Goffman's Stigma Revisited." *The Sociological Quarterly* 54(2): 229–253.

Orne, Jason. 2017. *Boystown: Sex and Community in Chicago*. Chicago, IL: University of Chicago Press.

Pais, Jeremy, Scott J. South, and Kyle Crowder. 2012. "Metropolitan Heterogeneity and Minority Neighborhood Attainment." *Social Problems* 59(2): 258–281.

Park, Robert. 1914. "The Concept of Social Distance." *Journal of Applied Sociology* 8: 339–344.

Portes, Alejandro, and Leif Jensen. 1989. "The Enclave and the Entrants: Patterns of Ethnic Enterprise in Miami Before and After Mariel." *American Sociological Review* 929–949.

Portes, Alejandro, and Min Zhou. 1993. "The New Second Generation: Segmented Assimilation and Its Variants." *The Annals* of *the American Academy of Political and Social Science* 530(1): 74–96.

Quillian, Lincoln, and Devah Pager. 2001. "Black Neighbors, Higher Crime? The Role of Racial Stereotypes in Evaluations of Neighborhood Crime." *American Journal of Sociology* 107(3): 717–767.

Rubin, Gayle. 1992. "Thinking Sex: Notes for a Radical Theory of the Politics of Sexuality." *Pleasure and Danger: Exploring Female Sexuality*. London: Pandora.

Saguy, Abigail C., and Anna Ward. 2011. "Coming Out as Fat: Rethinking Stigma." *Social Psychology Quarterly* 74(1): 53–75.

Seidman, Steven. 2002. "*Beyond the Closet.*" *Routledge*. London: Taylor & Francis Group.

Song, Miri. 2009. "Is Intermarriage a Good Indicator of Integration?" *Journal of Ethnic and Migration Studies* 35(2): 331–348.

Sosin, Kate. 2012. "Center on Halsted CEO on Controversies, Five-Year Anniversary." *Windy City Times*, April 18, 2012. http://www.windycitymediagroup.com/lgbt/Center-on-Halsted-CEO-on-controversiesfive-year-anniversary/37316.html

Whyte, William Foote. 1943. *Street Corner Society*. Chicago, IL: University of Chicago Press.

Williams, Christine, Patti A. Giuffre, and Kirsten Dellinger. 2009. "The Gay-Friendly Closet." *Sexuality Research and Social Policy* 6(1): 29–45.

Zolberg, Aristide R., and Long Litt Woon. 1999. "Why Islam is like Spanish: Cultural Incorporation in Europe and the United States." *Politics & Society* 27(1): 5–38.

Afterword

Somewhere beyond the Gayborhood

C. J. Janovy

Might it be possible for LGBTQ activists and their allies to transform a Trump Country town into a gayborhood? By the definitions used in this book, the answer is no. Gayborhoods are a metropolitan phenomenon, and Independence, Kansas—home to about 9,000 people—is by almost all measures rural. It's the Montgomery County seat, and some of its historic buildings retain the feeling of the frontier town it became in 1869, built by predominantly white settlers during the Westward expansion, after the removal of Osage Indians to what is now Oklahoma. The demographic composition of its population mirrors that of Kansas: around 84 percent of its residents are white, 74 percent of the voters in the area cast their ballots for Donald Trump in 2016, and the median family income is about $20,000 less than national average reported by the census. In their essay "Performative Progressiveness: Accounting for New Forms of Inequalitiy in the Gayborhood," Adriana Brodyn and Amin Ghaziani describe a thirty-nine-year-old resident of Chicago's Andersonville gayborhood who asks: "Is there anybody left in this country who actually has a problem with this? . . . . I can't believe that anybody would get upset about homosexuality in this day and age." If that question is serious, the Andersonville man should pay a visit to Kansas.

Located in the state's southeastern corner, Independence is an hour and a half north of Tulsa, Oklahoma (metro population around 766,000), the nearest big city where a queer person might more easily be expected to find community. The closest such cities in other directions are Wichita, two hours to the west (metro population around 527,000); Springfield, Missouri, two and a half hours to the east (metro population around 437,000); and Kansas City, three hours to the north (metro population around 2 million). Across the United States, small towns like Independence are lucky if their single business districts still have healthy storefronts instead of dusty antique stores and boarded-up windows—such towns are so depopulated and brain-drained that they would welcome any form of the gentrification that is troublesome in other places discussed in this book. Towns like Independence tend to be the types of places where, if there's any LGBTQ culture at all, it seems decades behind the times—if those "times" are defined by the standards of iconic urban gayborhoods such as Chicago's Boystown, the Castro in San Francisco, or Christopher Street in New York City's Greenwich Village. Even lesser known gayborhoods like that of the Grove in St. Louis, Westport in Kansas City,[1] or the Fruit Loop in Las Vegas seem light years away.

Still, many of the social dynamics discussed elsewhere in *The Gayborhood: From Sexual Liberation to Cosmopolitan Spectacle* influence the lives of people in Independence, suggesting the commonality of the queer lived experience throughout much (though not all) of the analysis contained in this book. I am a journalist, rather than a scholar,[2] but the act of journalistic reporting parallels field research; this chapter contains no quantitative research (which I am not trained to do) but rather describes the lived experience of an individual and his community. My reporting here then is best thought of as another narrative reflecting the ideas presented elsewhere in this book, and challenging them by calling upon readers to compare and contrast them to more rural locations.[3] Though it would take great poetic license to consider Independence, Kansas, a gayborhood, the town can, by some standards, be considered an oasis for lesbian, gay, and bisexual people in the extended rural neighborhood of southeast Kansas.

"Growing up, I always hated small towns," said Brandon West, who was born in 1988 in Cherryvale, Kansas (pop. 2,000), about ten miles from Independence. His Southern Baptist grandmother, who lived a block away, picked him up to attend church every Sunday morning. "I never saw myself in a small town, especially when I was struggling with my sexuality," West said. "I didn't see anybody like myself." Like many young people in small towns, West was active in his church. That changed around the time he entered middle school, when he realized he couldn't agree with what the minister was preaching. Like so many gay kids who grew up in similar environments, West figured he was going to hell because of how he felt.

Also like many isolated gay kids, West found some relief on television. "My aunt and uncle had HBO, and they were advertising that on Friday there was going to be a Cher concert. I really liked Cher, and I asked my aunt to record it for me." West's aunt set her VCR for three hours. As it turned out, the recording included the first episode of *Queer as Folk*, the TV series about five gay men living in Pittsburgh, Pennsylvania; based on a British series of the same name, the American version aired from 2000 to 2005. "I think I maybe watched the Cher concert once, but the first 30 minutes of *Queer as Folk* over and over again," West said.

That experience was helpful in some ways but not others. The small-town American expectation that a boy would grow up, find a wife at college, have 2.5 kids and a white picket fence was deeply ingrained, West said: "*Queer as Folk* made me know I wasn't alone, but it brought more issues through high school: nobody can find out, these urges are going to pass."[4]

Though he had stopped going to church, West stayed active in community organizations: the Boy Scouts, sports teams, Future Farmers of America, anything he could find to participate in, even though he knew he was different. He suppressed his identity throughout high school, engaging in the same sort of "impression management" Magdalena Wojciechowska observed in her study of lesbian mothers in Poland, where "awareness and self-comparison to heteronormative standards" causes people to "surveil their own behavior in order to remedy what can be seen as problematic." Wojciechowska, extending Goffman's framework here, reminds us of the origins of internalized homophobia that stem from living in a heteronormative world. As she further elaborates, "protecting oneself against potential symbolic sanctions" by the dominant culture "can free the individual from short-term anticipated consequences of disclosing one's deviation, it also creates internal conflict."

For West, that internal conflict began to ease after he graduated from Independence Community College and left in 2008 to study abroad in Amsterdam. The city felt like "an adult Disneyland," West said. "Amsterdam is such a free and accepting community, I thought, 'If I'm going to figure out who I am, this would be the place.'" Discovering his first gayborhood, a block of bars and other gay-oriented businesses, served the same crucial purpose for West in the early twenty-first century as Greggor Mattson describes for twentieth-century gay men, for whom "bars were the most important cultural institution where newly 'out' men were socialized, interpersonal contacts made, (and) social isolation alleviated" (2). However, West said, the Dutch people he met in bars were reserved. Taking him for a typical American, a group of regulars who hung around a bar called Café 't Leeuwtje were reluctant to let him into their social group. "Once they got to know me, they realized I wasn't just there for party," he said.

West's process of self-discovery took about a year. It was the early days of Facebook's chat feature, where he came out to some friends, all of whom took the news well. "A few even mentioned, 'It's about time. I've known for years,'" he said. West loved the life he was living overseas and hated coming back to the States. Those feelings were punctuated a few days after his return, which coincided with the death of superstar Michael Jackson. "Television was nothing but Michael Jackson's funeral, and my parents didn't have internet," he said. His cell phone had been cut off while he was overseas, so he couldn't call friends. In what West described as "a fit of rage," he came out to his parents one night over dinner. He'd figured his mother would be the more supportive one, but she told him he was going to hell. His father, with whom he'd grown closer during Skype calls while he was overseas, reassured him: "Dad said I was still his son and he was going to love me."

West earned an associates degree at Independence Community College and went on to Kansas State University in Manhattan (pop. 53,678). Planning to be a teacher, he majored in secondary education, speech and drama, but his student teaching experience convinced him that wasn't what he wanted. After college, he spent a summer interning with the youth arm of People for the Ethical Treatment of Animals. "I learned so much about activism, working and campaigning with PETA," West said. He was hired full time and spent the next six months touring college campuses and speaking on behalf of animal rights. His passion for activism grew, and he moved to Los Angeles with hopes of working for a big LGBT organization. "That was my dream: move to the coast and change the world," he said. "I tried my darnedest to make it in LA."

Despite his ambitions, he wasn't able to find a decent job. West came back to Independence, where he got a job as the public service manager at the Independence Public Library (he is now the development coordinator). "I realized the library was perfect, because you can do activism," he said. "I can give people equal access to information. I can use civil rights programming to help fuel conversations in my community." He hadn't given up on his dream of working for a big LGBT organization; his plan was to build his resume and move back to the coast. "I always associated being gay with 'you have to move to big city,'" he said, so moving from Cherryvale to Los Angeles had "made me feel like I was at home." Now he made frequent weekend trips to Kansas City, he said, "so I could have an escape. I felt more at home when I'd go on vacation to the city." West had become one of Mattson's "gay lifestyle commuters."

One evening in 2016, West was having drinks at a bar with "one of the older gay members of the community" who had traveled in his younger years. The two were comparing notes about how they never thought there would be much of a gay community in Independence. They began listing all the LGBTQ people they knew, and wondering why these people didn't know each other. "Our friend groups went out, but there was never any cohesion, never any intermingling between the groups," West said. They invited all of these separate friends to a Facebook group with an unwieldly name: the Montgomery County Lesbian, Gay, Bisexual, Transgender, Questioning and Allies Social Group. Four or five people showed up to their first meeting, which they figured wasn't bad. As Wojciechowska observed among lesbian mothers in Poland, part of the benefit of being queer is our ability to create spaces for ourselves and others. However, no one showed up to the group's second meeting; West speculates people were busy with a large annual festival that preoccupies the town every October. Once that was over, in November, fifteen or twenty people showed up to the group's next meeting. From there, attendance stayed steady for every meeting, which was twice a month at a local bar. "A lot of them were allies," West said of the regular attendees, "but occasionally a new LGBTQ person would show up." Eventually, they renamed the group Project Q&A, for queers and allies.

Despite its billing as a social group, this was not a place where "singletons" might face the sort of stigma Aliraza Javaid discusses in "Disappearing: The Gay Singleton in Gay Spaces." Such singletons are not immediately "surrounded by missed opportunities or missed lives with potential romantic others" because in Independence, there isn't any significant "social context of gay scenes by which the gay singleton dances, drinks and socializes." Most of that activity is on dating apps, West pointed out. Using a dating app in southeast Kansas, he noted, is "a really different scenario than say, using those apps in Kansas City where you could be 100 feet or a block away from somebody. Here you're miles away from someone." The dating dynamic plays out in another way that might be more common in small towns. "Often when allies find out you're single or are looking, they're like, 'I know this one gay person and you'd be perfect together.' It's that stereotypical, 'You're going to like my gay best friend.'" West said he joked that when he started Project Q&A, "it was to find a husband—but that was a minor joke. Project Q&A doesn't really serve that purpose." The group's purpose soon became planning for a Pride celebration. They considered various dates: April was too soon, and the traditional Pride month wouldn't work either, because two out lesbians in town owned a bakery and wouldn't be able to help because they were busy with June wedding orders. "In small towns," West noted, "you don't mess with church and school events." The group decided on September 2017.

Meanwhile, West had managed to build a network between small-town Kansas and Los Angeles. He'd made connections with the Los Angeles-based It Gets Better Project, a nonprofit whose mission is "to uplift, empower, and connect lesbian, gay, bisexual, transgender and queer youth around the globe," which offered to help sponsor their first pride. Through It Gets Better board members, word got out to other organizations, and the New York City-based Stonewall Inn Gives Back Initiative, a nonprofit that provides financial and other assistance to support LGBTQ advocacy efforts in small cities and rural communities, also made a financial contribution to Project Q&A's first pride.

The inaugural event was a three-day celebration: a social on Thursday; a family movie night on Friday (they showed *Kinky Boots*); a Saturday afternoon drag show at an art gallery on Main Street, featuring a drag queen from Brooklyn who'd grown up in nearby Chanute, as well as queens from Wichita, followed by a community potluck with a keynote speaker from Los Angeles (a woman who'd grown up in Thayer, about half an hour away) and a pub crawl.

Around 300 people attended the various events, West said, many of them more spectators than participants. "The pub crawl had maybe 30 or 40 LGBTQ people walking on Main Street, carrying Pride flags, raising a ruckus," West remembered. "This cowboy dude stepped out (of a bar), spit in his cup, and was like, 'What's going on here?' (People said) 'It's gay pride!' He said, 'Keep doin' doing what you're doing! High five!'"

Had the members of Project Q&A transformed a few blocks of Independence into a gayborhood for at least three days? It's arguable that they had. Intriguingly, although the celebrants were almost entirely white, they had participated in a kind of ephemeral queer place-making similar to the practices among communities of color that Theodore Greene describes in "The Whiteness of Queer Urban Placemaking." While the communities Greene describes might, for example, "transform singular nights in mainstream gay bars and nightclubs as spaces for communion," the members of Project Q&A transformed a small-town American Main Street into a space for communion not just among themselves but also with bystanders. Perhaps they had also expanded the definition of "collective intimacy" that Étienne Meunier and Jeffrey Escoffier explore in "The Triumph of Collective Intimacy—Gay Collective Sex in New York City from the Late 1880s to Today." The circumstances on Independence's Main Street were dramatically different from the sex clubs and cruising areas with which Meunier and Escoffier are primarily concerned. But as the two scholars note, "The increasing legitimacy and visibility of gay sexualities and communities would change the urban landscape." Project Q&A's effort was bringing similar changes to the small-town landscape. Considering Project Q&A's efforts through the lens of the sociologists' definition of intimacy—"a form of close association characterized by the shared knowledge of the other," in this case non-sexual—it seems that the participants in Independence's inaugural Pride were displaying the collective intimacy that Meunier and Escoffier say "has been and still is crucial for LGBTQ cultures and politics as a way to resist the hegemony of the heteronormative way of life."

Response has generally been positive, West said. Some owners of bars and restaurants who supported the effort "got a couple of letters" of complaint, he said, "but after that first year, nobody really said anything. I don't know if Pride truly changed (attitudes in Independence) or it just showed show who we really are." After that first Pride, the owners of a local candle and scent shop, two openly gay men, approached other businesses around town and asked them to fly rainbow flags from first of June through Flag Day—nearly twenty of them did, which might seem minimal to those in major cities but is a significant show of support in a small town. This was empowering, West said, reinforcing the feeling Vanessa R. Panfil describes in "Gayborhoods as Criminogenic Space." Though she does not live "in a gayborhood," Panfil writes, "I am very heartened and feel safer seeing other rainbow flags in my neighborhood, since I feel as though there are allies or people like me nearby who contribute to a more accepting culture."

After Project Q&A's first pride, its members planned an entire week of activities. "If big cities could do it, we could too," West said. More than 500 people attended the various events—carnival games at the park, movie night, family game night, an evening drag show on Friday night at a historic hotel, a Saturday afternoon drag show, educational workshops on Saturday morning, a Saturday afternoon drag show, the potluck and pup crawl, church on Sunday, then a picnic to unwind—but it was too much work for their volunteers, and West was the only one who showed up to the church service. Since then, they've kept the festivities to two or three days. (In 2020, they hosted a virtual event as part of the online Global Pride event amid the COVID-19 pandemic, and planned for a possible virtual Pride in September.)

All of this has changed the culture of Independence, said Nancy Kishpaugh, who works with West at the Independence Public Library. "Brandon has helped changed attitudes here," she said. "You see Pride flags flying not just during Pride but all the time. It keeps that in the front of people's minds. I think people have gotten to know gay men and women as people."

West's work at within the library has helped create that community as well. When he arrived there in 2013, he found that the only material on LTBTQ issues books from the 1990s about HIV and AIDS. He made it his mission to update the collection, adding nonfiction and fiction and getting grants to bring in speakers and host workshops on history and topics such as body positivity and how to understand LGBTQ teens. Kishpaugh said West has been courageous, "putting himself on the line in a rural Kansas town to encourage understanding, or at the very least tolerance. He is always patient and knowledgeable in answering questions and helping to educate the public, myself included. He displays deep empathy with families with questioning children and parents who love them and may or may not understand them."

For these reasons, Kishpaugh nominated West for the American Library Association's Gay, Lesbian, Bisexual and Transgender Round Table Award for Political Activism, which he won in 2018. West accepted the award at the American Library Association's (ALA) annual convention in New Orleans. It was his first professional conference, an opportunity to meet with LGBTQ authors and connect with other librarians who shared his passion. In general, he learned, "Small rural libraries don't get those vocal LGBTQ allies."

West's activism didn't just help educate other LGBTQ people's parents—
it improved his relationship with his parents. When he returned from Los
Angeles, West lived with them, figuring his time back in Independence was
temporary while he built his library resume and prepared to move back to the
coast. He ended up staying in their house for seven years, a period of time
that allowed the family members to come to terms with each other. When he
started Project Q&A, West said, his mother feared he was putting the family
in danger by calling attention to them; this caused fights. When his parents
didn't come to the first Pride, he was hurt because they'd always shown up
for everything he did. "It took a long time to forgive them, especially since
so many parents brought kids and came up and talked to me," he said. But
his mother has come to the last two Prides. "She realizes it's bigger than
just my family," West said. He came to understand that his mother's initial
resistance was based in fear. "She didn't want anything bad happening to
myself or our house," he said. "Also, she just didn't understand. She had two
gay brothers, which was never talked about in our family. She was OK with
having gay friends and relatives, but it was always one of those things you
don't talk about." West's activism was the opposite of "not talking about it."
Eventually, he said, "she realized it's OK to talk about it, that it actually helps
to talk about it. Now, at her work, when she needs a new employee and they
happen to be gay, she calls and says, 'Do you know this person?' I say, 'Mom
we don't know everyone. But tell them to come to project Q&A!'"

West's experience with his parents is not unique; it's one I heard over
and over again while researching my book *No Place Like Home: Lessons
in Activism from LGBT Kansas*, which chronicled how a decade of grassroots activism in a stereotypically conservative state contributed to dramatic
changes in public acceptance of LGBTQ people. "I always had a negative
view of Southeast Kansas until I started getting active," West said. "It's really
empowering to drive down Main Street and see Pride flowing throughout the
three-block stretch of small-town U.S.A., at the community college," West
said. "I never thought it would be possible in a small town to have an LGBTQ
community." In this way, West exemplifies symbolic interactionists' asser-
tions that social life happens due to the conscious action of other "doing,"
and thereby reminds us of the agency we all have to shape the social worlds
around us.

Some factors unique to Independence, however, have made that work
easier than it would have been in many other Kansas towns. Because
Independence is home to the playwright William Inge (1913–1973), the community college's William Inge Center for the Arts hosts a four-day festival
that brings in Pulitzer Prize-winners and other playwrights from around the
country for performances and workshops. Having an arts community helps
the town be more accepting, West said. Another factor: Oil magnate Henry

F. Sinclair was also from Independence. The Sinclair company was acquired by Atlantic Richfield Inc. in the late 1960s, and the Arco Pipeline Company's world headquarters was located in Independence until the 1990s. Having high-paying oil industry jobs in town, West said, created a class of employees who had the resources to travel and be exposed to other kinds of people. Finally, the town has a strong tradition of volunteerism, of people coming together as a community, evidenced by their hosting of the Neewollah festival. "We have a real strong sense of making our community better," West said. "We might not always agree with one another, but we come together to accomplish things. That sets us apart."

All of which means Independence is not necessarily a textbook case for how something approaching a gayborhood can be created in any small town. Independence has a strong leader with connections to national organizations that can provide financial assistance, and a handful of allies who are willing to put in the work. And one should avoid any tendency to romanticize small-town life based on a few rainbow flags flying year-round. Visibility for trans people in Independence is non-existent. "We have very few folks in our community that openly identify as trans or nonbinary," West said. "Those that do tend to stay home and are not involved with Project Q&A due to the visibility of the group." In this way, trans people in Independence may be feeling like those in Jonathan Jiménez "Evicted from the Gayborhood": left "to fend for themselves outside of the broader LGBT movement." Kishpaugh remembered that Independence had a greenhouse owned by a trans person "and she was very popular," but "most people didn't even know." The woman has since died. "She was in her 70s. I don't think it was always easy for her."

West also said Project Q&A had not been able to reach people of color in Independence, suggesting that it may be an example of "Queer Men of Color" Omar Ali Musthaq's "largely White dominated" queer community, where whiteness is "enacted systematically in that it (is) codified within LGBTQ institutions," to the extent that Project Q&A might be considered such an institution. According to U.S. Census figures from 2010, the city's population is 6.5 percent black and 6.5 percent Latino. West is a member of the town's Diversity Task Force, a group initiated through a leadership program sponsored by the Chamber of Commerce, to promote diversity overall. Kishpaugh said the town has a long way to go before people of color might feel as empowered as gays and lesbians. "Independence is a strange town because it's not part of the North but it's not exactly part of South, but from the Civil War on, Independence was more southern," Kishpaugh said. "The largest race riot in Kansas was here in 1920, when an African American man was accused of killing a white store owner. One of the main witnesses was a member of the KKK, who later became mayor. We still have hatred towards African Americans here in Independence." Kishbaugh said she believed attitudes were slowly improving. "We're not there yet, but I see much more acceptance."

With more work to be done, West has plans to expand the reach of Project Q&A. The organization has received nonprofit status and has been developing a board of directors. The goal is to expand throughout the Midwest "to any little town" while maintaining a headquarters in Independence. "I started realizing nobody was really fighting for small towns," West said. "There's an estimated 2.9 million LGBTQ individuals living in rural America who pretty much get left off of the map. The big organizations do a good job in a metropolis, but not in small towns."

West said he still plans to move back to a coast eventually, but can see himself staying in Independence for another ten or fifteen years.

"I've grown to love Independence and southeast Kansas," he said. "Never in a million years have I ever thought I would say that. But the more active I've grown, I see the value. You don't need to live in a big city to be able to be yourself without that fear, and there's always an inkling of fear even in a city. The more I get involved here, I think, 'Oh, it's a great community. We're in the middle of nowhere and the middle of everywhere.'"

NOTES

1. There is some debate on this. Some residents point to the fact that Kansas City gay pride was, for a time, held in the West Bottoms as a sign that the neighborhood has shifted. However, the longest running gay bar, Missy B's, is located in Westport.

2. The editors of this text would like to point out that the so-called early Chicago school comprised scholars using journalistic methods. Indeed sociology owes much to the journalistic mode for the development of its method, rather than anthropology whose ethnographic tradition developed independent of sociology as documented in Martin Bulmer's book published in 1984 titled, "The Chicago School of Sociology."

3. Particularly the research described by editors Christopher Conner and Daniel Okamura in an earlier draft of the introduction which is under review with *Sexualities* titled "Queer Expectations: An Empirical Critique of Rural LGBT+ Narratives." In it, they challenge assumptions made about queer modes of existence using a mixed methods approach.

4. This strain is something touched upon in sociology by Robert Merton and Robert Agnew as strain theory.

Index

Abramowicz, Marta, 170–71n1
"Accelerating Acceptance Report"
  (GLAAD), 18
acculturation, significance of, 215, 216
ACT UP. *See* AIDS Coalition To
  Unleash Power (ACT UP)
Adam4Adam app, 210
Addams, Jane, 1
Adonis Complex, 136
affect, 31–33, *34*
affection, significance of, 193
affection-image, 190, 191, 201; face
  in terms of, 201; meaning and
  significance of, 189–90, 194–96; as
  partial objects, orientations through,
  198–200; reflective, 197
ageing capital, 113
Agnew, Robert, 236n4
Ahmed, Sarah, 190, 198, 199
AIDS and collective sex crackdown,
  92–94
AIDS Coalition To Unleash Power
  (ACT UP), 58
Alcoholic Beverage Control (ABC) (San
  Francisco), 54
"Alienation, Ambivalence, Agency"
  (Simpson), 113
American Community Survey (2010),
  20

Andersonville (Chicago), 20, 23, 24, 26,
  36n2
anti-blackness, 135–37
anti-gay verbal and physical harassment,
  73–76
assimilation, in Boystown:
  discussion of, 221–23; enclaves
  and gayborhoods and, 208–10;
  gentrification and, 211–14
  (intertwined character, 214–16;
  sexual field restructuring, 216–21);
  meaning and significance of, 206–8;
  study methods, 210–11

Badlands (Castro, San Francisco), 57
bathhouses, gay, 88–89, 91
bear face, 195, 200
bears, significance of, 158n2
beat, significance of, 70, 72
Becker, Howard S., 10n3
Beemyn, Genny, 145
Belmont Rocks (Boystown), 221
Benjamin, Ruha, 6, 190
Berlant, Lauren, 99
"bigness," notion of, 137
BIPOC. *See* Black, Indigenous, and
  People of Color (BIPOC)
Black, Indigenous, and People of Color
  (BIPOC), 145, 147, 158n3

Black Metropolis (Drake and Cayton), 210

black queer. *See* erotic capital; queer people of color (QPOC); queer urban placemaking

Blue (Castro, San Francisco), 55

Blumer, Herbert, 202n4

bodies-under-glass, significance of, 193, 202n5

body, 8, 138, 150, 158n2, 177; affected, 193, 196; affecting, 193; affection-image and, 195, 196; cisgender, 179; contact, 97; dehumanized, 113, 114; face and, 9, 193, 196; finger and, 199; gay. *See* gay singleton; go-go dancing and, 132–34; Grindr app and, 191, 197, 199, 200; leaning of, 132–33; modification of, 131; muscular, 112, 121n5, 128, 135–37; non-white, 108, 136–37, 153; normative judgments about, 130; partial objects and, 197, 202; sexual, 97, 112, 196, 199; white, 108, 200, 201

Bourdieu, Pierre, 163

Boystown (Chicago), 1, 20, 24, 26, 36n2, 78, 100, 147, 152, 153, 157; positive loitering walk in, 79

Boystown (Orne), 208

Brennan, J., 110, 113

British ethnic minority (BEM), 114

Broadway Youth Center, 152

broken windows theory, 69

brownness, significance of, 114

Brown-Saracino, Japonica, 36n2, 212

buck, as hypersexuality, 132

Buck's (Boystown), 219

Bulmer, Martin, 236n2

Burgess, Ernest W., 68

Butler, Judith, 192, 198

Buttigieg, Pete, 5

Café (Castro, San Francisco), 55–56

Calhoun, Craig, 10n8

Callander, D., 135

Campbell, Elaine, 70

Castells, Manuel, 3, 145

Castro (San Francisco), 47; homonormativity resistance and, 57–59; metrosexual homonormativity of, 55–56; "sanitation process" in, 48–49; significance of, 51

Castro LGBTQ Cultural District, 62

Catacombs, 91

Cavalcante, Andre, 182

Center on Halsted, 79, 152, 153, 214, 220

Centner, Ryan, 48

charmed circle, notion of, 27, 207, 210, 215, 216, 218

Chasin, Alexandra, 3

Chauncey, George, 145

Chelsea (New York), 98

Cher concert, significance of, 228–29

Cherry Grove (New York), 91

Chicago, 19–20

Chicago Health and Social Life survey, 209

Choi, S. K., 174

Christopher Street (New York City), 78, 79

The Cinch (Polk, San Francisco), 61

Cinema 1 (Deleuze), 193

Cip Lounge (Soma, San Francisco), 54

City Hall Park (New York City), 88

closeted life, view of, 145, 146, 148, 149

Cobalt (Shaw/U Street neighborhood), 150

Cocktail (Boystown), 214, 216

Cohen, Stanley, 10n4

collective intimacy, 232; continued relevance of, 98–101; fostering, 94–98

collective sex practices, in New York City, 85–87; collective intimacy relevance and, 98–101; current situation of, 94–98; waves, 85, *86* (before Stonewall, 87–90; crackdown on collective sex, 92–94; Stonewall to early 1980s, 90–92)

Collingwood Park (Castro, San Francisco), 55, 56

Collins, Patricia Hill, 125

commodification, of sexuality, 111

Compton's Transgender Cultural District, 61

concentric zone theory, 68–69

contact hypothesis, 17, 33

Continental Baths (New York City), 91

cosmopolitanism, 7, 146; homonormative placemaking and, 45–48, 50–52, 54, 55, 59, 60; performative progressiveness and, 25, 26, 29, 35

courtesy stigma, 119, 121n7

CPTED. *See* Crime Prevention through Environmental Design (CPTED)

Crenshaw, K., 125

Crime Prevention through Environmental Design (CPTED), 69

criminogenic space: as contested space, 68–71; gayborhoods as defensible space and, 74–78; gentrification and gay gathering places and, 78–81; meaning and significance of, 67–68; victimization in gayborhoods and, 71–74

cruising, 9, 232; collective intimacy and, 87–89, 91–95, 98, 99; homonormative placemaking and, 55, 56, 58, 60; significance of, 87, 93–94

cultural archipelagos, 146

cultural capital, 126

cultural enclaves, 208–9

cultural geographers, 69–70

Daddy's (Castro, San Francisco), 56

Daley (Mayor of Chicago), 211

Daley, Tom, 110

Dank, Meredith, 174

dark/light contrasts, significance of, 193–94

D.C. Gay Men's Chorus, 155

Delany, Samuel, 101

Deleuze, Gilles, 189, 193–201

Denzin, Norman, 202n2

Department of Health and Mental Hygiene (DoHMH) (New York City), 93

"Designing Out Crime." *See* Crime Prevention through Environmental Design (CPTED)

Desmond-Harris, Jenee, 36

Detour (Castro, San Francisco), 56

deviance framework, 3, 10n3

digital trans neighborhood, 173–75; creation (new digital community, 184–85; trans self digital possibilities, 182–84); and exclusion, 178–82 (LGBT affirmation and, 179–80; racializing of LGBT spaces and, 180–82; transphobia in adult spaces and, 178–79); gayborhoods and, 175–76; study methods, 176–78

Dirty Goose (Shaw/U Street neighborhood), 149

Diva's (Polk, San Francisco), 52, 61

Diversity Task Force, 235

Doan, Petra L., 175

DoHMH. *See* Department of Health and Mental Hygiene (DoHMH) (New York City)

Dolores Heights (Castro, San Francisco), 62

Driftwood (Soma, San Francisco), 55

Dupont Circle (Washington D.C.), 154–57

Eagle (New York City), 95

Eagle (Soma, San Francisco), 54, 58, 61

Ebony (magazine), 146

Edge (Castro, San Francisco), 56

Edwards, Harry, 2

environmental criminology, 69

Erikson, Kai T., 10n3

erotic capital, 125–26; black
  masculinity, being tough, and getting
  bigger and, 134–37; hypersexuality,
  muscularity, and leaning out and,
  130–34; methods to study, 127–28;
  race, gym bodies, LGBT community
  and, 128–30; sexuality and, 126–27
ethnic cleansing, 111
ethnic nights, significance of, 130–31
ethnographic triangulation, 216
exclusion and digital trans
  neighborhood: LGBT affirmation
  and, 179–80; racializing of LGBT
  spaces and, 180–82; transphobia in
  adult spaces and, 178–79

face, 199–200; affection-image and,
  194–96; overcoding of, 197–98;
  primacy of, 193–94
"faces-within-a-face," 191, 198
Family of Choice in Poland project,
  170n1
finger, as body, 199
Finnie's Ball (Chicago), 146
Florida, Richard, 3–4
Frankfurt School, 4
front and backstage regions, distinction
  of, 117

The Gangway (San Francisco), 61
Gay and Lesbian Alliance against
  Defamation (GLAAD), 18
gay bars and night life. *See* San
  Francisco gay nightlife
"gay-blindness," 29–30
gayborhoods: meaning and significance
  of, 1; inequality in, 33–36; purposes
  of, 67; as social sites, 30; under
  threat, 3–4. *See also individual
  entries*
gay dating apps and affection-image,
  189–90, 194–96; app design and
  identity portrayal and, 191–93;
  approach of, 190–91; face primacy
  and, 193–94; microfascisms and,

200–202; and partial objects
  (orientations through affection-
  images as, 198–200; and overcoding,
  196–98)
gay Disneyland model, 213, 214, 217,
  219–21
gay liberation and collective sex, 90–92
Gay Liberation Movement, 145
Gay New York (Chauncey), 145
gay phantom phone syndrome, 202n7
Gay Shame (Polk, San Francisco), 58,
  60
gay singleton, 107–8; and gay couples
  compared, 108; heteronormativity
  and, 108–9, 114; "invisible" gay and,
  115–19; meaning and significance
  of, 109–12; social landscape and,
  112–15
GenderJUST, 220
gender nonconformity, significance of,
  182
gentrification, 4, 9, 26, 68, 86, 209, 228;
  and Boystown, 211–14 (assimilation,
  214–16; sexual field restructuring,
  216–21); gay gathering places and,
  78–81; homonormative placemaking
  and, 46–49, 53, 57–59, 61, 62; queer
  urban placemaking whiteness and,
  143, 144; stages of, 212, 217, 219
Ghaziani, Amin, 67, 80, 81, 146
Giuliani, Rudy, 94
GLAAD. *See* Gay and Lesbian Alliance
  against Defamation (GLAAD)
Goffman, Erving, 22, 36, 107, 108,
  115–19, 162–64, 177, 192, 202n9
Green, A. I., 125, 126, 128–31, 134,
  136, 137
Greene, Theodore, 78
Greenwich Village (New York),
  89, 98
Griffin, C., 112, 113, 115
Grindr app, 9, 110, 135, 178, 189–91,
  202n11, 210; affection image
  and, 194–95; design and identity
  portrayal in, 191–93; finger as

body in, 199; message notification of, 202n8; microfascism and, 201; normativity on, 197; partial objects on, 197, 198; penis images on, 196; perverse facialized surface on, 198; as space promoting normativity, critique of, 200; torso shots on, 196. *See also* gay dating apps and affection-image

group sex, 91–92

Grow Up Queer (Robertson), 182

Guattari, Felix, 189, 193, 197–201

gym vernacular, 132

HAART. *See* Highly active antiretroviral treatments (HAART)

habitus, 126, 163

Haines, Shaun, 62

Hanhardt, Christina B., 73, 77

Hayward, Keith J., 69

Hell's Kitchen (New York), 98

Hennen, Peter 158n2

heteronormativity, 108–9, 114, 120, 163, 169

heterosexuals, 35, 81, 128, 161–62, 174; assimilation and, 207, 212, 223; collective intimacy and, 90, 93, 101; gay singleton in gay spaces and, 109–11, 113–15, 120; homonormative placemaking and, 46, 53–55, 75; performative progressiveness and, 18, 25, 28

Higgins, Harrison, 175

Highly active antiretroviral treatments (HAART), 100

Hole in the Wall (Soma, San Francisco), 58

Holt, M., 112, 113, 115

Home (Castro, San Francisco), 55

homonegativity, 34, 36; meaning and significance of, 17

homonormativity, 7, 9, 99, 114; assimilation and, 207; metrosexual, 55–56; in San Francisco, 47–49 (resistance of, 57–59)

homophobia, 58, 76, 114, 129, 229; performative progressiveness and, 29, 32, 35; queer urban placemaking whiteness and, 146, 148, 151, 154; two-mother families and, 162, 165, 169, 170

homosexuality. *See individual entries*

hooks, b., 127, 134

hook up culture, 215–16

hot spots policing, 69

Howard Brown Youth Center, 79

The Huffington Post (newspaper), 22

Humphreys, Laud, 2, 88

hypermasculinity, 47, 52, 138, 190, 192, 218; nonconformist, 53–55. *See also* masculinity

hypersexuality, 131–32

Icard, L. D., 129

imagined contacts, significance of, 17, 22

impression management, 229

Independence (Kansas), 227–34

indirect questioning technique, 22

interactive performance, significance of, 18

intersectionality, 125, 205, 210

intersectional knot, 205–6

intimacy, sociologists on, 97

"invisible" gay, 115–19

Jaspal, R., 114

Jet (magazine), 146

Kishpaugh, Nancy, 233, 235–36

Kitsuse, John I., 10n3

Kochanowski, Jacek, 163, 169

Kuhn, Thomas, 2

Lacan, Jacques, 192

Lady Gaga, 4

Latino Mission district, 48

Latinx Pride (Washington D.C.), 143

Latinx queer, 147, 148, 150, 154–57

Lawrence v. Texas (2003), 72

Leather Alliance (Castro, San
    Francisco), 62
"Leather and LGBTQ Cultural District"
    (Soma), 61
leather culture, 91, 158n2;
    assimilation and, 211, 215, 218;
    homonormative placemaking and,
    50, 53–58, 61–62
Leather Image (Castro, San Francisco),
    56
Legacy Business Registry and
    Preservation Fund, 61
Lemert, Edwin M., 10n3
Levine, Martin, 2, 92, 145
LGBTQ+. *See individual entries*
Light, B., 192–93
linguistic relativity, 27
Loftus, Jeni, 17
Lone Star Saloon (Soma, San
    Francisco), 61
Lucky Horseshoe (Boystown), 217

Mailman, Bruce, 91
Manhattan, 89
Marcuse, Herbert, 4
masculinity, 8, 9, 55, 71, 121n4, 158n2,
    185; affection-image and, 191, 194,
    195, 198; erotic capital and, 127,
    128, 130, 132–34; homoerotic, 189;
    racialized, 134–38, 200, 201. *See
    also* hypermasculinity
Massumi, Brian, 193
Mattachine Society, 4
Mattson, Greggor, 229
McDiarmid, David, 189, 191, 195, 197,
    201
McKenzie, Roderick D., 68
Men as a Class are the Fetish
    (McDiarmid) (painting), 189
Merton, Robert, 236n4
microfascism, 190, 191
micropolitics, 201
Midler, Bette, 91
Midnight Sun (Castro, San Francisco), 55

Mineshaft (New York City), 91
Mizielińska, Joanna, 170–71n1
Moby Dick (Castro, San Francisco), 55
Monaghan, L. F., 132, 137
Monto, Martin A., 17
Moore, Darnell, 78
Moore, Mignon, 129, 208
Moskowitz, Peter, 73, 78
Mumford, Kevin, 87
Murray, Stephen, 2, 145
Muslim queer, 154–55, 157
Muslim Women's Policy Forum, 155
My Place (Soma, San Francisco), 54, 58

naked intimacy, 98
Nellie's (Shaw/U Street neighborhood),
    149
New St. Marks Baths (New York City),
    91, 93
New York Times (newspaper), 21
non-normals, 120–21
non-person treatment, 116
non-white people and erotic capital,
    129–31; stereotyping of, 130–36
No Place Like Home (Janovy), 234
normal, 120–21
normativity, and Grindr as space, 200
N'Touch (Polk, San Francisco), 53
NVivo software, 22

Obama, Barack, 143
Obergefell v. Hodges, 9
objectification: feeling of, 217–18;
    significance of, 110
One-Dimensional Man (Marcuse), 4
Orne, Jason, 98, 112
Out Magazine, 207
overcoding, significance of, 197–98

Park, Robert E., 17, 68, 206
partial objects: orientations through
    affection-images as, 198–200;
    overcoding and, 196–98
Pelaez Lopez, Alan, 154

Pendulum (Castro, San Francisco), 56, 57

penis, as affection-image, 196

performative progressiveness, 6, 15–16; armchair allies and, 18; attitudes, actions, and placemaking, 16–19; research design and data, 19–23 (interviewing strategies, 20–22; pattern-making exercises, 22–23); significance of, 18; study results (affect, 31–33; attitudes towards homosexuality, 23–24; political absolution, 29–31; rhetorical moves, 27–29; spatial entitlements, 24–27)

"Performative Progressiveness" (Brodyn and Ghaziani), 227

Peterson, J., 129

Pew Survey study (2013), 8

physique, altering of, 132–33

Piccone, Paul, 6

Pines on Fire Island (New York), 91

Plante, Rebecca F., 10n2

Plato's Retreat (New York City), 93

Plummer, Ken, 109, 117, 118

poker-faces, 195, 196

political absolution, 29–31, *34*

Polk (San Francisco), 47, 49, 58; homonormativity resistance and, 58, 59; nonconformist homosexualities of, 51–53

Portes, Alejandro, 206

"positive loitering walk," 79

post-gay, view of, 5

The Presentation of Self in Everyday Life (Goffman), 117

private sex clubs, 95–96, 101; and bathhouses compared, 96; fostering physical intimacy, 97; play area of, 97; protection, against intrusions, 96; social area of, 96

Project Q&A, 231–33, 235–36

public bathrooms, for homosexuality, 88

Pulse nightclub (Orlando, Florida), 153

Pulse Vigils (Dupont Circle, Washington D.C.), 154–57

QPOC. *See* queer people of color (QPOC)

queer digital frontier, 5–6

Queer Eye for the Straight Guy, 4

queer people of color (QPOC), 208, 212, 214, 219–22

Queer Phenomenology (Ahmed), 190, 198

queer urban placemaking, 143–45; deviance as, 150–53; *Presente!* and, 155–57; subtlety of, 148–50; as way of (white) life, 145–48

racial consequences and assimilation, 219–21

racism, 32, 79, 114, 181; assimilation and, 211, 220, 221; charges of, 57; erotic capital and, 125, 132, 134, 136; facial arrangements and, 199; Grindr app and, 200; sexual, 127, 131; straight, 29; white face model, 194; without racists, 36

rainbow flags, significance of, 72, 233

Rechy, John, 89

responsive conversation, significance of, 191

reverse discrimination, 28; as unconvincing, 29

rhetorical moves, 27–29, *34*

Ringold Alley (Soma, San Francisco), 61

Robertson, Mary, 182

Roscoe's (Boystown), 214, 217

Rosenberger, R., 202n7

Rubin, Gayle, 61, 207, 215

RuPaul, 4

Saint (New York City), 91, 93

Sanford, Jesse Oliver, 62

San Francisco, sex clubs in, 91

San Francisco Chronicle (newspaper), 20

San Francisco gay nightlife, *47*, 60–62; and gay bars, *47* (distributions,

51); and homonormativity, 47–49 (resistance of, 57–59); significance of, 45–47; stylistic diversity decline and, 50–56; stylistic practices and erotics and, 49–50

San Francisco Human Rights Commission, 57

Schnur, Dan, 36

Schulman, Sarah, 49

Scott, S., 107, 116

Seattle Neighborhood Greenways, 81

secular intimacy, in public, 87–90

Seidman, Steve, 192

self, significance of, 192

7-Eleven (Broadway), 152

sexual assimilation, 215–16

sexual fields, 209, 215, 222; restructuring of, 216–19 (racial consequences, 219–21)

sexual prejudice, 18

sexy community, 98

Shaw/U Street (Washington D.C.), 147, 149

Sidetrack's (Boystown), 214

Silver, Nate, 207

Simpson, P., 113

Sinclair, Henry F., 234–35

smartphones, 199; affection-images and, 201–2; significance of, 193, 202n5

Smith, Dusky Lee, 10n8

social capital, 163

social disorganization theory, 69

social landscape and gay singleton, 112–15

sociological imagination, queering of: culture, community and, 3–4; digital frontier and, 5–6; post-gay and, 5; significance of, 1–3

sociology of culture, 2

solidarity, significance of, 30–31

Soma (San Francisco), 47, 49, 51, 58; homonormativity resistance and, 57–59; nonconformist hypermasculinity of, 53–55

Somewhere Beyond the Gayborhood (Janovy), 228

Sosin, Kate, 220

spatial capital, 48

spatial entitlements, 25–27, *34*; liberal sensibility and, 26

Sri Lanka, 73

Stasińska, Agata, 170–71n1

stereotyping, of non-white people, 130–34; altering of physique and, 133; black masculinity and, 135; impact, on sociality, 136; physical and psychological price of, 133; "thicker" ideal of, 132; toughness and, 134

stigma, 162, 169; by association, 119; as effective, 119; embodying, 118; of non-white bodies, 128; significance of, 107–8; strategies to deal with, 164–65; trans digital neighborhood and, 180, 182, 183, 186

Stonewall Inn, 73

Stonewall Inn Gives Back Initiative, 231

Stonewall Riots, 68, 145; anniversary, significance of, 4

straights, 6, 75, 89; gay singleton in gay spaces and, 110, 112, 115, 121n4; homonormative placemaking and, 47, 48, 55, 56, 58, 60; queer urban placemaking and whiteness and, 143, 144, 146; sexual and racial character and assimilation and, 206–8, 212–19, 222. *See also* performative progressiveness

strain theory, 236n4

Street Corner Society (Whyte), 210

Street Patrol (San Francisco), 76–77

stroller set, 216

strolls, significance of, 70, 72

Stud (Soma, San Francisco), 61, 62

subcultural practices/capital, 113, 126, 127, 218; collective intimacy and, 89–92, 96–98; homonormative placemaking and, 47, 48, 50, 51, 58, 60; queer urban placemaking

whiteness and, 143, 147, 157, 158n2; sociological imagination queering and, 2, 3, 8, 10n7
Supinski, Jessica, 17
Sycamore, Mattilda Bernstein, 58, 59
symbolic interactionist approach, 2, 3, 10n2
symbolic violence, 117–18, 163, 171n2

Take Back Boystown event, 211, 214, 219–22
Tannenbaum, Frank, 10n3
Tenderloin (San Francisco), 51, 61
Thornton, S., 126
A Thousand Plateaus (Deleuze and Guattari), 197, 201
Times Square/42nd Street (Manhattan), 89
torso shots, significance of, 196, 202n10
trans digital neighborhood. *See* digital trans neighborhood
transphobia, in adult spaces, 178–79
triangulation principle, 21, 216
Trump, Donald, 154
Tumblr app, 182
two-mother families and social invisibility, in Poland, 161–62; as group, 166–67; informal groups as support groups and, 168–69; and normality (desire for, 165–66; social construction of, 162–64); passing and covering consequences and, 167–68; strategies to deal with stigma and, 164–65; study methods, 165

urban diversity, 28, 35
urbanization, 127, 130, 228, 232; collective intimacy and; 85, 87–89, 91, 92, 98; criminogenic space and, 67, 68, 72, 73, 81; homonormative placemaking and, 45–49, 55–57, 59–60; performative progressiveness and, 16, 18, 19, 23, 26–28, 31–35; sociological imagination queering and, 1–4, 7, 8. *See also* queer urban placemaking

Valle, Modesto Tico, 220

"walking while trans" strategy, 73
Warner, Michael, 99, 163
Warren, Carol A. B., 2
Waskul, Dennis D., 10n2
Weeks, J., 111
Weinberg, Martin S., 2, 89
West, Brandon, 228–36
West, C., 127
West Side Piers (New York City), 91
West Village areas (New York City), 79
white face model, 194
whiteness, significance of, 114, 129, 131, 134, 137, 138, 235
White Swallow (Polk, San Francisco), 52
Williams, Colin J., 2, 89
Windy City Times (newspaper), 220
Wojciechowska, Magdalena, 229, 230

Young Men's Christian Association (YMCA), 88

Zhou, Min, 206
Žižek, Slavoj, 6
zone of transition, 68–69
zoning resolutions, for adult establishments, 94

About the Editors

Christopher T. Conner is visiting professor of sociology at the University of Missouri, Columbia.

Daniel Okamura is instructor of sociology at the University of Nevada, Las Vegas.

About the Contributors

Adriana Brodyn is a doctoral candidate at the University of British Columbia and a researcher at the Center for Interdisciplinary Inquiry and Innovation in Sexual and Reproductive Health (Ci3) at the University of Chicago.

Jeffrey Escoffier is a research associate at the Brooklyn Institute for Social Research.

Amin Ghaziani is professor of sociology at the University of British Columbia.

Theodore Greene is assistant professor of sociology at Bowdoin.

C. J. Janovy is a Kansas City-based journalist and the author of *No Place Like Home: Lessons in Activism from LGBT Kansas.*

Aliraza Javaid is senior lecturer in criminology at the University of East London.

Jonathan Jiménez is a doctoral candidate at the University of Nevada, Las Vegas.

Greggor Mattson is associate professor of sociology at Oberlin College.

Étienne Meunier is associate research scientist in the Department of Sociomedical Sciences at Columbia University.

Omar Ali Mushtaq is an independent researcher and scholar.

Jason Orne is assistant professor of sociology at Drexel University.

Vanessa R. Panfil is associate professor of sociology and criminal justice at Old Dominion University.

Tom Penney is lecturer in the School of Design at RMIT University Australia.

Magdalena Wojciechowska is assistant professor of sociology at the University of Łódź, Poland.

www.ingramcontent.com/pod-product-compliance
Lightning Source LLC
Chambersburg PA
CBHW050637280326
41932CB00015B/2689